Elizabeth Phillips Dip. Arch RWA, RIBA is the senior partner in Architect's Information Services. She was trained at the Royal West of England Academy School of Architecture, and her career includes design and supervision of projects in both large and small architectural practices, a mid-career research fellowship, followed by research and development for the Health Service in Scotland and England, and at the end of her service with the NHS she was secretary to Regional Architects Information Exchange. Current work includes a consultancy for RIBA Services Practice Data Law series, and general information services for the construction industry.

Meyricke Serjeantson BA Dip.Lib., MIInfSc is an information scientist, currently working for RIBA Services Ltd on a wide range of legal and technical information services for the construction industry. He also runs a free-lance consultancy providing technical writing, indexing and public relations services in the areas of construction and CAD.

Butterworth Architecture Management Guides

1 The Architect's Guide to Running
  a Job
  Ronald Green
2 Standard Letters in Architectural
  Practice
  David Chappell
3 Standard Letters for Building
  Contractors
  David Chappell
4 The Architect in Employment
  David Chappell

Butterworth Architecture Legal Guides

1 Professional Liability 2nd edition
  Ray Cecil
2 Building Contract Dictionary
  Vincent Powell-Smith and David
  Chappell
3 JCT Intermediate Form of Contract
  David Chappell and Vincent
  Powell-Smith
4 Small Works Contract
  Documentation
  Jack Bowyer
5 JCT Minor Works Form of
  Contract
  David Chappell and Vincent
  Powell-Smith
6 Building Contracts Compared and
  Tabulated
  Vincent Powell-Smith and David
  Chappell

Construction Law Reports

Volumes 1–11 edited by Michael
Furmston and Vincent Powell-Smith

Legal Reminders for Architects

**Elizabeth Phillips and
Meyricke Serjeantson**

With a Foreword by Sir Andrew Derbyshire
Chairman of RMJM

Butterworth Architecture

London   Boston   Singapore   Sydney   Toronto   Wellington

Butterworth Architecture
is an imprint of Butterworth Scientific

First published 1988

© 1988 Elizabeth Phillips and Meyricke
Serjeantson

British Library Cataloguing in Publication Data

Phillips, Elizabeth
    Legal reminders for architects,–
    (Architectural press legal guides).
    1. Architects – Legal status, Laws, etc. –
    Great Britain
    I. Title   II. Serjeantson, Meyricke
    344.103'7872   KD2978

ISBN   0-408-50001-8

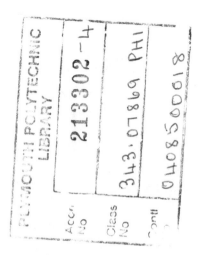

Typeset by S&P Business Systems,
Chipstead, Surrey
Printed in Great Britain by Biddles Ltd,
Guildford and King's Lynn

Contents

Where (bcd) appears in the text, it refers to "Building Contract Dictionary" by Vincent Powell-Smith and David Chappell: (qv) denotes an internal cross-reference, which may be found in the index of this book.

Foreword

Our profession has been getting a bad press lately from critics who do not begin to understand the complexity of our work. Designing buildings is difficult enough; but navigating the design and its implementation through the tricky waters of legislation demands of the architect a wider range of skills than most other professionals are expected to deploy.

Nevertheless there are increasing numbers of competitors in the industry professing such skills as project management, and trying to attract clients away from architects as the natural leaders of the team. The best way of tackling such competition is to refresh and refurbish some of the non-design skills which we may have disregarded.

Several years ago we discovered in my practice that we were having problems with planning applications – we were taking longer than we should penetrating the maze of planning legislation and obtaining speedy consents.

This book is exactly the kind of response to the tangled web of law which architects have to understand and unravel if they are to serve their clients well, discharge their public responsibilities with competence, and care for their staff as good employers. It thus covers a much wider field than our *RMJM Guide to Planning Applications* which we published last year. However a similarity does exist in that an exploration of existing literature drew a blank in both cases: similarly, both are directed at exactly the same target – the improvement of the architect's performance to society as a whole.

I am therefore greatly encouraged to see in this book an experienced architect joining with an expert in building industry communications to produce a guide to the law which architects need to know – simply and clearly presented.

If we take heed of these precepts – which we are all too inclined to neglect for the fascinations of design – we will face the future with that extra confidence which our clients and their other advisers look to us to provide. It follows that this is a book to be taken seriously and kept close to the other essential references for the complete architect.

Sir Andrew Derbyshire   *January 1988*
Chairman, RMJM Ltd

Preface

This book is intended as "an early warning system" for architects, which will enable them to negotiate the maze of legislation which encompasses all planning and building work. It should prepare the reader against unpleasant legal suprises but it is not a legal text book. Professional decisions must not be made on the basis of the information in this book; if the reader is in any doubt about the legal position professional advice must be sought. Students in the construction professions will find that the book provides a good basic introduction to the range of legislation which will affect their chosen careers.

The law cited is limited to that for England and Wales only. It has not been possible to include the law of Scotland and Northern Ireland in a publication of this size. Each entry gives the gist of the law as it may affect an architect, and where appropriate, suggests a suitable procedure which may be followed. The less well known planning, building and employment terms are explained. What, for instance, is "bad neighbour development", an "established use certificate", or a "period of incapacity for work", and when is a footpath a footway or even a walkway?

The book is divided into nineteen chapters, Town and Country Planning, Development Control, Building Types, Employment: Payments and Benefits etc. Subjects are set out in alphabetical order within each chapter, cross references are given to other entries, and there is a full alphabetical index of other important terms. For those who prefer their law raw there are Tables of Statutes and Statutory Instruments.

With a few exceptions, such as the Building (Disabled People) Regulations 1987 which were laid before parliament on the 20 August, the law stated is as known to us on 31st July 1987. As the law is continually changing, however, the provident architect should use all of the "current awareness" services which are available. The RIBADATA service from RIBA Services Ltd is a good source of abstracts of new legislation, whilst the full text of the law may be found in the microfiche services available from both RIBA Services Ltd and Barbour Index plc. The technical press should also be consulted to provide leads to new legislation.

Cross-references within this book are signalled by (qv) or "see also": readers should use the index to trace the heading in question. References followed by (bcd) are to entries in "Building Contract Dictionary" by Vincent Powell-Smith and David Chappell (Architectural Press).

We are grateful to David Reade LLB, of the Middle Temple, Barrister, who monitored the book for inaccuracies, to Francis Goodall MA FRIBA FCI Arb AA Dipl, who made comments from the architect's viewpoint, and to the staff of the British Library, Holborn Law Library and Croydon Reference Library for their help in unearthing some of the more elderly Statutes and Orders. Above all, we thank Kate Fortlage, without whose assistance we would not have been able to complete this work. We will also be pleased to receive any constructive comments on the book so that changes may be incorporated into the next edition.

Elizabeth Phillips
Meyricke Serjeantson

The Law

"The law is a ass - a idiot" or so thought Mr Bumble in Oliver Twist. Sir Edward Coke, leading parliamentarian of the seventeenth century was more charitable, speaking of "The law, which is the perfection of reason". Lastly, Edmund Burke, another parliamentarian, used an architectural metaphor, which sums up the essence of the law and the problems which it causes. "Laws, like houses, lean on one another".

Unfortunately, whilst the law has been described in a large variety of ways, many of them far from complimentary, it has a far reaching effect upon all of us, both in our professional and domestic environments. The architect is likely to be an applicant for many types of permission or certificate both in his own right and in that of a client. These permissions will cover buildings being designed, buildings being maintained or demolished and the buildings in which the architect's own business is performed. The architect will be an employer, an employee or a sole proprietor, all of which require extensive involvement with employment and financial law. The architect has a contractual relationship with his client and a duty of care both to that client and to the public at large. The architect may well be unfortunate enough to discover just what a wide range of people have the right to inspect his work, premises, records and finances.

All of this should suggest that the architect will have an extensive acquaintance with the law in all of its forms. That is, of course, far from the truth. Most architects, in common with most other members of the community, have little idea of the structure of the law and even less of most of the small print. This book does not aim to be a comprehensive guide. Only a lawyer can hope to offer that, and the architect who does not have ready recourse to good legal advice is tempting

providence. Our aim is to make the reader aware of some
of the areas in which the law operates so that advice may be
sought before it is too late.

We have tried to identify those areas which are currently
least well covered by existing sources of information. For
this reason, we have not attempted to interpret the Building
Regulations, which all practitioners should possess, and
which have had many books written about them. We have,
similarly, excluded the main forms of contract, partly
because there is no shortage of information about them and
partly because they are not actually the law. The contracts
are, in fact, model agreements which satisfy the law of
contract and provide a consistent relationship between the
various participants in the construction process.

The law covers a myriad of subjects and comes in a variety
of forms. Some documents emerge from Parliament and
have obvious legal significance. Other documents emerge
from sources completely separate from the government but
may still be considered in a law court to have a significance
on a par with the outpourings of the Houses of Parliament.
Stage one is, therefore, to examine the workings of the law
and to offer guidance on the documentation and the sources
of information.

The United Kingdom may have a single form of government
(even this would be disputed in the Channel Islands and the
Isle of Man) but it does not have a unified legal system.
Scotland and Northern Ireland have entirely separate
systems and, whilst some legislation is common to the whole
of the UK, in many areas, notably planning and building
control, the law is totally separate. This book is only relevant
to England and Wales, the law of the Principality being the
same in almost all instances. It should also be remembered
that, even within England, there are many local bye-laws
and local acts (qv), which govern a single local authority
area.

Acts or Statutes

These are the main elements in the legal system which
contain the substance of the policy of the government of the
day. They receive the Royal Assent following a series of
readings in both the Commons and the Lords. Every Act
has a title, a year and a chapter number: eg The Factories
Act 1961, c 34. This title is a unique identifier and should

always be used when citing Acts. Just using the title can be misleading. It should be admitted, however, that for reasons of brevity, in the text of this book we have only cited the title and the year. The full reference may be found in the Tables of Statutes and of Statutory Instruments. The simplest abbreviation is to use the year and the chapter number. This is often done when citing one act in another. Public acts relate to England and Wales, whilst local acts (qv) relate only to a specified area.

Agency Law

An agent, in legal terms, is a person who acts on behalf of someone else and has the power to take actions which are binding upon that other person. The architect will often be in that position on behalf of his client, whilst also having the professional duty to act fairly between the parties. For a more detailed definition, see ''Building contract dictionary'' by Powell-Smith and Chappell, hereafter noted thus: (bcd).

Amendment

When a British Standard is purchased from BSI the copy bought, errors excepted, is the latest available text, containing any amendments which may have been made since the document was first published. This does not apply to the law. The document purchased will be the same as it was when it gained the Royal Assent many years previously. The onus is on the user to establish what changes have been made to it since that date. This is an extremely difficult task and has provided a meal ticket for the lawyers (and the authors of books such as this) since time immemorial. The practitioner must rely upon the published information sources and upon professional advisors. There is no easy way round this problem, the important thing being to remember that the printed word is not to be taken at face value.

British Standards

A British Standard has no legal significance unless it has been awarded to it by another document (see also Codes of practice). As with the Highway Code, however, failure to comply with any British Standard, be it specification or code of practice, may well be considered by a court to constitute a breach of the duty of care.

Building Regulations: Approved Documents

The Building Regulations 1985 introduced a range of documents specifically produced for the purpose of explaining good practice. These replaced the "deemed to satisfy" clauses which had appeared in the previous Regulations. In addition to the guidance which they contain, it is intended that they will draw upon information in many other documents. Currently, British Standards form the vast majority of cited documents, although it is highly likely that this will soon change.

Case Law

Statute law is open to interpretation by the judiciary. The important features of any cases decided in court are then used as precedents for future cases. Thus, a system of "case law" is built up. This type of law is a study in its own right and is not the central subject of this work. Essentially, case law will decide exactly what is meant by "as soon as is reasonably practicable" or another of the many tests of reasonable behaviour which form a vital part of statute law.

Codes of Practice

The best known code of practice is the Highway Code. This has no legal standing at all but is accepted as the official guide to good practice on the road. The best defence against a charge of driving without due care is to show that the recommendations of the Highway Code were being followed to the letter and that, therefore, the driver could not be held to be negligent. Unfortunately, anyone can produce a document and call it a code of practice, so that it is important to assess the status of the document's source before relying upon its recommendations.

In recent years, certain codes of practice have been singled out for special attention by being cited in legislation. The advantage of this is that it enables legislation to be effectively updated, without the parliamentary process having to be followed each time, by relying upon the producing body to update its document in line with new developments or requirements. The two most common sources of this sort of guidance are the Health and Safety Executive and the British Standards Institution. The Control of Noise (Codes of Practice for Construction and Open Sites) Order 1984 introduces BS 5228: "Code of practice for noise control on construction and open sites" as the means of satisfying the legal requirements. Similarly, the Health and Safety (First Aid) Regulations 1981 rely upon a code of practice produced by the Health and Safety Executive to define the exact requirements for first-aid provisions in the workplace.

Commencement

Once an Act or a Statutory Instrument has appeared in print, it is often assumed that it is in force. This is not so. In each, there will be a section entitled "commencement". This states the day on which the legislation comes into force. This may be on the day that it receives the Royal Assent or on a day named in the text. In many cases, however, it merely says that the document will come into force on a day to be appointed. Another piece of legislation will then be required to state the day on which commencement will take place. This may be a separate SI, known as a commencement order or, in some cases, another piece of legislation. It is common for different clauses of the same act to come into force on different dates.

Common Law

There are many areas of law based upon what has been the custom rather than upon any piece of legislation produced by Parliament. The more complex areas of building and planning law have been developed in Parliament but in the area of contract law, there are many "customs" dating from the Middle Ages which still control our activities. The judiciary acts as interpreter and guardian of this law.

Contract Law

A contract is a binding agreement which creates a relationship between two or more people or organisations and sets out both rights and duties. It must be enforceable by law and must be entered with the intention of creating a legal relationship. Contracts are not the law themselves, merely agreements which must comply with the law. Thus documents such as the JCT forms are only model forms of contract which agree with the laws of England and Wales. For a more detailed definition, see "Building contract dictionary" (bcd) by Powell-Smith and Chappell.

Guidance Material

There has yet to be a case which defines the full range of material that the practitioner should have read in order to have fulfilled the duty of care. The publications of all Government departments are sources to which special attention should be paid, it being unwise to argue in court that Her Majesty's Government does not know what it is doing - irrespective of what the individual may think. Department of the Environment Circulars and Building Research Establishment Digests are obvious examples of this category of information.

Negligence

The area of tort (see also Tort) with which the architect will be most familiar is negligence. This is an immensely complicated area of law but there are some important basic principles:

— the defendent must owe the plaintiff a duty of care;
— the defendent must breach that duty;
— the plaintiff must suffer a loss.

A duty of care suggests a relationship between the two parties. There can be no doubt that the architect has this relationship with the client. There are many other cases, however, where this relationship is not so obvious. The main underlying principle is that a duty is owed to anyone who could be reasonably expected to be harmed by any act or omission.

Official Guidance

The law, as outlined, depends to a considerable extent upon the concept of the "reasonable" action. In many areas of law, such as contract, there is a body of case law built up which defines the reasonable action. In other areas which are subject to more frequent change, such as building technology, there is a need for guidance from official and other well informed sources. The construction industry is well equipped with guides of all shapes and sizes, ranging from official codes of practice produced by Government departments to small guides to good practice produced by product manufacturers. In any charge of negligence relating to a design decision or similar, the architect will need to show that he fulfilled the duty of care by using the best skills available. This may well mean being able to show that the correct documentation had been studied and that its recommendations were followed.

Repeal

Legislation does not last for ever and each act and SI will eventually be withdrawn as obsolete. This will be done by noting in another piece of legislation that it has been repealed or revoked. In some cases, this will be done in an obvious way. The Building Regulations 1976 were, for instance, revoked by the Building Regulations 1985. There is, however, no guarantee that the document and the one which revokes it will be connected in any way.

Statute Law

This is the law which emerges from a process in the Houses of Commons and Lords and which may be purchased from Her Majesty's Stationery Office or its agents.

Statutory Instruments

These contain the detail of the legislation and each one is empowered by an Act. Legally speaking, they are delegated legislation, in that they are produced not by Parliament but by a minister or a Government department. The minister is only given this power by an Act. If the Act which empowered a statutory instrument is repealed, the instrument itself, will cease to have effect unless some measure has been taken to "save" it under the powers of another act. The title of each instrument consists of a title, a year and a serial number: eg Building Regulations 1985. SI 1985/1065. The simplest abbreviation is the year and the serial number. In this book, we have only used the title and year. The full reference may be found in the Table of Statutory Instruments. Before 1947, statutory instruments were known as statutory rules and orders. There is no effective difference between a regulation, a rule and an order. ALL MUST BE OBEYED!

Tort

Tort is a wrong which can be put right by the law. It is civil rather than criminal law so, that it affects two individuals or organisations, rather than the interests of the state. It is most easily recognised in the form of an action for damages, with one party seeking to receive financial recompense from the other. In order for such a case to be proved, the defendant must be shown to have

— done something that should not have been done (or failed to do something that should have been done);
— made this act or omission deliberately, negligently, (ie with such a lack of care that a reasonable man could not have done the same), or in breach of the law;
— caused the plaintiff to have suffered a loss.

If the plaintiff is successful, the court will order a payment for damages to be made. There are numerous variations in the law of tort but these principles are the ones upon which it is based.

Town and Country Planning

Introduction

This chapter deals with legal reminders on the broader aspects of town planning; the detailed legislation on individual planning applications is in chapter 2 on Development Control. There are currently many areas in England and Wales which are subject to special planning control; so much so, that one third of all land is now subject to these controls. National Parks and Areas of Outstanding Natural Beauty are the largest and most obvious of these controlled areas, but minor ones such as Marine and Nature Reserves may cover quite a small area and they, like mushrooms, have the habit of appearing overnight. Always check the current position with the local planning authority, as rural sites in sensitive areas can so easily be adjacent to a controlled area. The right that the public have of access to the countryside is a contingency that should be planned for, as public rights of way can devastate a client's privacy within his own property. There are many restrictions on development in the more attractive parts of England and Wales, but there are also many encouragements to build in the less attractive areas; the architect should point out these factors to developer clients.

More detailed advice is given in "Planning Applications and Appeals" by Charles Mynors (Architectural Press).

Access to the Countryside

There are three sets of maps which show land to which the public have access.

— review maps with a minimum scale of 1in to 1 mile (1:50,000);

— access order maps with a minimum scale of 6in to
1 mile;(1:10,000)
— rights of access maps with a minimum scale of $2^1/_2$in
to 1 mile (1:25,000).

Access maps show the land comprised in the access order
by means of a green edging, land subject to to restrictions
on access is indicated by green dots and excepted land is
shown by green vertical hatching.
Review and rights-of-way maps show land subject to an
access agreement order or land acquired for access by the
local authority or r .iister, and these are indicated by green
edging and the relevant symbols. Review maps also show
open country by green diagonal hatching, land subject to
restrictions imposed by access agreements or orders themselves is indicated by green dots, and areas excluded because
of danger to the public are shown as green cross-hatching
edged in green.
National Parks and Access to the Countryside Regulations
1950

Agricultural and Forestry Development in National Parks etc

Where it is proposed to develop any agricultural buildings
and works (Class VI) or Forestry buildings and works (Class
VII in the General Development Order 1977) (see Use
Classes) within a National Park, or one of the areas listed
below, the developer or his agent must comply with the
following procedure.
Where development consists of the erection, alteration or
extension of any building or the forming or alteration to a
"private way" (defined in the 1977 GDO as highway or
footpath which is not a highway maintainable at public
expense), the developer or his agent must provide the local
planning authority with a written description of the proposed
development including a list of the materials to be used and
a plan showing the site of the proposed works.
Development must not start until 28 days has elapsed from
the time the local planning office have received this
statement. If within the 28 days the local planning authority
give the developer a written statement stating that the
development shall not begin without prior approval of the
authority as to the siting and means of construction of any
private way and the siting, design and external appearance

of any building to be erected, altered or extended; then the developer must comply with these conditions.

Development may then be carried out at any time within the next five years as long as it complies with the approved details. Areas affected include:

— all National Parks (qv);
— the following areas in Wales outside the boundaries of the National Parks:
communities within the boroughs of Aberconway, and Arfon;
communities within the districts Meirionnydd, Arfon, Dwyfor and Glyndwr.

For further details and the effect of boundary changes refer to the original document. Architects with farm or forestry projects on the drawing board should take note.

Town and Country Planning (Agricultural and Forestry Development in National Parks etc) Special Development Order 1986

Agricultural Land: Development

As a result of the surplus of agricultural products within Western Europe, the Secretary of State for the Environment is advising planning authorities to encourage a more diversified rural economy by allowing development which will result in greater and more varied employment opportunities. They are, however, reminded that once used for development, land is not easily returned to agriculture.

Wherever an architect is involved in the development of agricultural land, he should check its class in relation to the Agricultural Land Classification for England and Wales: Class I land is prime agricultural and will almost certainly be refused for development. Class II is good quality land and unlikely to be released for development. Classes IIIa, IIIb and IV are liable to a certain amount of adjustment but Classes IIIb and IV are the most likely candidates for development. Obviously, further restraints occur in National Parks, AONBs etc. It is, for example, the Class IIIb and IV land on Exmoor and Dartmoor which gives these areas all the qualities which caused them to be designated as National Parks in the first place.

Areas of Outstanding Natural Beauty

When the Countryside Commission is intending to create an Area of Outstanding Natural Beauty, they must consult with every authority in whose area the proposed AONB is situated. And before making an order they must publish in the London Gazette and in one or more local papers a notice of their proposals. The notice must indicate the effect of the order, the time limits and the manner of making representations to the Commission.

National Parks and Access to the Countryside Act 1949

Areas of Special Scientific Interest

There are many classifications of areas of the countryside that come under tight planning control; one of these is termed an Area of Special Scientific Interest. These areas have been and can still be designated by the Nature Conservancy Council if in their opinion the land has particularly interesting or rare flowers, animals, rock formations and so forth.

If the client is in or near one of these areas it is worth while checking if operations as superficial as landscaping, land drainage from a septic tank or swimming pool, or tree planting operations may be carried out near the SSI, as these could well upset the ecology of the area.

Anyone who is actually the proud owner or even occupier of an SSI must be notified and be given a list of the rarities in or on it. He will also find that he is very unlikely to be allowed to carry out "harmful operations" on, in or over his land.

If any part of the client's site is about to be designated an Area of Special Scientific Interest the Nature Conservancy Council must give three months' notice, so that objections and representations may be made to them and given their careful consideration.

Wildlife and Countryside Act 1981 and Wildlife and Countryside (Amendment) Act 1985

Common Land

All common land including town and village greens is now registered, and the registers are held by the local authority, usually in association with the Land Charges Register (qv).

Local authorities now have wide powers of control over common land.

The local authority may provide any recreational facilities they think appropriate on common land, and they can also exercise compulsory purchase powers on adjoining land if it is required to make the facilities practicable. Facilities include not only sports pitches, but buildings, playgrounds, lakes and camping sites, though it is an offence to park a caravan on open common land.

It is worth checking the local authority's plans for recreational development if the client's site adjoins a common.

Commons Registration Act 1965

Conservation and the Countryside

There is an increasing national concern with the conflict between agriculture, horticulture and food production and the conservation, and enhancement of the natural beauty and amenity of the countryside.

The main Acts on these subjects tend to be general in nature, and are supplemented by regulations spelling out detailed requirements as to footpaths, rights of way, and country recreation.

The better known country conservation areas are:
— Areas of Outstanding Natural Beauty (qv);
— Areas of Special Scientific Interest (qv);
— Environmentally Sensitive Areas (qv);
— Green Belts;
— Heritage Coasts;
— Marine Nature Reserves (qv);
— National Nature Reserves (qv);
— National Parks (qv);
— Sites of Archaeological Interest (qv);

These areas cover approximately one third of all land in England and Wales, and are subject to special planning controls; this means that the architect with a client or developer seeking out-of-town sites will have little scope for exercising his flair in design in exotic materials and in many cases will be fortunate if he can design any new buildings at all.

Agriculture Act 1986

Conservation Areas

If the planning authority consider that whole areas should be preserved or enhanced because they are of special architectural or historic interest, they can designate them as conservation areas. This gives them extra control over the area, and all applications for planning permission must be advertised in the press.

No building within a conservation area whether listed buildings (qv) or not, may be demolished without consent. Similarly trees, whether covered by tree preservation orders (qv) or not, may not be felled or lopped without six weeks notice being given. The architect should check if his client's development is in a conservation area, and if so, what extra controls the local authority can exercise. These often take the form of Design Guides; they are not statutory, but compliance with them is likely to be a condition of planning consent.

Town and Country Planning Act 1971 and amendments

Crown Land

Crown land is defined as:

— land belonging to Her Majesty in right of the Crown (bcd) and forming part of the Crown Estate. These matters are dealt with by the Crown Estate Commissioners;

— land belonging to Her Majesty in right of the Duchy of Lancaster. These matters are dealt with by the Chancellor of the Duchy of Lancaster;

— land belonging to the Duchy of Cornwall. These matters are dealt with by the offices of the Duchy of Cornwall;

— land belonging to a Government department or held in trust for Her Majesty for the purposes of a government department. These matters are dealt with by the appropriate authority, that is the Department of Transport, the Department of the Environment, and so forth. Also included is land belonging to the Health Authorities and the Metropolitan Police.

In certain contexts, the definition of Crown Land can change. Where there is any doubt on Government Department ownership of land the question is referred to the Treasury.
Town and Country Planning Act 1971

Derelict Land

Grants are available for the improvement of derelict, neglected, or unsightly land, and may be given for environmental as well as economic reasons. Reclamation may be carried out by private companies or by the nationalised industries, and there are also a number of schemes run under the Employment and Training Act 1973 which provide unskilled volunteer labour for clearing sites where the community interest is served.

The Town and Country Planning Act 1971 provides for grant aided acquisition and clearance of land by local authorities as a preliminary to developing large areas or providing new open spaces. Local authorities can compel owners to clear up vacant sites under the Civic Amenities Act 1967 in addition to their public health powers to get rubbish removed for health reasons.

It should be possible for the enterprising architect to tap one or more of these sources if his project involves areas of derelict land.
Civic Amenities Act 1967, Town and Country Planning Act 1971 and Derelict Land Act 1982

Development in Areas of Outstanding Natural Beauty, National Parks etc

In certain parts of the country, such as Green Belts, National Parks, Areas of Outstanding Natural Beauty, Conservation Areas designated by the local planning authority, areas specified by the Secretary of State and the Ministry of Agriculture Food and Fisheries, additional planning controls are in force. In these areas the new regulations modify the General Development Order and its amendments as follows:

— Class I.1 (dwellings): Main changes include additions allowed up to 50 m^3 or 10% whichever is the greater to max. 115 m^3 if the ground covered by the extension does not exceed 50% of the free site.

It also limits the height to that of the highest point of the original roof, nor must extensions project beyond the building line to the highway or be more than 4 m high within 2 m of any boundary. The erection of a garage, stable, loosebox, coach-house etc. within the curtilage will be treated as an enlargement to the dwelling.

— Class I.2A: allows the installation of satellite antennae which do not project beyond the building line.

— Class VIII.1 (certain industrial undertakers): main changes include cubic capacity not to exceed 10% of original or 500m^2 of aggregate floor area. Architects working within these areas should check current Special Development Orders for any changes to development control.

— Class XXVIII (extensions and alterations to warehouses): restricts increases of the original building to 10% of cubic content or to 500 m^3 over the existing floor area.

Town and Country Planning (National Parks, Areas of Outstanding Natural Beauty and Conservation Areas etc) Special Development Orders 1985 and 1986

Development Plans

There are two main types of development plan which replaced the original development plans; structure plans and local plans.

Structure plans (qv) are the responsibility of the County Councils, while local plans (qv) are prepared by District Councils. Since the demise of the GLC and the Metropolitan County Councils a new system for "unitary development plans" has been introduced. All development plans are subject to statutory public participation procedures, which cover objections, public inquiries and time limits. The policies contained within these plans form the basis for all planning decisions, and the architect is advised to acquaint himself with these plans before embarking on any major project.

Town and Country Planning Act 1971

Environmentally Sensitive Areas

The Agriculture Act 1986 allows the Secretary of State in consultation with the Countryside Commission and the Nature Conservancy Council to designate Environmentally Sensitive Areas (ESAs).

Of the fourteen ESAs originally selected for designation, six have been confirmed by the Secretary of State; these are;

— the Broads;
— the Pennine Dales;
— the Somerset Levels;
— West Penwith;
— South Downs (eastern end);
— Cumbrian Mountains (northern and southern sections).

These areas are defined on maps which may be inspected at the local offices of the Ministry of Agriculture Fisheries and Food (MAFF) or at MAFF headquarters in London.

The object of this Act is twofold; firstly, to conserve and enhance the natural landscape together with its flora, fauna, and notable geological and archaeological features; secondly, to promote the enjoyment of the countryside by the public, whilst establishing a balance between farming and conservation. This may well have an effect on those hoping to build within these areas, and the architect should check with the local planning authority whether additional areas have been designated. Remember too, that these are in addition to National Parks (qv), Areas of Outstanding Natural Beauty (qv), Areas of Special Scientific Interest (qv), Sites of Archaeological Interest (qv), and Designated Areas.

Agriculture Act 1986

Green Lanes

This is the name often given to tracks which are between two hedges, and they can be of ancient origin. ''Green Lane'' has no legal meaning, so that any lane of this type that is in dispute must be designated in some other way, for example a right of way (qv), footpath (qv), or bridleway (qv).

Inner Urban Areas

In 1978 the Inner Urban Areas programme was put forward as an attempt to speed up planning procedures in certain areas within England and Wales where inner city decay was severe. The planning legislation was, and is, supplemented by social and economic measures intended to revitalize these areas. Local authorities were empowered to invest in designated areas and to make grants and loans for the development of new industry and commerce.

Subsequent orders have designated many areas under this heading, and architects whose practice lies in inner cities should check what grants or other help is available to their clients.

Inner Urban Areas Act 1978 and subsequent Orders

Limestone Pavement Orders

This is yet another little order which could have repercussions on the client or on the architect as a specifier of limestone. If the Nature Conservancy Council consider that an area of limestone pavement is of special interest because of the flowers, animals, geology and general land form, they must inform the local planning authority. And if the Secretary of State considers that it would be detrimental to the area to remove or disturb the limestone, he may make a Limestone Pavement Order designating the land. Once the order is in force, it is an offence to remove or disturb any limestone on or in that area.

Wildlife and Countryside Act 1981

Local Plans

These plans are prepared by district councils and set out in detail the general policies stated in the structure plan. A local plan will consist of policy, key proposals and key diagrams, together with explanatory notes. Local plans can deal with general planning matters, but they may also take the form of an action area plan for the comprehensive development or upgrading of a specific area, or a subject plan which deals with a particular planning subject such as transport, recreation or industry.

These development plans are subject to statutory public participation procedures, which cover objections, public inquiries and a time limit for making representations, which is six weeks. Local plans affect nearly all future planning decisions and the architect should check both policies and maps. Subjects to be noted include policies on car parking provision, height restrictions on buildings, land uses, design policies, plot ratios, conservation generally, tree preservation, and change of use.

The policies set out in the local plan form the basis of the local authority's stand in relation to planning decisions and public inquiries.

Town and Country Planning Act 1971

Marine Nature Reserves

The client may possibly own or occupy land containing land that is always covered by tidal water or the sea, or at least covered for part of the time. Once again the Nature Conservancy Council may consider that it contains flowers, animals or geological features that it considers worth conserving, or that would provide special conditions for research and study. If the Secretary of State considers that the NCC have made a valid case, he will designate the area a Marine Nature Reserve. This then allows the NCC to make byelaws which may contain prohibition on the depositing of rubbish; killing, taking, molesting or disturbing any animals or plants; and possibly restricting the entry of certain private vessels or people. Any hope that the client may have of developing a boat harbour or marina is then likely to be doomed.

Wildlife and Countryside Act 1981

National Nature Reserves

This is another case where the architect is advised to check if the client has land within an area which the National Conservancy Council have or are likely to declare as a National Nature Reserve. These reserves are generally already being managed as a nature reserve under an agreement or by the NCC, but because of their importance to the nation they are upgraded to National Nature Reserves.

These too carry restrictions as to their use, for example if the area contains a mill pond, and the clients wants to run a working mill, it is quite likely that he will be restricted as to the amount of water that he can take from the pond at any one time, thus reducing the productive capacity of the business.

Wildlife and Countryside Act 1981

National Parks

In a National Park, planning matters are dealt with by the county planning authority, or joint authorities where the park crosses county boundaries. The authorities are required to produce and update a National Park Plan setting out their policies, and it is useful to consult this plan before submitting a project to them.

The following areas are scheduled as National Parks:

— Breacon Beacons National Park
— Dartmoor National Park
— Exmoor National Park
— Lake District National Park
— Nothumberland National Park
— North York Moors National Park
— Peak District National Park
— Pembrokeshire Coast National Park
— Snowdonia National Park
— Yorkshire Dales National Park.

Development control (qv) is much stricter in National Parks, both as regards the amount of permitted development (qv) and the appearance of buildings; the architect should check these constraints at an early stage.

Town and Country Planning (National Parks, Areas of Outstanding Natural Beauty and Conservation Areas etc) Special Development Order 1985

New Towns

New Towns are normally under the control of a Development Corporation during their inception and growth. Once the New Town is fully grown and capable of functioning without special support, its assets and management are transferred to the Commission for the New Towns; the water authority takes over sewerage and water management, and other functions are exercised by the district authority who usually take over the housing authority role. Eventually the Commission is destined to hand over all new towns to normal local government control. The architect who is involved with projects in New Town areas may find it necessary to deal with several different bodies if the town is in a transitional stage.

Town and Country Planning (New Towns) Special Development Order 1985, Town and Country Planning (New Towns) Special

Development (Amendment) Order 1977 and New Towns and Urban Development Corporations Act 1985

Planning Blight

Planning blight is a term used to describe the effect on land of development plan (qv) proposals. Such land is likely to be reduced in value because of the effect of compulsory purchase (qv) by the local authority or other bodies having powers of compulsory purchase. The local authority may buy land subject to planning blight up to ten years before it is needed, the object being to help owners, who cannot sell land because of the planning blight, to realise the market value of the property. The most frequent case arises when the highways authority seeks to acquire land for new roads or road widening. An owner-occupier can in certain conditions serve a "blight notice" on the local authority requiring them to buy the property.

The architect might well be asked to advise a client whose property is suffering from blight, but he should be aware that the procedure is fraught with many hazards and that compensation is rarely as high as the client would wish.

Town and Country Planning Acts 1959 and 1971, Land Compensation Acts 1961 and 1973

Recreation in the Countryside

The public has right of access to certain waterways and woodlands, and there are a number of bodies who are empowered to provide country parks, camping and picnic sites, and toilet facilities in these areas. Footpaths and bridleways (qqv) must also be signposted. Bodies responsible for these provisions are local authorities, the Forestry Commission and the National Parks authorities.

Architects dealing with country projects may find that the site is affected by some of these provisions.

Countryside Act 1968

Simplified Planning Zones

Simplified planning zones are areas where planning permission is automatically granted for specified developments or specified classes of development, though planning conditions and exceptions may be set by the local authority. Such conditions may affect any or all of the developments

permitted by the Simplified Planning Scheme; these conditions may also include the requirement that the consent of
the local planning authority is needed for particular types of
permitted development. Planning permission for developments not covered by the scheme must be sought in the
normal way.

Simplified planning zones have a ten-year life, at the end of
which planning control reverts to the normal procedures.
Certain classes of land may not be included in a scheme.
These are national parks, conservation areas, AONBs,
ASSIs and green belts. The architect should check with the
local planning authority that his client's proposed development comes within the scheme.

Housing and Planning Act 1986

Sites of Archaeological Interest

These are defined in the amendment to the General
Development Order of 1977 as: "Land included in the
schedule of monuments compiled by the Secretary of State
under the Ancient Monuments and Archaeological Areas
Act 1979 or which is within an area of land which before
March 1986 was designated as an area of Archaeological
Importance under the same Act or which is within a Site
registered in the County Sites and Monuments Record
before that date."

The developer or his agent must give the local authority six
weeks notice of his intention to start operations on sites
within these areas. Exempt from this requirement are:

—   agriculture, horticulture or forestry not below 600 mm;
—   landscaping not below 600 mm;
—   tunnelling or mining below 10 m underground;
—   repairs to roads, footpaths, water, drainage and other
services generally not below 600 mm.

The local authority usually has records of ancient monuments (bcd) and scheduled sites, and if not, the Historic
Buildings and Monuments Commission should be able to
provide the information. If permission to build on such sites
is given, the building owner may be required to allow
enough time for a "rescue dig" to take place, and this
possibility should be remembered.

*Operations in Areas of Archaeological Importance (Forms of Notice
etc.) Regulations 1984, Areas of Archaeological Importance (Notifica-*

tion of Operations) (Exemption) Order 1984 and Town and Country Planning General Development (Amendment) (No. 2) Order 1985

Structure Plans

Structure plans prepared by county councils consist of a written statement of general policies, supported by diagrams. These have to be approved by the Secretary of State. The requirement for structure plans was first introduced in 1968 and most of these are now in force for England and Wales. Local planning authorities may collaborate to produce a "Joint Structure Plan" which is subject to the same rules as an ordinary structure plan. They must be kept up to date and publicised so that any representations may be made before the review is adopted.

With the demise of the GLC and the Metropolitan County Councils a new system for "unitary development plans" has been introduced. All structure plans are subject to statutory public participation procedures, which cover objections, public inquiries and time limits.

Where the architect is involved in large scale development he would be wise to check the contents of the written statement in relation to such subjects as transportation, housing, education, industry, and recreation, as these may well affect the availability of labour in the area and therefore the viability of the project.

Town and Country Planning Act 1971 and subsequent legislation

Tree Preservation Orders

It pays to take Tree Preservation Orders seriously, because if trees are removed or wilfully damaged by topping or lopping ¯in a manner likely to damage the tree without permission, the culprit may have to pay a fine of £400 or twice the value of the tree whichever is the greater. On conviction the culprit is liable to a fine equal to the financial benefit he is likely to make out of destroying them. Developers of heavily treed sites having TPOs on them beware.

Under normal conditions the local authority require five day's notice of a request to remove a tree. If however the tree has become a danger to the public or the neighbouring buildings through storm damage or decay, the owner may have the tree topped, lopped or if necessary cut down or uprooted.

The architect should inspect the local authority's map showing the location of preserved trees, and if his client wishes to place a TPO on any trees he must make an application to the local authority who are also responsible for cancelling TPOs.

Town and Country Planning (Tree Preservation Order) Regulations 1969 and 1981

Trees in Conservation Areas

Most though not all trees in a conservation area are likely to be the subject of Tree Preservation Orders. There are exemptions to this protection but it is advisable to check the plans held by the local planning authority before deciding on the best solution to developing or extending buildings in conservation areas which are close to trees.

Remedial work to trees is usually exempt from control but notice must be given to the local authority before work is carried out.

Town and Country Planning Amenities Act 1974 Town and Country Planning (Tree Preservation Order) (Amendment) and (Trees in Conservation Areas) (Exempted Cases) Regulations 1975

Trees in Woodlands

Amendments to section 62 of the Town and Country Planning Act 1971 may well be of interest to those dealing with development sites within woodland areas. Originally the Act required trees that had been removed, uprooted or destroyed to be replaced in the same position, but this amendment allows for the same number of trees to be replaced either on or near the place where the trees originally stood. As a further option, if the the owner and the planning authority can agree on an alternative piece of land, the requisite number of trees may be planted there.

The Forestry Commission also has authority to require the restocking of land with trees after unauthorised felling, and the trees maintained in accordance with good forestry practice for ten years.

Town and Country Planning Amendment Act 1985, Forestry Act 1986 and Forestry (Felling of Trees) (Amendment) Regulations 1987

Unitary Development Plans

The new planning structure for Greater London is by means of unitary development plans prepared by the 33 London boroughs. Strategic planning guidance to the boroughs will be provided by the Secretary of State for the Environment. This guidance will be based on strategic advice submitted by the London Planning Advisory Committee. The boroughs have a statutory requirement to take the Department of the Environment's strategic guidance into account when preparing unitary development plans. The London Planning Advisory Committee will also deal with issues affecting areas adjoining Greater London in co-operation with the local planning authorities.

The effect of this legislation is to centralise all planning guidelines under the aegis of the Department of the Environment, with the exception of purely local issues.

The adoption of a unitary development plan automatically cancels previous structure plan decisions.

Local Government Act 1985

Urban Regeneration

In order to speed up the process of urban regeneration, the Secretary of State may make grants, loans, guarantees or spend money for the purpose of assisting the upgrading of specific run-down city areas. The term ''regeneration'' in this context covers acquisition of land or buildings, conservation or demolition of existing buildings, providing plant and equipment, services, infrastructure and environmental improvements.

This is a general statement of policy and the architect should check with the local authority if any of his client's development qualifies for financial aid.

Housing and Planning Act 1986

Development Control

Introduction

The aspects of planning law most frequently met by the architect are those concerned with the detailed control of buildings and site development. The more obvious controls on uses and sizes of buildings are well known, but there are many other controls on particular classes of development which are less common. The limits of permitted development are also constantly changing, and the architect should make sure of the current limits before preparing designs.

There has been a system in England and Wales for the control of development for many years, but the first serious steps to exercise control over all the land by granting or refusing planning permission was taken by the Town and Country Planning Act 1947.

Since then this exercise of control has been taken over by the Town and Country Planning Act of 1971 and by the General Development Order of 1977. Whatever the developer may feel about restrictions, these two pieces of legislation in particular have prevented urban sprawl, endless unsightly caravan sites along the coast, and a sprouting of factory chimneys in the valleys.

Over the years legislation on development control has increased in its complexity and the time taken to get a final grant or refusal of planning permission on a scheme has lengthened. The types of development which require notification in the press have also multiplied: so much so, that the client and his architect are much more likely to find themselves defending a contentious development against vociferous pressure groups than ever before. The message that comes across here is to understand all the aspects of development control and to consider any project as part of the local community. Good public relations with local groups at an early stage will do much to reduce the number of objections which are likely to delay the project once official notification has been given.

More detailed advice is given in "Planning Applications and Appeals" by Charles Mynors (Architectural Press).

Advertisement Control for Business Names

Not all advertising signs require permission from the local planning authority before they can be displayed. Those that are exempted from planning permission (qv) are divided into classes, and include:

Class II: Advertisements relating to the identifying of businesses, direction or warning. Signs giving identification, or warning; maximum area of sign is 0.2 m^2. Name advertisements (one for each name or business); maximum area for each sign is 0.3 m^2.

Class IV: Business names (qv) advertisements, only allowed if the premises include a shop window and then no higher than the bottom of the first floor window. In areas of special control these allowances are reduced.

Class V: Advertisements on forecourts; maximum area 4.5 m. If the forecourt fronts onto two roads, two notices are allowed, one facing each road.

Within these classes no letters may be over 750 mm high. No advertisement may be placed higher than 4.6 m above the ground, though if part of the building is to let or for sale the advertisement may be placed higher than this. Advertisements visible through a window are subject to these regulations. The illumination of advertisements is controlled. Additional constraints are imposed in "areas of special control" (qv), conservation areas (qv), national parks (qv) and areas of outstanding natural beauty (qv).

Architects designing commercial buildings should remember to confirm the position of all advertising material which forms part of the building contract.

Town and Country Planning (Control of Advertisements) Regulations 1984

Advertisements on Building Sites

The erection of hoardings (bcd) round building sites is controlled by the Highways Act 1980, and the local authority have powers to specify the type and height of hoardings and the arrangements for pedestrians.

Town planning regulations only allow a limited amount of advertisements on sites unless planning approval is applied for. Those that are exempt from planning permission are divided into classes, and the following are likely to be used on building sites.

Class III: Site notice boards. One name can cover an area of 2.0 m^2 but each extra name can only cover an area of 0.4 m^2. (There must be a moral here somewhere) If however the notice board is placed 10 m from the boundary one name can be 3 m^2, and each extra name 1.6 m^2. Any one involved in the siting of the boards can spend many happy hours deciding which option to go for.

Class VII: Advertisements on hoardings around building sites. In all cases no advertisements are to contain letters over 750 mm high.

The illumination of signs is controlled. The building contractor usually puts up advertising boards, but it is a good idea to make sure that the architects' name board at least does not infringe the regulations.

Contravention of these regulations can prove an expensive exercise as the fines have recently been doubled.

Town and Country Planning (Control of Advertisements) Regulations 1984 and Town and Country Planning (Control of Advertisements) (Amendment) Regulations 1987

Advertisements on Buildings

There are various advertisements which are allowed to be attached to a building, and which do not require planning permission (qv). Occasionally, however the local planning authority may define an area as ''an area of special control'' and this makes it almost impossible to display any advertisements externally and any which are visible from outside are likely to be restricted. The following classes are exempted from planning control:

Class II: Covers all types of building uses including:

—　religious, educational, recreational, and medical buildings, public houses, blocks of flats, clubs and boarding houses.

In order to keep within the exempted limits, advertisements must not cover an area greater than 1.2 m^2 for each premise; though if the building has entrances off two different streets, one is allowed at each entrance.

The illumination of signs is subject to control, but where they are required to direct patients to a surgery and so forth sufficient lighting to carry out this function is allowed within the exemption. The local planning authority should be consulted when in doubt as to the limitations on advertisements, or on the definition of an advertisement such as business names advertisements (qv).

Town and Country Planning (Control of Advertisements) Regulations 1984

Bad-Neighbour Development

The construction of buildings or use of the land for any of the following nine classes are listed as the types of development which could be considered to be "bad neighbours":

— 1. buildings used as a public convenience;

— 2. buildings or use of land for the disposal of refuse or waste material or a a scrap yard or coal yard or for the winning or working of minerals;

— 3. buildings or the use of land for the retention, treatment or disposal of sewage, trade waste or sludge. This does not include septic tanks or cesspools serving single dwellings and normally used by a maximum of ten people;.

— 4. buildings or the use of land for the purpose of a slaughter-house or knacker's yard or for killing and plucking poultry;

— 5. buildings used as a casino, funfair, a bingo hall, an amusement arcade, a pin-table saloon, a theatre, a cinema, a music hall, a dance hall, a skating rink, a squash court, a swimming bath or gymnasium (not being part of a school, college or university), a Turkish, vapour or foam bath;

— 6. buildings used as a shop for the sale of hot food;

— 7. buildings or land used as a zoo or for the business of boarding or breeding cats or dogs;

— 8. buildings or land used for motor racing;

— 9. land used as a cemetery.

The building owner or the architect as his agent must advertise the planning application in the local press and post a notice on the site.

Town and Country Planning General Development Order 1977

Building Preservation Notices

If the local planning office consider that any non-listed building has special architectural features, or is of historic interest and is in danger of alteration or demolition, it may serve a "building preservation notice" on the owner or occupier. This has immediate effect, and prevents any work being carried out for the next six months. The object is to give breathing space for a decision to be made whether or not to list the building. This is a useful procedure which enables conservation architects, who are trying to preserve minor buildings of interest, to gain time for the preparation of a good case for listing.

Certain buildings are exempted from building preservation notices and "urgent works" action. These include ecclesiastical buildings in use or ancient monuments.

Town and Country Planning Act 1971 and Housing and Planning Act 1986

"Calling-in" Planning Applications

The Secretary of State has the power to "call-in" any applications for planning permission which he considers should be dealt with by him rather than by the planning authority. This also applies not only to a particular application, but to applications for a whole class of buildings or other development. Local authorities too are subject to this procedure in respect of their own development proposals. Either the applicant or the local planning authority may wish to make representations, in this case both parties can put their case to an inspector in much the same way as in an ordinary planning inquiry, and the decision of the Secretary of State's decision is final.

Town and Country Planning Act 1971 and General Development Order 1977

Captive Balloons for Advertising

If the client, or indeed the architect, feels like advertising in a big way without having to apply for planning permission (qv), he can fly a captive balloon not exceeding a certain size and not more than 60m high above the ground level, whether it is on a building or not. However if he wishes to fly it for more than ten days in any one calendar year, or if the site is within a national park or area of outstanding natural beauty (qv) he will have to apply to the local planning authority for planning permission. Bear in mind the RIBA Code of Conduct on advertising. "Free flying" balloons do not come within local authority planning control. *Town and Country Planning (Control of Advertisements) Regulations 1984*

Caravan: Definitions for Planning Purposes

There are two distinct definitions for caravans, depending upon where they are sited. It is important to know the difference. The definition given in the 1960 Act is for the case where caravans are kept on a site licensed for human habitation by the local authority; here they are defined as any structure other than a tent, or railway carriage standing on a railway, which has been designed or adapted for human habitation and is capable of being towed or transported from place to place.

The definition given under the 1968 Act is not applicable to sites licensed under the 1960 Act, as it allows for caravans of the mobile home variety which when assembled are capable of being moved by road.These include twin-unit caravans in which the total dimensions do not exceed 60 ft in length, 20 ft in width and 10 ft in height. Any twin-unit structure larger than that is not a caravan.

Caravan Sites and Control of Development Act 1960 Caravan Sites Act 1968

Caravan Sites

No land can be used as a caravan (qv) site until the owner or occupier has been issued with a licence by the local authority. As members of the Caravan Club will be aware there are exceptions, but this is the general rule. If an architect is asked to put in an application to use a piece of land as a caravan site, he must first of all apply for planning permission; the planning authority in turn have a duty to consult with the site licensing authority before granting permission. Once this hurdle is passed, obtaining a licence (qv) is more or less automatic. However, and this is the rub, it can have attached to it any number of conditions.

These conditions, however onerous they may seem to the developer, must relate to the interests of the caravan dwellers on the site, or any other class of persons, or the public at large. The local authority also have the right to impose conditions which restrict the occasions on which occupied caravans are stationed on the land, as well as the total number of caravans stationed there at any one time. They may also control the type of caravan on the site, in relation to its size, state of repair etc.; though they cannot impose any condition as to the material used in the construction of the caravan. The licensing authority can also call for the building and maintenance of adequate amenities, ie sanitary, laundry facilities and so forth, together with proper measures for the detection and fighting of fires, and may require that the equipment is properly maintained.

Finally they have a right to impose conditions that will enhance the amenity of the site; these include planting trees and bushes, and regulating the position in which occupied caravans are placed. Architects who are commissioned to design caravan site buildings should check the licence conditions.

Caravan Sites and Control of Development Act 1960 Caravan Sites (Licence Application) Order 1960 Model Standards for Caravan Sites

Caravan Sites Licence

All caravan sites (qv) must be licensed in addition to being given planning permission. The licence application must include full details of the site layout showing:

—   roads and footpaths;
—   the position of toilet blocks, stores, laundries etc.;
—   the position of foul and surface water drains;
—   sewage and waste water disposal arrangements;
—   water supply and water points;
—   fire fighting points;
—   refuse disposal facilities;
—   recreation spaces and car parking arrangements.

The architect should discuss the requirements with the local authority before completing the site layout drawings and applying for planning permission.

Caravan Sites (Licence Applications) Order 1960

Caravan Sites on Crown Land

Where the occupier of the Crown Land is not the owner he must apply for planning permission for a caravan site (qv) and apply for a licence from the local authority in the normal way.

Caravan Sites and Control of Development Act 1960

Change of Use

This means a "material" or "substantial" change of use of a building or site from one type of use to another. The use classes (qv) are the basis of deciding whether or not a change of use will take place if the development or alteration goes ahead. A change of use from one class to another, with some exceptions, requires planning permission. As an example, a building once used for light industrial purposes can be used for a different type of light industry without requiring planning permission, but not for recreation or shopping; strangely enough, if a single dwelling is to be divided into flats planning permission will be required.

If the architect is not sure of the position, he should first study the current Use Classes Orders and, if the proposed building is not covered by a well-defined use class he should then consult the local planning authority.

Town and Country Planning Act 1971. Use Classes Order 1987

Churches and Burial Grounds

The client may have commissioned plans for alternative uses for:

—   a church;
—   a churchyard;
—   any other building previously used as a place of worship;
—   any consecrated land used as a burial ground.

It is essential to check that he has obtained permission to do so from the Bishop before embarking on the project. If the development involves a church or other place of worship which still contains fixtures and furnishings there is guidance in the regulations on the method of disposing of them. Where development is proposed on a disused burial ground guidance is given on the press notices to be served. The owners of the burial ground will decide what arrangements must be made for re-burying or cremating human remains; the memorials must also be disposed of.

Disused Burial Grounds (Amendment) Act 1981 and Town and

Country Planning (Churches, Places of Religious Worship and Burial Grounds) Regulations 1950

Compensation for Planning Constraints

Generally compensation is payable by the planning authority if they revoke or alter planning permission after granting it. The planning authority may also be liable to pay compensation if they refuse planning permission for development which is within the current use of the land, or if they impose restrictions on this type of development.

In the case of new development which is outside the current use of the land, and there is an unexpended balance of ''development value'', the whole argument over compensation is best left firmly in the hands of the client's lawyers, since there is a long and complicated history of legislation on the subject. However, the architect may be asked to prepare material for submission to the planning authority, or in case of dispute, to the Lands Tribunal (qv).

Town and Country Planning (Compensation) Act 1985

Crown Land: Development

The Crown does not apply for outline or full planning permission in the normal way, but it does have a duty to notify and consult with local planning authorities before starting on any development or carrying out a material change of use (qv). It does not pay a fee for this service. Theoretically the Crown has to abide by the rules set out in the General Development Order with regard to local planning matters; both the county and district planning authorities may request further information and consult with all relevant authorities on matters of transport routes and so forth.

Once a planning authority has collected all this information it can be assessed, and the proposals accepted or objected to. The local planning authority may publicise a bad neighbour development (qv) and the Secretary of State may agree to a non-statutory public inquiry. Once the development has been accepted work must start within five years and in the case of outline planning acceptance the Crown authority must submit full details within three years and start work within two years from that date.

Town and Country Planning Act 1971 and Town and Country Planning (Crown Land Applications) Regulations 1984

Crown Land: Sale of Land

An authorised authority owning Crown land (qv) may now sell it with planning consent including:

— listed building consent;
— conservation area consent to demolish an unlisted building in a conservation area;
— a determination under Section 53 for definition of development;
— general planning consent to develop land.

Where the Crown authority does not apply for planning permission for itself applications may be sought by an authorised person, for example a consultant architect. If the local planning office wishes to preserve trees or woodland on Crown land likely to be sold to, or developed by, a private developer it may do so but the order will not have effect until the land is sold or developed privately.

In general when the Crown disposes of land, the use of the land carried out by the Crown can be continued lawfully by the purchaser, and any building erected by the Crown can be retained lawfully.

Town and Country Planning Acts 1971 and 1984

Deemed Planning Permission

A local planning authority may usually give themselves "deemed" planning permission for development. This may be for development by the authority on land owned by themselves, or for development on land owned by them but which is to be developed by others. The proposals must be publicised and any objections considered in the same way as ordinary planning permission. They must apply for consents such as listed building consent (qv) from the Secretary of State.

Town and Country Planning General Regulations 1976 and Town and Country Planning General (Amendment) Regulations 1981

Development and Material Change of Use

The term development is defined in the 1971 Act as, "the carrying out of building, engineering, mining or other operations in, on, over or under land or the making of any material change in the use of any buildings or other land.'' It then goes on to list those operations or uses of land that do not constitute development, briefly these are:

— internal maintenance, improvement or alteration to any building as long as the exterior is not materially affected;
— any building or land within the boundary of a dwellinghouse may be used for any purpose that is incidental to the enjoyment of the house. (If, for example, the site contains a hut at the bottom of the garden, it may be used as an author's retreat, or a play-house for children, but it may not be used for breeding dogs for commercial purposes). Buildings on a site containing other buildings or land already used for a specified ''use class'' (qv) may be used for the same purpose.

Where a house currently used as a single dwelling is divided into two or more dwellings, this does constitute a ''material change of use'' and will therefore require planning permission. The interpretation of this undefined term has lead to many court cases, but generally it has been agreed that to be a ''material change of use'', the new use must be substantially different from the old use. As always there are exceptions to these rules, particularly in sensitive areas such as National Parks (qv) or AONBs (qv).

There is a tendency to apply for planning permission ''just to be on the safe side'', but there is no reason why the planning authority should not be asked to give a ruling without committing the client to an expensive and possibly time-consuming process unless it is really necessary.

Town and Country Planning Act 1971

Development as defined in the Town and Country Planning Act 1971

1. The carrying out of building operations, engineering operations, mining operations or other operations in, on, over or under land, or
2. The making of any material change in the use of any buildings or other land.

In order to avoid any doubt the Act states that the use as two or more separate dwellinghouses of any building previously used as a single dwellinghouse involves a material change in use of the building and therefore constitutes a development. The deposit of refuse or waste material on existing sites constitutes a development if the superficial area of the dump

is extended, or if the height of the deposited material exceeds
the level of the land adjoining the site.
Town and Country Planning Act 1971

Development Corporations

In addition to the previous Urban Development Corporations (qv), the policy of special development control has now
been extended to cover areas which cannot be designated as
urban areas.

The most recent areas designated include the Black Country,
Teeside and Tyne and Wear. The boundaries of these areas
are shown in the individual orders setting up the Development Corporations. The powers of these Corporations may
include housing, development control, environmental control and industrial development. These powers may be
varied from time to time. If his project lies within one of
these areas, the architect should check what controls are
operative and what powers are exercised by the local
authority and by the Development Corporation.
*Local Government, Planning and Land Act 1980 and subsequent
Government Orders.*

Enforcement Notices

Enforcement notices are served on the owner by the local
planning authority who consider that the development in
question is unauthorised, and constitutes a breach of
planning control. This notice requires the owner to remedy
the breach and takes effect not less than 28 days after it has
been served.

Enforcement notices must specify the alleged breach together
with notice of how they, the planning authority, expect the
breach to be remedied. They must be served within four
years from the date of the breach. At worst they can demand
that the development be demolished and the land restored
to its original condition. It is possible to appeal. There are
numerous reasons for serving enforcement notices including:

— development that has been carried out without planning permission;

— development that has failed to comply with the
conditions or limitations upon which planning permission
was granted;

— changing the use of any building for use as a single dwelling.

The latter case is to stop owners turning barns and other farm buildings into dwellings. The best way to avoid enforcement notices being served is to make sure that all planning conditions have been complied with before the contract starts. Registers of enforcement notices must be kept by local planning authorities, and it is advisable to look at the register in case enforcement notices are in force for the site before making a full planning application (qv).

Town and Country Planning Act 1971 and Town and Country Planning (Various Inquiries) (Procedure) (Amendment) Rules 1986

Enforcement of Planning Controls

When any development has breached a planning condition, or is unauthorised development, the local authority may serve an enforcement notice (qv) on the owner. In general the planning authority is encouraged to help those developing a small business by reaching a compromise rather than serving an enforcement notice. The notice must specify the nature of the breach and the remedial action to be taken and the time limit.

The enforcement notices are often served where reserved matters (qv) have not been implemented, or where a section 52 agreement (qv) has been broken, or an unauthorised change of use has taken place. The architect is likely to be involved in providing evidence when an owner wishes to appeal against an enforcement notice.

If the enforcement is considered by the local authority to be a matter of urgency, it may serve a stop notice (qv).

Town and Country Planning (Amendment) Act 1977

Enterprise Zones: Local Government

Enterprise zones are intended to encourage commercial and industrial development in selected areas. Areas are chosen from schemes that have been put forward at the request of the Secretary of State, and then publicised for comment. Once designation has taken place, it affects all stages of development by allowing certain relaxation on controls and finance; however the designation does not allow relaxations of any control on matters of pollution or health and safety.

Eleven Enterprise Zones were created in 1981-82, fourteen in 1983-84, and three of the first zones were extended in 1983-85. The benefits obtainable in enterprise zones are available for 10 years from the date that the zone was established for new and existing industrial and commercial enterprises. The benefits are:

— no industrial or commercial rates;

— capital allowances for industrial, commercial and hotel enterprises, available for corporation or income tax purposes. Land is excluded;

— 100% of construction expenditure on industrial, commercial and hotel buildings can be set against tax;

— no levy or information required by the Industrial Training Board.

— automatic planning permission for development specified in the zone authority's scheme. All other planning controls apply;

— faster administration. Normally 14 days for planning and building control approvals. Priority service can be expected from statutory undertakers for making connections to services;

— firms are exempt from making most compulsory government statistical returns;

— relief from customs duties and import/export charges arising from the Common Agricultural Policy (CAP). Easier custom control on bonded warehouses.

Although the decision whether or not to build in an enterprise zone is a matter for the client, an understanding of the advantages enables the architect to contribute more usefully to the project costing.

Local Government, Planning and Land Act 1980

Fees for Planning Applications

The local planning authority make charges for applications for planning permission, and the fees are payable at the time of submission. Fees are payable for the following types of application:

— planning permission;

— approval of reserved matters;

— consent to display advertisements;

— deemed permission in connection with enforcement notices (qv) and established use certificates (qv);

— on-shore natural gas and oil exploration.

Currently fees are not required for:

— alterations or extensions in or around existing dwelling houses where these provide access or other facilities for disabled residents;

— provision of access for disabled persons to public buildings;

— development within the classes listed in Schedule 1 to the General Development Order 1977;

— change of use where the change is within the same use class (qv) but planning permission is required because of planning conditions.

Concessions are made where fees are payable for:

— alternative applications for the same site have been made within twelve months;

— the application is for playing fields and changing rooms etc, and the applicant is a parish council, a community council or a non-profit-making organisation;

— revised applications for planning approval are submitted within 28 days;

— revised applications for approval of reserved matters.

Applications across boundaries:

— only one set of fees is payable if the project lies across local planning authority boundaries;

— one and a half times the standard fee is payable if the site lies across county boundaries.

Town and Country Planning (Applications and Deemed Applications) Regulations 1983, 1985 and 1987

Flagpoles and Forecourts

There are many occasions when the designer may wish to cheer up a forecourt with flagpoles, but unless the following rules are adhered to, planning permission (qv) must be sought.

Exemptions are classed as follows:

— Class V advertisements on forecourts: maximum area of total display must not exceed 4.5 m^2;

— Class VI flags: one flagpole and flag with the name or logo of the occupier attached in a vertical position on the roof of a building.

(Strangely enough no maximum size is given for the flagpole or flag).

*Town and Country Planning (Control of Advertisements) Regulations
1984*

General Development Orders

The Secretary of State has powers to make General
Development Orders; the first and most important of these
is dated 1977, though it has been updated many times since.
Amongst other provisions in the 1977 GDO, Schedule 1 sets
out the classes of permitted development (qv) for which
planning permission is not required, and these include most
types of small scale extensions and alterations to buildings.
The architect should therefore keep a watchful eye on the
technical press for news of any changes to the General
Development Order, since from time to time the chief
development order is amended to bring into line various
classes of development that were not contemplated in 1977.
As an example, the 1977 Order has been amended by adding
two new classes to Schedule 1 (development permitted by the
order), Class XXIV (development by telecommunications
code system operators) and Class XXV (installation,
alteration, or replacement of satellite antennae etc. on
buildings and other structures).

The latest amendment takes note of the new Use Classes
(qv) by introducing a new Class III to Schedule 1 permitting
premises used for the sale of food and drink (Class A3) and
for the sale and display of motor vehicles to be used as shops
(Class A1). It also allows business premises (Class B1),
general industrial (Class B2) and storage and distribution
(Class B8) to be interchanged as long as the floor space does
not exceed 235 m^2.

Town and Country Planning General Development Orders 1977 - 87

Historic Buildings

Lists of buildings of special architectural or historic interest
that have been compiled for the Secretary of State are
deposited with the planning departments of local authorities
and are held in the local Land Charges Register (qv).

Once listed, these buildings cannot be altered or extended
without permission, therefore before any work is started a
listed building consent (qv) must be obtained from the local
planning office. All proposals are advertised locally before a
decision can be taken.

To demolish all or even part of a listed building without permission is a serious offence. If it has to be demolished permission is required in the same way as for alterations but in addition the Historic Buildings and Monuments Commission (English Heritage) must be notified as well.

If any unauthorised work, whether demolition or alterations are carried out on listed buildings without permission the local planning authority can call for its restoration. Work on listed buildings is sure to attract attention from local conservation societies, and it is wise to make sure that all the necessary consents and permissions have been obtained before starting work; it is a matter of courtesy to inform the conservation societies at an early stage.

Town and Country Planning Act 1971

Industrial Development Certificates

Until January 1982 industrial development certificates were required for most industrial developments, and were obtained from the Secretary of State for Industry and had to be produced when applying for planning permission. The object of the exercise was to enable the Secretary of State to regulate the distribution of industry over the whole country. Although these regulations were superseded in 1981 they could be resurrected at any time.

Town and Country Planning Act 1971 and Town and Country Planning (Industrial Development Certificates) Regulations 1981

Landscaping

Landscaping is defined in the General Development Order of 1977 as:

— the treatment of land being the site or part of the site in respect of which an outline planning permission (qv) is granted, for the purpose of enhancing or protecting amenities of the site and the area in which it is situated. Landscaping includes screening by fences, walls or other means, planting trees, hedges, shrubs or grass, formation of banks, terraces or other earth works, laying out of gardens or courts, and any other amenity features.

Landscaping requirements are often dealt with under the heading of reserved matters (qv) and this can prove a very costly exercise and may well make the proposed development uneconomical; it is therefore advisable to ascertain the

planning authority's attitude to landscaping before completing the design stage of the project.
Town and Country Planning General Development Order 1977

Lay-bys: Development by Snack Vans etc

Placing mobile snack bars and refreshment vans on a lay-by constitutes development. Where lay-bys form part of a trunk road the land belongs to the Crown and therefore should the local planning authority consider it expedient to issue a "special enforcement notice", they must apply to the Crown (in this case the Ministry of Transport) before doing so.
Town and Country Planning Act 1984

Listed Buildings

It is an offence to demolish, alter or extend a building of special architectural or historic interest without obtaining listed building consent from the local authority. This consent may be granted subject to conditions such as special architectural or historical features. Emergency repairs can be carried out without penalty, but the local planning authority must be notified as soon as possible.

Minor alterations which do not affect the character of the building may be exempted, but the architect is advised to check with the local planning authority if there is any doubt. The local conservation groups are often the first people to object to any alterations to this type of building being altered or extended, and it is sensible to keep them in the picture in order to reduce opposition to the minimum.

The procedure for making an application is given in the 1987 regulations, as are applications to vary or discharge conditions attached to listed building consents. In both cases, the local planning authority must advertise these applications.

All applications and appeals must be accompanied by one of the following certificates signed by the applicant or his agent stating that:

a) the applicant was the owner of the building 21 days before the application date;
b) the applicant has notified any person who owned the building 21 days before the application date;

c) the applicant is unable to issue the required certificate, but tried all reasonable means to do so;
d) the applicant has been unable to issue any of the required certificates but has tried all reasonable means to do so.

The procedure for dealing with appeals to the Secretary of State for the Environment against a local planning authority is given, as is the procedure for dealing with buildings in National Parks. The regulations also cover the procedures for demolishing unlisted buildings in conservation areas.

Also covered by the term "listed building" are any objects or structures within the curtilage of a listed building which have been there since 1 July 1948, together with such objects which are fixed to the building. The purpose of this legislation is to ensure that all the statuary and ornaments that enhance the building are not sold off.

The definition of "urgent works" carried out to listed buildings in the Housing and Planning Act 1986 has been more precisely set out and the architect who is involved in such work should ensure that he has complied with the new requirements by checking with the local authority or the Historic Buildings and Monuments Commission (English Heritage) before starting work.

It should be noted that listed building consent may contain certain conditions specifying details of work to be treated as reserved matters. The local planning authority, the Secretary of State or the Historic Buildings and Monuments Commission may also carry out urgent work required to preserve a listed building, although they may only do so to parts of the building not in use, and costs may be recovered from the building owner. The Secretary of State can also take similar action on unlisted buildings in a conservation area. (See also Historic Buildings).

Town and Country Planning Act 1971, Housing and Planning Act 1986 and Town and Country Planning (Listed Buildings and Buildings in Conservation Areas) Regulations 1987

Mineral Working

If the client operates mineral workings, he may possibly receive an order which has the effect of:

— revoking, modifying, requiring the discontinuance of, or prohibiting the resumption of, his mineral workings which have ceased;

— imposing requirements in relation to the site where mining operations are temporarily suspended.

In these cases the architect may advise his client that he may be entitled to apply to the planning authority for compensation.

Town and Country Planning (Minerals) Act 1981 and Town and Country Planning (Compensation for Restriction on Mineral Workings) Regulations 1985

Office Development Permits

Until August 1979 an office development permit was required from the Secretary of State before an application for planning permission could be processed. It did not apply to small offices, but the minimum limit varied from 3000 ft^2 to 30 000 ft^2 before the order was finally repealed. The object of the exercise was to restrict new office blocks from being built in areas where too many already existed.

Town and Country Planning Act 1971 and Control of Office Development (Cessation) Order 1979

Outline Planning Permission

A developer may wish to test the formal reactions of a planning authority to developments on several different sites. The most economical way to do this is by applying for outline planning permission; this method allows the principle of the development to be considered without going into full design drawings.

Planning permission if granted is likely to be subject to reserved matters (qv). If the planning authority are of the opinion that they cannot consider the application without further detailed information, they are entitled to call for such details as are listed under reserved matters (qv) and in the meantime withhold their decision.

Once a planning authority has committed itself to allowing development based on a specific application for outline planning permission, they are also committed to allowing development to proceed, subject to any reserved matters stated in the permission granted being satisfactorily covered by the drawings submitted with the full application.

The application for full planning permission based on the reserved matters must normally be made within three years of the granting of ''outline'' approval. An architect who is commissioned to prepare an outline planning submission would be wise to consider the detail planning design even though this is not submitted, since reserved matters may include planning requirements which could have a major effect on the design. The planning authority will usually be helpful in advising the architect on the likely requirements. *Town and Country Planning Act 1971*

Permitted Development

The General Development Orders specify certain classes of development for which planning permission is not required: known as "permitted development". The classes change from time to time and it is essential to check the latest development orders and to consult the local planning authority if in doubt.

It is a waste of time and effort to apply for planning permission when it is not needed. The definition and conditions of each class of permitted development is complicated, and only the main headings are given here.

— Class I: development within the curtilage of a dwelling-house (qv);

— Class II: sundry minor operations such as boundary walls, gates and fences;

— Class III: change of use for industrial buildings and for shops;

— Class IV: temporary buildings;

— Class V: use by members of recreational organisations, for camp sites etc;

— Class VI: agriculture buildings on land over one acre; (see also Agricultural and Forestry Development in National Parks etc; and Agricultural Development in AONBs);

— Class VII: forestry buildings and works;

— Class VIII: development for industrial purposes carried out by an industrial undertaker;

— Class IX: repairs to unadopted streets and private ways;

— Class X: repairs to services by public authorities and undertakers;

— Class XI: war damaged buildings etc.;

— Class XII: development under local or private acts or orders;

— Class XIII: development by local authorities; minor works;

— Class XIV: development by local highways;

— Class XV: development by drainage authorities;

— Class XVI: development by water authorities;

— Class XVII: development for sewerage and sewage disposal;

— Class XVIII: development by statutory undertakers (qv);

— Class XIX: development by mineral undertakers;

— Class XX: development by National Coal Board (British Coal);

— Class XXI: uses of aerodrome buildings (British Airports Authority);

— Class XXII: use as a caravan site (in specified circumstances);

— Class XXIII: development on licensed caravan sites (qv);

— Class XXIV: development by telecommunications code system operators;

— Class XXV: installation, alteration or replacement of satellite antennae etc. on buildings and other structures;

— Class XXVI: Mineral exploitation;

— Class XXVII: Removal of material from mineral-working deposits;

— Class XXVIII: Warehouses;

— Class XXIX: Amusement parks;

— Class XXX: Development by the Historic Building and Monuments Commission for England.

Town and Country Planning General Development Order 1977 -1987

Permitted Development: Dwelling Houses

The original classes of permitted development are revised from time to time and the latest General and Special Development Orders should be checked for amendments. Currently, allowances now include:

— All houses other than terrace houses may be enlarged by 70 m^3 or 15% whichever is the greater.

— Terrace houses may be enlarged by 50 m^3 or 10% whichever is the greater.

Both these are subject to a maximum of 115 m^3.

With regard to dwelling houses, there are limits imposed on the amount of ground which may be covered by new development. Only one half of the ground may be covered, and the heights of extensions are limited to 4 m where they are within 2 m of the boundary. This height restriction does not apply to roof and roof window alterations.

New garages and coach-houses within 5 m of the house will count towards the additional cubic content.

There are special limits of permitted development in National Parks (qv), AONBs (qv) and Conservation Areas (qv) which are more restrictive. Currently, additions may be 50 m^3 or 10%, whichever is the greater, to a maximum of of 115 m^3, but the ground covered must not exceed 50% of the free site. The erection of a garage, stable, loosebox, coach-house etc within the curtilage is treated as an enlargement to the dwelling. Height restrictions are also imposed.

Once a dwelling has been enlarged to the full extent of the permitted development, no further extension can take place unless planning permission is sought, otherwise buildings could go on being enlarged indefinitely. Check whether the limits of permitted development have already been reached before starting on extensions or enlargements. ie if there has been any "permitted development" since 1981 it will, almost inevitably, be necessary to apply for planning permission for any further enlargement.

As the General Development Order is amended at frequent intervals, the architect should check with the local planning authority that he is conversant with the latest amendments.
Town and Country Planning General Development (Amendment) Order 1981

Permitted Development: Industrial Buildings

Planning permission is not required for a factory or warehouse if the extension does not exceed 1000 m^2 or 25% of the volume of the existing building. The new extension should not be higher than the original one.

If the factory or warehouse is in a conservation area (qv), national park (qv), area of outstanding natural beauty (qv), or the Norfolk Broads, currently the extension must not exceed 500 m^2 or 10% of the volume of the existing building. It is now permissible to change the use of the building from industrial to warehousing and the other way round, as long as the area to be changed does not exceed 235 m^2.

Other typical changes of use which are permitted are from a general industrial building to a light industrial building, from a hot food shop, pet shop or shop used for selling motor vehicles to an ordinary shop.

Adjacent or continuous buildings, for example a row of terrace units, with different uses but forming part of a single business can change uses without seeking planning permission.

If in doubt, the advice of the local planning authority should be sought before submitting a planning application.

Town and Country Planning General Development and Use Classes Orders 1972 onwards

Planning Appeals

Appeals against planning decisions may only be made by the applicant within six months of the refusal of planning consent. Objectors to the project have no right of appeal, though they may make representations to the local planning authority before any decisions are taken.

The 1987 amendment to the General Development Order requires specific documentation to accompany a notice of appeal to the Secretary of State. Appeals made under Section 36 of the 1971 Town and Country Planning Act must give notice to the Secretary of State on the required form available for English sites from the DoE office at Bristol and for Welsh sites from the Welsh Office at Cardiff.

Appeals may also be made against;

— failure to give a planning decision;
— enforcement notices;
— planning conditions;
— advertisement control.

Appeals are heard by Inspectors appointed by the Secretary of State and they may be by means of written representation or by means of a public inquiry if the Inspectorate agrees that the matter is of public concern. Both appellant and objectors have to make a written representation of their case to the Inspector, who may call additional evidence if he thinks fit.

When an appeal is heard by written representation there are new procedures which are carefully programmed with the object of speeding up planning appeals, although the 1987

Regulations do allow the Secretary of State to extend the time limits at his discretion.

When public inquiries are held, the public have a right to attend unless the Secretary of State decides that it is against:

— national interest;
— national security;
— security of premises or property.

Where the architect represents the appellant at a public inquiry he must make himself conversant with the rules governing the procedure for the inquiry and for any agreed site inspections. The whole procedure is lengthy and complicated and if the architect is representing his client he must carry through all procedures correctly, including preparing a proof of evidence (bcd), posting of notices, sending in written statements and so forth before the inquiry. The proceedings at the inquiry itself are subject to rules not unlike those governing formal court procedure and the architect must be prepared for expert cross-examination.

An inspector may now make an order as to costs and to whom those costs are to be paid.

Town and Country Planning Appeals (Determination by Appointed Persons) (Inquiries Procedure) Rules 1974, Planning Inquiries (Attendance of Public) Act 1982, Town and Country Planning (Various Inquiries)(Procedure)(Amendment) Rules 1986, Town and Country Planning (Determination of Appeals by Appointed Persons) Regulations 1986 and Town and Country Planning (Appeals)(Written Representations Procedure) Regulations 1987

Planning Applications Registers

Planning authorities must keep registers of statutory planning applications; these are normally set out in two parts:

Standard Applications for Planning Consent
Each register should give:

— Part I: copy of the application and any application for approval of reserved matters together with plans of the proposed development;
— Part II: a further copy of the applications, together with:
particulars of any directions;
the planning authority's decisions and their dates;

dates and details of any Secretary of State decisions such as appeals and inquiries;
dates of any subsequent approval on reserved matter and so forth.

Notices of proposed development by Crown Authorities
Each register should give:

— the name of the Department and the date of submission of the "notice" together with details of the development;
— a note of any decision made and any agreed conditions;
— the date and outcome of any reference to the Department of the Environment;
— the date and outcome of decisions on detail matters.

The developing Department must warn the authority if any submission is to be kept confidential for security reasons. Each register must contain an index and be kept at the local planning office.
Town and Country Planning General Development Order 1977

Planning Gains

This expression, though fully understood, is officially and more tactfully described as "obligations and benefits which extend beyond the development for which planning permission has been sought". It is often used to describe work carried out by a developer which is not strictly part of his development but which will be of benefit to the community. Planning gains are agreed between the planning authority and the developer; broadly the principle is that if a developer is likely to benefit considerably from planning consent to his proposals, he ought to make some return to the community. Guidance from the Department of the Environment indicates that planning gains must be closely related to the planning submission, and not a separate development; for example, it would be reasonable to request a developer to improve an access road which serves both his project and the neighbouring community, but not to contribute a community building on another site.

Register of Planning Applications

Once they have been made, all planning applications (qv) must be registered by the local planning authority. The register is in two parts as follows:

Part I of the register, which contains applications for approval, must have copies of every application and of any application for the approval of reserved matters. In either case any drawings sent with the application must be attached.

Part II of the register must contain a copy of every application and the plans attached to it, any decision made, the date of the decision and the name of the local authority. If the application has been the subject of an appeal this part of the register must contain details of any decision and the date at which it was taken.

Entries in both parts of the register must be made within 14 days of an application or decision. Both parts of the register must be available for inspection by the public at all reasonable times, and it is worth while checking the register for the result of previous applications for the site before preparing a new one, as the previous planning decisions and conditions, including Section 52 agreements (qv) may bear on the project.

Town and Country Planning Act 1971 and General Development Orders 1977 to 1987

Reserved Matters within Planning Permission

If an application has been made to the local planning authority for outline planning permission (qv), they reserve the right to give planning permission (qv) subject to the list of "reserved matters" appended being satisfied.

These reserved matters are defined as siting, design, external appearance, means of access and landscaping of the site. However the reserved matters appended to a specific application must be matters relevant to the proposed building and its site, and be for detailed information not given with the application.

If the local planning authority considers that it is not possible to make a decision without consideration being given to the reserved matters they can give notice to this effect within one month of the receipt of the application, and the applicant then has to give the detailed information requested. It is not unknown for compliance with reserved matters to be so costly as to make the development uneconomic, and usually the planning authority will be willing to discuss their standards of landscaping and so forth before the reserved matters are actually dealt with. However it is unwise to rely entirely on this approach, and the reserved matters should be limited as far as possible in order to avoid revisions or additions to the project.

Town and Country Planning General Development Orders 1977 to 1987

Retrospective Planning Permission

Where a client has carried out development which requires planning permission but has failed to apply for it, the local planning authority will either ask for an application to be submitted for the work already done, or they will serve an enforcement notice (qv). When the authority grant permission for existing work they may impose conditions which are difficult to comply with, and it is usually at this stage that the architect is called in to advise how best to overcome the problems.

If on the other hand an enforcement notice is served, this will contain the steps that the local planning authority expect the building owner to take in order to remedy the breach of regulations. The really unlucky client may be ordered to demolish the development, though he has the right of appeal. No compensation is payable in these circumstances.

Town and Country Planning Act 1971

"Section 52 Agreements"

The local planning authority may enter into an agreement with a landowner restricting or regulating the development or use of a piece of land. This agreement may be permanent or for the time stated in the agreement.

Section 52 Agreements are restrictive in nature and they can go with the land, and can therefore be passed on to the next owner of that land. Before carrying out any work on an existing building the architect should enquire whether a Section 52 Agreement is in force, as it may well make void the development which the client wishes to carry out. When obtaining planning permission for a project, a Section 52 Agreement can be made with the planning authority as a

planning condition and while this will enable the development to go ahead, it could inhibit any future ideas that the
client may have for his site.
Town and Country Planning Act 1971

Sight Lines

Sight lines giving a safe view of traffic at the junction of an
access road or driveway with a highway are usually set by
the local planning authority, and are determined when the
planning application is submitted. The highways authority
may be consulted if the access is onto a major road, but there
is normally a standard local layout and boundary height for
domestic accesses onto minor roads.

Check the requirements at an early stage of the site design,
as the splay may cut into the site frontage to a considerable
extent if the site is on a bend or near a road junction. If the
road is likely to be widened in the future, the highway or
local authority may ask for provision to be made for longer
sight lines to suit the new carriageway.
Highways Act 1980

Site Notices

If any proposed development is defined as a "bad neighbour" (qv) development, the local planning authority must
require the owner or his agent to post a notice for not less
than seven days during the month immediately preceding
the application for planning permission.

The notice must be written in the form given in Schedule 3
of the General Development Order 1977, and displayed
where it is easily visible to the public without going on the
site. The normal procedure is to place the form in an
inverted sturdy plastic bag and nail it to a post or tree.
Although the owner or agent cannot be held responsible if
the notice is vandalised, or removed, he is expected to make
it tough enough to stand up to inclement weather.
Town and Country Planning General Development Order 1977

Special Control Areas

These are areas designated by the local planning authority
where the use of advertisements on buildings (qv) is strictly
controlled. Often no advertisements at all are allowed, and
even advertisements inside buildings are controlled if they

can be seen from outside. These areas are usually conservation areas or unspoilt rural areas. It is worth while checking
if a proposed development is in an area of special control if
advertisements are likely to form part of the design.
Town and Country Planning Act 1971

Statutory Undertakers

These are defined in the Building Act as "persons authorised
by an enactment or statutory order to construct, work or
carry on a railway, canal, inland navigation, dock harbour,
tramway, gas, electricity, water or other public undertaking".
Much of the development carried out by them is covered by
Planning (Permitted Development) Classes XIV to XXI and
includes improving of land abutting highways, laying drains,
water supply pipes and repairing them, the construction of
buildings to house plant etc. Statutory undertakers (bcd)
may also carry out accommodation works (bcd) to provide
accesses, bridges, and so forth for the benefit of adjoining
owners.
The procedure to be followed by them in opening up streets
is set out in the Public Utilities Street Works Act 1945. This
sets out the procedure to be followed when undertakers
propose to open the streets; they must give details to the
highway authority or in the case of private streets (qv) they
must give details to the person managing them.
*Public Utilities Street Act 1945, Building Act 1984 and General
Development Orders 1977 to 1987*

Stop Notices

If the local planning authority have served an enforcement
notice (qv) in respect of a breach of planning conditions, and
no action has been taken by the owner, they may serve a
stop notice before the enforcement notice takes effect.
When the local planning authority considers it essential to
halt an unlawful activity to land, they have the authority to
serve a stop notice as well as an enforcement notice.
This notice must refer to the enforcement notice, and takes
immediate effect; the intention is to prevent the owner (or
contractor) getting to a point where the enforcement notice
cannot be complied with.

If the enforcement notice is subsequently withdrawn, the owner is entitled to claim for compensation against the planning authority. Registers of stop notices must be kept by the local planning authority.

The architect should endeavour to make sure that all planning conditions are complied with, so that neither enforcement nor stop notices are served.

Town and Country Planning Act 1971 and Town and Country Planning (Amendment) Act 1977

Street Lamps

The local authority is entitled to fix street lamps to buildings, but they do need the owner's consent before doing so. As these could have an adverse effect on the elevations of the building, the architect should endevour to agree a position with the authority. When dealing with listed buildings the architect will appreciate that as it is an offence to alter a listed building unless there is listed building consent, the design and position of such street lamps becomes a delicate matter.

Public Health Act 1961

Urban Development Corporations

The Secretary of State is empowered to set up Urban Development Corporations, which are similar to New Town Development Corporations. They are not intended to be permanent replacements for the local authorities, but to act as catalysts to accelerate development in special areas. They have powers to take over:

— housing;
— planning;
— development control.

They may be given additional powers such as:

— building control;
— public health;
— fire precautions.

They may act as full scale housing authorities for the time being. The full extent of their powers is not always explicit; the architect who has a project in one of these areas should

check the division of control over development between the Corporation and the local authority in order not to fall foul of one side or the other or - most probably - both.
Local Government Planning and Land Act 1980

Use Classes

Use Classes are classifications of buildings, and in certain circumstances the land around them, which enable the planning authority to control their use. The object is to ensure that new development or changes of use are compatible within a given area and with the policies of the development plans (qv). Where a building and the land attached to it was used for the same purpose and it is proposed to change the use of both to another use within that class, it may be changed without obtaining planning permission.

The use classes were completely reorganised by the 1987 Use Classes Order and the 1972 Use Classes Order and its amendments are revoked. There are now sixteen classes grouped into four parts:

Part A covers shops, financial and professional services and food and drink;

Part B covers business, industrial processes and storage and distribution;

Part C covers hotels and hostels, residential institutions and dwelling houses;

Part D covers non-residential institutions, assembly and leisure activities.

Each part contains two or more classes. No class allows for the manufacture, processing, storage or use of a notifiable quantity of a hazardous substance. There is also no class listed to include a theatre, an amusement arcade, a taxi or car-hire business, a scrap yard, a yard for the storage or distribution of minerals or a car-breaker.

The object of this new order is to reduce the number of classes, whilst retaining control over changes of use that have environmental consequences and to ensure that each class is broad enough to accept changes which do not normally need to be the subject of specific control.

When the architect is commissioned to design or convert a building he must check if the project is permitted development (qv) and if not, consult the planning authority to ascertain whether the proposals come within the acceptable use classes.

Town and Country Planning (Use Classes) Order 1987

Use Classes: List in Alphabetical Order

Assembly and Leisure Class D2:
Formerly contained in Classes XVII and XVIII. The new class now includes Cinemas, Concert Halls, Bingo Halls, Casinos, Dance Halls, Swimming Baths, Skating Rinks, Gymnasia or areas for other indoor or outdoor sports or recreations not involving motorized vehicles or firearms.

Business Class B1:
This was partly contained in the former Classes II and III. The new class includes offices (except those used for professional and financial services serving the public), research and development of products and processes, any industrial process, as long as these businesses can be carried out in a residential area without causing detriment to its amenity. This class should open up a useful opportunity to integrate housing with certain office businesses and light industry, so creating a more balanced community.

Dwelling Houses Class C3:
This is a new class not contained in the 1972 Order. It covers use as a dwelling house, whether as the main home or not, and which is used by people living as a family unit; or by not more than six people living together as a single household -this last category includes any household where care is provided for residents.

Financial and Professional Services Class A2:
A new class, although it does include parts of the former Classes I and II. These are services provided for the public, not private offices, and include financial services, professional services (but not health or medical services). Also in this class are any other services, including betting shops, which are suitable for shopping areas.

Food and Drink Class A3:
Another new class which covers the sale of food or drink consumed on the premises. It does not cover hot food ''carry-outs'' or ''take-aways''.

Hotels and Hostels Class C1:
Not unlike the former Class XI, except that it does not cover any premises providing a significant amount of care for the residents. The class includes hotels, boarding houses, hostels and guest houses.

Industrial processes: General Class B2:
Similar to the former Class IV, it covers industrial processes which are not covered in Class B1 or B3 to B7.

Industrial processes: Special Group A Class B3:
Similar to the former Class V and covers any work registerable under Alkali Works Etc Regulations Act 1906. It excludes any processes within Classes B4 to B7.

Industrial processes: Special Group B Class B4:
Similar to the former Class VI. This class lists six metal-working processes which cover both large and small works. It also includes the process of recovering metals from scrap or waste, unless the work is part of quarrying or mining operations.

Industrial processes: Special Group C Class B5:
Similar to the former Class VII. It lists seven processes including burning bricks, pipes, lime or dolomite; the production of zinc oxide, cement or alumina; and the production of carbonated or hydrated lime, unless the process is part of quarrying or mining operations.

Industrial processes: Special Group D Class B6:
Similar to the former Class VIII. It lists ten processes ranging from distilling, refining and blending oils (not petroleum), boiling linseed oil, stoving enamelled ware and the production of rubber from scrap to producing or using cellulose or other pressure-sprayed metal finishes.

Industrial processes: Special Group E Class B7:
Similar to the former IX. Lists some 26 trades, all of which are noxious, including blood and bone boiling, fat melting and extracting, fellmongering and making manure from animal and vegetable products.

Non-residential Institutions Class D1:
Similar to the former Classes XIII, XV and XVI. It includes any of the following which do not have a residential use; provision of medical and health services; a creche, day nursery or day centre; schools; art galleries; museums;

public libraries; public halls and exhibition halls; churches and other religious buildings.

Residential Institutions Class C2:
Formerly Classes XII and XIV. Covers the provision of residential accommodation for those in need of care except for those falling within Class C3); hospitals; nursing homes; residential schools; colleges and training centres.

Shops Class A1:
Some but not all of these categories are listed in the former Class I. Includes shops (other than hot food shops); post offices; travel agencies; cold food ''carry-outs'' or ''take-aways''; hairdressing; display of goods for sale; hire shops for domestic or personal goods; cleaners and undertakers.

Storage or Distribution Class B8:
Formerly Class X except that it now includes the use of open land for storage and distribution centres.
Town and Country Planning (Use Classes) Order 1987

Use Classes: Outline Definitions

The 1987 Use Classes Order lists the following definitions which should help the architect to decide in which class the proposed development may fall. These definitions have been somewhat simplified from the original Order.

Care
is defined as the personal care required by people who are elderly or disabled, or have or who have had a dependance on alcohol or drugs, or who have or have had a mental disorder. In class C2 it includes the personal care of children and medical care of treatment;

Day Centre
is defined as premises which are visited during the day and provide care as well as re-habilitation or occupational training, social or recreational facilities;

Hazardous Substances and Notifiable Quantities
are as defined in the Notification of Installations Handling Hazardous Substance Regulations 1982;

Industrial process
is defined as a process incidental to any of the following, in the course of any trade or business other than agriculture, mining or quarrying:

a) making of any article or part of an article (including a ship or a vessel, a film, video or sound recording);

b) altering, repairing, maintaining, ornamenting, finishing, cleaning, washing, packing, canning, adapting for sale, breaking up or demolishing an article;

c) getting, dressing or treatment of minerals.

Town and Country Planning (Use Classes) Order 1987

Compulsory Purchase

Introduction

Although this is not strictly the concern of the traditional architectural practice, it may affect the architect when he works in conjunction with a developer or a design-and-build organisation. Under normal circumstances the architect will only be involved on the fringe of any compulsory purchase proceedings, as for example, preparing evidence for his client to submit to the local authority or to the Lands Tribunal (qv).

The Compulsory Purchase Act 1965 is the main act dealing with this subject and it is supported by numerous rules and regulations which also cover compensation. It is a complex subject normally dealt with by the client's lawyer, but the architect will find it useful to have a basic understanding of the principles involved.

Certificate of Appropriate Alternative Development

Where a compulsory purchase order is made on:

— land or buildings which are not provided for in the Development Plan (qv), or

— are scheduled for any development other than residential, commercial, or industrial;

then the owner may apply to the local planning authority for a certificate of appropriate alternative development. The application for this certificate sets out the type of development which the owner, or the architect as his agent, considers to be appropriate for the area. Applications may include the development of land not belonging to the client if it would result in a more advantageous scheme; there is no bar to putting forward imaginative or unusual proposals since land of this type is often "white land" for which the planning authority has no specific use.

If the local planning authority concurs with the proposals it may issue the certificate for the stated development, or it may issue a certificate for development of their choice. The development stated in the certificate is then the basis of compensation of compulsory purchase of the land.

Land Compensation Act 1961 and subsequent Government orders and regulations

Compensation for Compulsory Purchase

The architect's client will be deeply interested in this subject, and the architect may be involved with any negotiations and almost certainly with the preparation of plans and surveys to be used as the basis for compensation claims.

Compensation for compulsory purchase is based on three elements:

— the value of the land;
— severance and devaluation of remaining parcels of land;
— disturbance to the business.

The Lands Tribunal (qv) are the authority for assessing compensation for all compulsory land acquisitions and when calculating compensation the value of the land is assumed to be that of any development that is specified in a development plan (qv) for that area. If there is no development plan provision the owner may apply to the local authority for a Certificate of Alternative Development (qv). Compensation takes no account of increases or decreases of the value of the land which would occur if the local authority's project were carried out; for example if the land currently contains warehouses and is shown in the development plan as housing, then the value will be that of the warehouses and not that of the housing. (The Pointe Gourde decision 1947).

Compulsory Purchase Act 1965 and Land Compensation Acts 1961 and 1973

Compulsory Purchase Powers

Compulsory purchase powers must be used within three years from the date that the order becomes operative. Acts under which compulsory purchase can be made include:

- the Acquisition of Land Act 1981
- the Town and Country Planning Acts;
- the Water Acts;
- the Housing Acts;
- the Pipe Lines Act 1962;
- the Post Office Act 1969;
- most statutory undertakings and various bodies such as the Housing Corporation have limited compulsory purchase powers to enable them to carry out their functions effectively.

The Secretary of State for the Environment may acquire "any land necessary for the public service"; this includes rights over easements (qv). He may also authorise county or London borough councils to acquire listed buildings (qv) which are in need of repair together with the contiguous land.

There are many other compulsory purchase powers vested in bodies such as the Ministry of Defence and the airport operators, and the architect will need to keep in touch with local developments on this subject.

When the purchasing authority only want to purchase part of the property, the owner may require the authority to buy the whole lot. Owners can require the local authority to purchase their land if it becomes subject to planning blight (qv) or if it becomes no longer viable because of adverse planning decisions. This latter point is not easy to prove.

A parish or community council may ask the district council to compulsorily purchase land for "authorised purposes" if they are unable to obtain it by agreement.

All private rights over land are extinguished when the land is compulsorily purchased, but public rights of way (qv) can only be extinguished by the Secretary of State.

Compulsory Purchase Act 1965, Town and Country Planning Act 1971 and Housing and Planning Act 1986

Lands Tribunal

This is the national body set up under the Act to adjudicate on the questions of compensation (qv) and compulsory purchase (qv) of land under the Town and Country Planning Acts and similar legislation. The Lands Tribunal has power to discharge a restrictive covenant (qv) and where the client wishes to do so, he must apply to the Lands Tribunal.

Compensation is based largely upon assumptions as to the planning future of the land and the surrounding areas, but the rules governing compensation are extremely complex, and the level of compensation is not easily predictable. The architect should therefore not try to forecast his client's awards.

Lands Tribunal Act 1949 and Law of Property Acts 1925 and 1969

Highways

Introduction

The law of the highway is based on many ancient statutes, and complaints about "purprestures" (encroachments on the highway) were as prevalent in Stow's Elizabethan London as they are now in England and Wales.

The architect should acquaint himself with the basic knowledge of highway law, as any project is invariably involved with access from the highway, boundaries and building lines as well as planting or conserving trees.

The legal definition of footpaths, bridleways, walkways and so forth can be important when it comes to public rights of access near or even through buildings, and the architect should be able to keep his client well informed on any highways regulations relevant to the project.

Highways and their Like

Footway

This is defined as a way comprised in a highway which also comprises a carriageway and over which the public have a right of way on foot only. The more common term used by architects and laymen alike is pavement, but in the Highways Act it is always referred to as the footway.

Street

A street includes any highway and any road, lane, footpath, square, court alley or passage whether a thoroughfare or not. It includes any part of a street. (The Building Act 1984 includes highways over a bridge)

Private Street

A street that is not maintainable by the highway or local authority. Under the private street works code the authority may make up a private street (qv) and apportion part of the cost to the fronting owners. Private street works expenses are a charge on the premises. If new buildings are erected in a private street the local authority require a sum to be deposited that will meet the cost of street works. The conditions under which the private street works code are operated are complicated.

Footpath

This is defined as being a highway, which is not a footway, and over which the public have a right of way on foot only.

Bridleway

This is defined as a highway over which the public have a right of way on foot, on horseback or leading a horse. The Countryside Act 1968 gives cyclists the right to ride over bridleways, but the highways authority do not have to upkeep a public right of way to cycling standards. Cyclists must give way to pedestrians and horsemen.

Carriageway

Carriageways are highways or part of a highway over which the public have a right of way for the passage of vehicles. It does not include a cycle track.

Cycletrack

This is a highway or part of a highway over which the public have a right of way on pedal cycles. It may also include a right of way on foot, but it does not allow the use of motorised cycles.

Walkways

A walkway is a way over, through or under a building. They are made by an agreement between the owner and the local highway authority; their use can be the subject of local byelaws and other regulations. There are statutory requirements for their safety and maintenance, including temporary closure and works by statutory undertakers. Notice is required if the building owner intends to stop off the walkway.

Walkways Regulations 1973, Walkways (Amendment) Regulations 1974 and Highways Act 1980

Access to Premises: Stopping Up

There is a procedure whereby the Secretaries of State or the local highways authorities may stop up an access to premises.

It is quite a complex procedure requiring owners and occupiers to be notified, notices to be published in the press, and time allowed for hearing all objections etc. If the procedure goes through, the relevant authorities will serve a notice on the owner and occupier. This situation is most likely to arise when road improvements are proposed, for example, making a dual carriageway road out of a single road. It is worth checking whether any such road improvements are imminent before designing the access to the project.

Stopping up of Access to Premises (Procedure) Regulations 1971

Barbed Wire Fences

It is an offence to have a fence made of or containing barbed wire next to a highway where it is in a position likely to be injurious to animals or people lawfully using the highway. The highways authority or the local authority may serve a notice on the occupier requiring them to remove the barbed wire within one to six months of serving the notice.

Highways Act 1980

Building Lines

The local planning authority specify the line beyond which no part of a building or other structure may project. This line is normally parallel to the highway, but as one of its main objects is to ensure satisfactory sight lines (qv) it may obviously reduce any development on a corner or road junction. An early consultation on building lines (bcd) with the planning authority is advisable as the exact position of the line may be varied at their discretion.

Building Materials Delivered on Highways

Any contractor wishing to have building material or rubbish deposited in the street temporarily must obtain the consent of the highway or local authority before doing so. These materials must be properly lit during the hours of darkness. The requirement to obtain consent also applies to making temporary excavations in the highway, but in this case the excavations must be properly fenced as well as lit, in the approved manner. This is the contractor's responsibility, but it is sensible to draw his attention to any breach of the

regulations (preferably in writing) since liability for fatal accidents is a serious matter.
Highways Act 1980

Constructions Over Highways

A licence must be obtained from the highway authority before constructing a bridge or any building over any part of a highway (qv). The licence will contain conditions which have to be adhered to, and will most likely specify the minimum height clearance under any part of the construction, and the type of lighting required. The licence conditions also allows the authority to make the owner remove or alter the bridge in order to comply with road improvements at any future date. Road improvements can obviously upset the original design, and the architect is advised to check whether there are any road improvements planned for the foreseeable future.
Highways Act 1980

Damage to Road Surfaces

It is an offence to mix mortar, concrete, cement or any material liable to stick to the surface of the highway directly on the road surface. Mixing boards or bankers may be used as long as they do not mark the road or allow the run-off to block drains or sewers. It is also inadvisable to allow any material to obstruct the gutters; since the authorities can charge for digging up, clearing and reinstating the blocked length of drain; a penalty which has been known to cost nearly half the contract sum on a small job.
Highways Act 1980

Discharges onto Highways

It is an offence to allow water to run off a roof or any other part of a building on to pedestrians using the highway, or as far as is practicable to allow surface water to flow onto or over the footway (qv).
The highways authority or the local authority may serve a notice on an occupier requiring them to deal with the matter within 28 days by constructing and maintaining channels, gutters downpipes, etc. It is also an offence for the owner or occupier of any land adjoining a public highway to allow soil

or refuse to fall onto the street and allow it to block any sewer or gulley.

This is not likely to happen with a completed building, but the architect should keep an eye on water and site material falling onto the road during construction.

Highways Act 1980

Doors Opening onto the Street

Doors opening out onto a street (see Highway) are not allowed unless both the highway and local authorities have given their consent. These consents usually concern public buildings which have emergency exits with gates or bars leading onto a street. Remember to get these consents if the project include this type of exit.

Highways Act 1980

Fires near Highways

It is an offence to light a fire on or near a highway which could, from smoke or any other nuisance, cause injury to the users of the highway, or to endanger or even to interrupt their safe passage on the highway. This could apply to demolition and site fires. If fires have to be lit near a highway advice should be sought from the local authority.

Highways (Amendment) Act 1986

Hedges and Trees

The owner or occupier of a property may be required to cut, prune, or pleach a hedge; or prune or lop a tree, which is damaging a carriageway. But no requirement can make the owner cut or prune a hedge before the 30 September or after 1 April: ie outside the dormant season. A further section restricts the planting of trees in or near a made-up carriageway (qv), or within 15 ft of the centre of that carriageway. If trees are planted in these illegal positions the highway authority or local authority may require the owner or occupier of the land to remove the offending trees within 21 days.

Where a hedge, tree, shrub or any other kind of vegetation obstructs vehicles or pedestrians, blocks the driver's view, or obscures a lamp, on any public road or footpath (qv); then the local authority may make the owner lop, cut or otherwise deal with the offending vegetation within 14 days.

(See also Tree Preservation Orders and Trees in Conservation Areas)
Highways Act 1980

Noise Insulation from Highways

The highway authorities have a duty to carry out insulation or make grants where the noise level from traffic is, or is likely to be, above the stated levels. There is a complicated table of distances from the highway related to noise levels which sets the eligibilty of the affected property. Buildings may also be insulated against construction noise during highway working if it is proved that the noise level seriously affects the enjoyment of the building.

The only buildings likely to benefit are existing dwellings and other residential buildings not more than 300 m from the nearest point of the highway. Exceptions include buildings subject to compulsory purchase (qv), closing, or demolition orders (qv), buildings first occupied after the "relevant date" for the highway construction.

There are very detailed specifications for the sound insulation work set out in the regulations and the architect must follow these in order that the work may qualify for the grant.
Noise Insulation Regulations 1975

Parking: Goods Vehicles

Procedures have recently been laid down whereby the local authority may control the parking of vehicles in areas used for loading and unloading goods vehicles. Before this can be done, the local authority must seek permission to do so from the owner and occupier of the loading area, and put press notices in the local paper so that any objections may be considered. If this hurdle is passed, the local authority serve an official notice on the owner, and the authority then put up the necessary signs in the loading area to control parking. The area then becomes a "controlled parking area".
Control of Parking in Goods Vehicle Loading Areas Orders (Procedure) (England and Wales) Regulations 1986

Private Streets

Private streets are streets that are not highways maintainable at public expense. There is a Private Street Works Code which allows for the execution of street works in private streets anywhere in England and Wales. Where a private street is not up to a satisfactory standard, the streets works authority have power to carry out essential work, and the cost of that work is apportioned between the premises fronting onto that street. Street works are defined as works required for:

— sewering;
— levelling;
— paving;
— metalling;
— flagging;
— channelling;
— making good of a street;
— proper provision of lighting.

Outside Greater London the county councils are the streets works authorities; within Greater London these are the London Boroughs, and in the City the, Common Council. *Highways Act 1980*

Projections over the Street

The highway or local authority may serve a notice on an occupier of a building requiring him to remove or alter any porch, shed, projecting window, step, signpost, sign bracket, show board, window shutter, wall, gate, fence, or any other conceivable obstruction which has been put up in front of a building so as to cause an obstruction. They may also serve a notice on any decrepit part of a building likely to fall onto somebody's head or vehicle. *Highways Act 1980*

Public Footpaths

A public footpath or bridleway (qv) can be closed or diverted by means of an application by the owner or occupier. The relevant authority may be the highways authority, the local authority or any other controlling body. The closing or diversion order is subject to confirmation by the Secretary of State. The authority must satisfy themselves that the alteration is in the interest of the applicant or in the interest of the public, and the owner or occupier may be required to contribute towards the cost.

Where the architect has been asked to deal with alternative routes for a public path he must apply to the highway authority or district council on behalf of his client for a diversion order.

Public Path Orders and Extinguishment of Public Right of Way Orders Regulations 1983

Retaining Walls

Where a retaining wall is to be built;

— on or within four yards of the street and;
— any part of it is more than 4ft 6in above the ground at street level;

plans, sections and a specification for the proposed wall must be approved by the local authority, and where applicable the highway authority, before work is started.

If an existing retaining wall of this type is in bad repair and likely to endanger the public, the local authority may serve a notice on the owner or occupier requiring them to carry out remedial work. Where the retaining wall is next to a street maintained by a London Borough plans must be submitted to them.

Highways Act 1980

Road Humps

There are strict regulations for the dimensions, position and frequency of road humps on public roads, this includes their relationship to road junctions and bends. They must also be lit and signposted and can only be used where there are speed restrictions.

As humps are often used on private roads it is advisable to consult these regulations before preparing working details, as compliance with the designs reduces the chances of any actions for damages. Sectional prefabricated road humps are available. Where bus routes or specific vehicles are involved the firms controlling them should be consulted.

Highways (Road Humps) Regulations 1986

Stiles and Gates

Any owner who has a footpath (qv) or bridleway (qv) across his land must maintain any stile, gate or similar structure in a safe condition. As this obviously includes kissing-gates, it

is understandable that they should be kept in such a condition as not to interfere with the rights of users.
Highways Act 1980

Yards and Passages

The local authority can compel an owner to pave any court, yard, or passage which gives common access to classes of buildings in order to provide proper drainage of the surface. Buildings subject to this requirement are;

— houses;
— industrial buildings;
— commercial buildings.

This applies to courts etc that are not public highways. It is also illegal to reduce or close an entrance to a court or yard serving two or more houses (in such a way as to reduce the ventilation) without the consent of the local authority
Building Act 1984

Site Appraisal

Introduction

This is an enormous subject, and one which the architect is well advised to spend a considerable time studying for each individual project. This chapter deals with the legal reminders on a few of the numerous factors which the architect should bear in mind when appraising individual or alternative sites. The client may have employed a lawyer to check many of the items discussed in this chapter at an earlier stage, and it is essential that the information obtained should be passed on to the architect so that he may interpret any findings in the light of his design proposals.

It is all too easy to place a proposed building thoughtfully on the site plan giving due consideration to aspect, prospect and so forth, and then find that it is sitting neatly over a thirty inch public sewer. A pristine urban site plan should always be treated with suspicion, and the architect should check with the water and other statutory undertakers what services exist underground. Even in rural areas gas and oil pipelines have a nasty habit of clipping chunks of land off an otherwise adequate site.

Abatement Notices

The local authority may serve an abatement notice on the person responsible for a statutory nuisance (qv), or if he cannot be found, on the owner or occupier of the premises. Any nuisance which deals with the structural condition of the building must be served on the owner. If the owner or occupier is not responsible for the nuisance, the local authority may abate the nuisance itself. The notice normally sets out the work necessary for abating the nuisance.

Noise from a building which amounts to a nuisance may be the subject of an abatement notice. Areas may also be designated as noise abatement zones. Noise control (qv) is dealt with elsewhere.

The architect should check that any building he is altering is not the subject of any abatement notices. Even if the building is due to be demolished, an abatement notice may be served on the premises.

Public Health Act 1936 and Control of Pollution Act 1974

Access from the Highway

Neither the Planning or Highways Authority have a duty to check that any proposed development has a right of way from the public highway over private land onto the site. Thus there can be just a narrow strip of land between the site and a public highway that can cause a serious hiccup in getting the development underway. If there is any doubt where the nearest public highway is, check with the highways authority, as they have to keep a list of them. Once this has been ascertained, a Local Land Register (qv) search will inform the client if the land beside the roadway is the responsibility of the highways authority or not.

If an easement (qv) is required, the architect should satisfy himself that the terms allow his client and his sucessors to have right of access. If it is intended to change the use over the land from - for example - domestic traffic to heavy commercial traffic, the easement may not be valid.

Highways Act 1980 plus case law

Badgers

Badgers are very strictly protected, and if the site contains an inhabited badger sett which is close to the proposed development, the architect will have to proceed with caution. Planning permission (qv) may be refused, or the development curtailed, if there is no way to protect the sett from interference or no alternative accommodation available for the badgers. This also applies to their territory and tracks, as they do not easily change their traditional patterns of life. It is also illegal to dig up the setts or to injure or even to disturb the badgers in any way, and the fines are very severe. It is advisable to consult the local Badger Society branch as early as possible.

If it is agreed that there is no alternative to killing the badgers if development is to proceed, a permit will have to be

obtained from the Ministry of Agriculture Fisheries and
Food to have the badgers trapped or gassed.
Badgers Act 1973

Bats

Bats of all species are heavily protected under the Wildlife
and Countryside Act and its statutory instruments. In
addition to protection in all other types of buildings, bats
enjoy the freedom to live in a house as long as they are not
actually resident in the living areas. Their winter and
summer roosts are protected, and if the owner insists on
getting rid of them, the Nature Conservancy Council must
be informed before any action is taken. The Nature
Conservancy Council will state what if any measures may
be taken; this could even mean that the owner is not
permitted to destroy or expel the bats. Fines for destruction
or disturbance of bats are severe.
Wildlife and Countryside Act 1981

Boundaries

The precise positions of boundaries are normally defined in
the title deeds and shown on an accompanying plan, and the
ownership of a fence or hedge is indicated by a "T" mark.
The Land Registry bases its plans on the ordnance survey
maps; as these invariably show any boundary lines down the
middle of a feature, this is not very helpful to the client or
his architect who is trying to determine the exact position of
a boundary. If a boundary has been moved over by the
adjoining owner, without any payment or other acknowledg-
ment being made to the rightful owner, the "squatter" may
be able to claim that land when he has remained in adverse
possession (bcd) for twelve years or, in certain cases, for a
longer period.
Where the site is bounded by a public road, the site
ownership extends to the centre of the road, but this does
not include the road-base or surface. In the case of a railway,
the land belongs to the railway.
Determining the boundary which consists of a hedge or fence
is difficult, but as a general rule where hedges exist on a
boundary line the owner of each half must maintain and
repair his own half, doing so in any way he likes. By
convention, where the hedge has a ditch both belong to the

same owner; the boundary line is taken to be the far side of the ditch from the hedge. Where a fence is made up of posts and wire or panel infill, the fence is assumed to belong to the "post-side" owner.

If the boundary is formed by a non-tidal river or stream, then the boundary is assumed to be down the centre of the watercourse.

The whole area of legislation surrounding boundaries is a highly contentious one and too often leads to litigation. The architect is strongly advised to check the ownership and rights attached to any site boundary with the client's lawyer before any work proceeds.

Builder's Skips

These regulations require a builder's skip, any part of which is placed on any part of the highway except a footway or verge, to be fitted with the prescribed "heavy vehicle" type markings; these plates are to be fitted as near to the edge of the skip as possible. All plates are to be kept clean and clearly visible to highway users. The plates are to comply with BS AU 152:1970 "Rear Marking Plates for Vehicles".

The owner of the skip (the person from whom the skip is hired) is responsible for complying with these regulations. He is also responsible for obtaining a licence for the skip from the local council.

Builder's Skips (Marking) Regulations 1984

Building and Improvement Lines

The highway authority may lay down a building line for one or both sides of a public highway. These lines are registered as a Local Land Charge (qv), and where they are in force no construction except a boundary wall or fence is allowed. The highway authority may revoke part or all of a building line which is no longer relevant. Building lines should be checked with the planning authority at an early stage of the project, since the position of the adjoining property will not be reliable as a guide if highway alterations are proposed, or have taken place since the original line was laid down.

Highways Act 1980

Building Surveys

This is often part of the service which architects perform for clients looking for a suitable property to buy or lease. If a general survey is done, based on inspection of those parts of the building to which the architect has ready access, then the report made to the client should make this absolutely clear, otherwise the architect may be held negligent (qv) for unseen defects. The architect should then ask his client if he wishes to go to the expense of having parts of the building opened up for inspection; for example breaking into roofs which do not contain traps and checking around "dry areas" in old buildings. This is particularly important if he suspects dry rot behind panelling, rising damp, beetle in the roof etc.

If the architect does take on this task, and is brought to book for negligence, he will be judged by the standard of a "reasonably competent" surveyor and not as an architect.

Mostly case law

Coal Mining Areas

Before starting on any development in coal mining areas the architect should check with British Coal what past, current, and future workings are listed for the area. Applications to inspect coal-working plans and any further information on the subject should be addressed to the local Area Surveyor at British Coal's area office. Under the Coal Industry Act 1975 the coal authority had a statutory right to "withdraw support from the surface"; they must give three months notice of withdrawal and publicise their intentions in the London Gazette and in the local press, as well as posting notices on the site and serving a copy on the local planning authority. The notice must contain a either map or grid references. Before a building owner starts work on his site he must notify British Coal of his proposals and if requested, he must submit drawings showing details of the foundations; British Coal have a right to inspect foundations before backfilling. They may pay compensation for damage or may make good with the owner's consent. It is important to find out what the authority's proposals are as regards disused workings.

Coal Industry Act 1975

Contributory Negligence

If the injuries sustained in the course of a site visit or inspection are caused partly by the architect's own carelessness, then the courts will allow him damages only to the amount due to the other party's culpability. There is considerable difficulty in apportioning blame for negligence; the best answer is to check that all site safety precautions are being properly carried out (including hard hats, eye and hearing protection), and to be careful when on site or on survey.

Law Reform (Contributory Negligence) Act 1945

Covenants

The covenants do not always run with the land, but where they do, and a piece of land is sold or changes hands, then the covenant (bcd) stays with the land and anyone wishing to develop that land must normally abide by it. Most covenants are restrictive (qv) in nature, and all should be entered in the Land Charges Register (qv). Some of the most common covenants are attached to housing estates which are on land previously held by a single owner, they can for example restrict the height of buildings and the type of fence to be used on boundaries.

Exceptions occur where land is the subject of compulsory purchase (qv) and covenants are overridden if it is the public interest to do so. The Lands Tribunal (qv) is empowered to cancel covenants and to award compensation in certain circumstances.

Law of Property Acts 1925 and 1969

Discharge of Restrictive Covenants

As areas change in use and character some restrictive covenants (qv) become outdated as far as their benefit to the owners of the adjoining land are concerned, or they may conflict with planning policy. In this case it is possible to have them discharged by the Lands Tribunal (qv) if the Tribunal is satisfied that the covenants are genuinely obsolete and of no value to the person entitled to benefit.

When checking the existence of restrictive covenants with the client's lawyer at the start of the project, remember to ask if the client wishes to discharge any of them, as the procedure could take some time, and the Tribunal's decision cannot be foreseen. The client's lawyer may not always appreciate the effect of a restrictive covenant on the design.

Restrictive covenants may also be discharged by agreement between the parties concerned.

Law of Property Acts 1925 and 1969

Easements

An easement must benefit the land and not an individual, and concerns;

—   the land for the benefit of which the right is excercised, referred to as the "dominant tenement";

—   the land over which the right is exercised, referred to as the "servient tenement".

An easement (bcd) gives the holder a right to make use of land adjacent to his site, for example, when he has a right of way (qv), a right to light (qv), or a right to support (qv). If the building is part of an estate there may well be easements allowing rights to use roads, drains and so forth in common with other building owners on the estate. These rights go with the land and are passed on to successive owners.

There can be no right of view, privacy, or general flow of air, or to have a property protected from the weather. So if a design makes use of an adjacent building to give privacy and shelter there is no right to have these privileges replaced if that building is demolished.

The existence of easements can be checked through the Land Charges Register (qv), or the deeds of the property or land. Not all easements have to be registered; legal easements are subject to registration but equitable easements are not.

Although the client's lawyer is usually responsible for checking these easements, it is sensible for the architect to ensure that he has been told everything relevant to the project, since it is not always apparent to the layman what effect an easement may have on the design. (See also bcd Prescription).

Law of Property Act 1925

Established Use Certificates

An owner or occupier who wishes to establish the use class of his property may apply to the planning authority for an established use certificate. The property must:

— have had a particular use before 1 January 1964 and have always since had that use and;
— have been begun and used without planning permission or;
— have been used in breach of planning conditions or;
— the use class has not changed to one requiring planning permission.

A property with a certificate cannot be served with an enforcement notice (qv) on the matter of use class.

The rules governing the established use certificates are complicated, and certificates cannot be granted for land used for a single dwellinghouse. The architect should check if an established use certificate has been given for the existing use.
Town and Country Planning Act 1971

Information Available to the Public

Recent legislation has made it mandatory for local authorities, and in some cases, police, fire and authorities, to provide more information on local government and similar matters. These authorities have also to provide easier access for the public to council and committee meetings at the authority's office.

Agendas and minutes must be made available and can normally be seen in the local authority's offices or the public library. The local authority must also supply copies of certain documents on request dealing with specific subjects, those likely to interest the architect include matters dealing with town planning, highways and the control of pollution. Obviously some items are excluded from the public domain, and these include:

— personal information on employees, tenants and persons under care;
— financial information on tenders and contracts; legal matters;
— notices being served.

The local authority must also keep a list of its principal officers specifying their duties and powers.

The architect may find that attending typical sessions of committees concerned with planning and building control is a useful way of testing the climate for any projects which he may have in hand.
Local Government (Access to Information) Act 1985, Local

Government Act 1972 and Local Government (Inspection of Documents) (Summary of Rights) Order 1986

Information for the Client

Whilst the architect can check many items, such as planning and building control requirements and the position of services, he must look to his client's lawyer for information to be gleaned from the Land Charges Register, the Local Land Charges Register (qv), the deeds of property and so forth. In particular, he must ask for any information on building lines (qv), tree preservation orders (qv), smoke control areas (qv), rights of light (qv), rights of way (qv), rights of support (qv) and any other restrictive covenants (qv) on the use of the land or buildings that it is proposed to develop.

Once the architect has assimilated this information into a clear site appraisal he must discuss the outcome with his client, who will then decide whether or not to proceed with the proposed development.

Mostly case law

Information from Unauthorised Sources

If an architect accepts information from an ''unauthorised person'', and that information is proved to be wrong, then the architect will be held to be negligent. It is therefore advisable to check the source of any data before acting on it. This applies not only to private sources, but also to informal information obtained from the local authority, which is subsequently found to be incorrect.

Case law

Land Charges Register

The Land Charges Act 1925 introduced a system for registering charges on land and the 1972 Act initiated the present system for unregistered land. The Registers of Her Majesty's Land Registry are the most important documents to search; they may be searched by visiting the offices at Croydon or Plymouth, or by completing the relevant forms and sending them to the Land Registry in London. If the matter is urgent, it is possible to obtain information by telephone or telex. The searches are normally carried out by the client's lawyer and, in all cases, a registration or search fee must be paid.

The Land Charges include such subjects as:

— value of improvements on agricultural land;
— Capital Transfer Tax;
— estate contracts;
— restrictive covenants after 1925;
— equitable easements made after 1925.

Registration of land normally occurs when property changes hands, although it can be done at any time, as compulsory registration is not yet in force. Under the Land Registration Acts, the Registrar is enabled to convert certain leasehold and freehold titles as absolute if the conditions are complied with.

The charges listed are in general those which run with the land, but they may not appear when the title deeds search is being made. Most land is now covered by the Land Registry and a search should be made to see if the land is indeed registered, and whether there are any charges on it. The Local Land Charges Register (qv) held by the local authority is more likely to contain details immediately relevant to the development, and it is wise to make sure that both registers are searched.

Land Charges Act 1972. Land Registration Acts 1925 and 1986 and subsequent Government orders

Local Land Charges Registers

Local land charges run with the land and are binding on the owner and all subsequent owners. The charges are supposed to be recorded in the Local Land Charges Register held by the local authority, but they are not invariably entered, so it is advisable to confirm that the register is up to date. Both private owners and specified public bodies can enter charges in the register, such as rights to light (qv) and tree preservation orders (qv), and a fee is payable for registration and also for searching the register.

Many of these charges will affect the potential for developing a site, and the architect should check that the client is aware of such restrictions. Typical charges entered in the register include:

— private street works code;
— rating surcharges;
— planning charges which place restrictions on the use of the land;
— compensation previously paid;
— new towns charges;
— civil aviation charges;
— listed building charges;
— light obstruction notices;
— drainage scheme charges;
— open cast coal charges;
— Agriculture (Miscellaneous Provisions) Act 1941 charges;
— enforcement notices.

Local Land Charges Act 1975 and subsequent Government orders

Mining Subsidence

British Coal (formerly the National Coal Board) has certain responsibilities with regard to damage caused by mining subsidence to buildings and the area around them, together with all service pipes, and wires. As a rule, they will either execute remedial work themselves, or pay a builder to do the work for them. In either case the building must be made fit for the purpose that it was used for immediately before the damage occurred, including decorations. In the case of dwellings, alternative accommodation must be found for the occupiers whilst the remedial work is carried out. Information is required by British Coal before construction takes place in coal-mining areas (qv).
Coal Mining (Subsidence) Act 1957

Occupier's Liability

Where an architect or for that matter any other person enters a building in order to survey it or carry out an inspection, the occupier is expected to make sure that he will be reasonably safe whilst in the building. This means that the occupier must point out any part of the building that is unsafe, for example a broken tread or handrail to a staircase, rotten floor boards or faulty electrics.

However as in this case the ''visitor'' is assumed to appreciate and guard against certain risks because of his profession or trade, he is expected to be reasonably competent in noting any special hazard connected with his work. One of the authors still has memories of falling through the floorboards of a "tallet". Stepping on a hay-covered floor is risky business!

As far as construction sites are concerned, the person in control has a duty to ensure that all reasonable precautions are taken to prevent risk of injury to visitors or others entering the site; this includes general warning notices and notices to parents, posted on site boundaries.

The duty of an occupier to persons other than his visitors also applies to the Crown (bcd). (See also bcd Occupiers' Liability).

Occupier's Liability Acts 1957 and 1984

Party Walls

As far as Inner London is concerned, Part VI of the London Building Acts (Amendment) Act 1939 still applies to party walls (bcd). They are defined as "a wall which forms part of a building and stands on lands of different owners. Projection of any artificially formed support on which the wall rests onto land of any adjoining owner does not make the wall a party wall...[and]...any part of any other wall as separates buildings belonging to different owners". There is a complicated sequence of notices to be served whenever one owner wishes to carry out any of the permitted operations on a party wall.

Any works carried out under the provisions of the Act must comply with the following conditions:

— must not cause unnecessary inconvenience to the adjoining owner;

— must protect the adjoining owner's property during the works;

— must comply with the Building Acts and Building Regulations;

— must be carried out in accordance with plans agreed with the adjoining owner.

The architect who encounters a party wall problem is advised to apply to the RICS who will put him in touch with surveyors specialising in party wall arbitration and who are prepared to act as "third surveyor".

All party wall law is based on common law, and in general these walls are assumed to be divided down the middle between adjoining owners. Each owner has the right to support from the other, and if one owner removes his structure he must waterproof the exposed section of the party wall. If an owner intends to build an extension on a party wall the structure must only bear on his half of the wall. There are rules governing the proportion of costs to be borne by each owner.

Any architect working on Inner London projects should make himself familiar with party wall law, as it is one of the most fruitful sources of litigation.

London Building Acts (Amendment) Act 1939

Pipe Lines and Transmission Lines

In this instance, pipe lines means a pipe, or a system of pipes, together with any apparatus and works associated with them for the conveyance of anything other than air, water, water vapour or steam. Amongst other exclusions, drains and sewers are not counted as pipe lines. Before cross-country or local pipe lines can be laid, authorisation must be obtained from the Secretary of State and once a specific route has been agreed, no deviations are allowed without further consent.

Certain pipe lines are considered a security risk and maps showing their position are not available to the public. However if the architect thinks that there are pipe lines of this category on or near his site, he may apply to the planning authority for information.

Overhead power transmission lines have an easement (qv) to cross land, and they also require a strip of land to be kept clear of any obstruction on each side of the line itself. Where overhead lines are on or near any proposed development the architect should check with the Central Electricity Generating Board what clearances are required; these vary according to the voltage and height of transmission lines.

Pipe Lines Act 1962 and Petroleum Act 1987

Prohibition Notices

The local authority may issue a "prohibition notice" to prevent the recurrence of a statutory nuisance (qv). It will normally state the work to be carried out in order to clear the matter up. Prohibition notices may be served if no action has been taken on an abatement notice (qv), but it may also

be served on its own or in conjunction with an abatement notice.
Public Health Act 1936 and Public Health (Recurring Nuisances) Act 1969

Protected Plants

It is an offence intentionally to pick, uproot or destroy protected plants. These are listed in schedule 8 of the Act, and cover thirty or so plants ranging from the Least Lettuce, through to the Greater Yellow Rattle. If the architect has been warned that some of these plants are on his client's site, he would be advised to contact the local Natural History Society for further information as to the action that may be taken.
Wildlife and Countryside Act 1981

Public Nuisance

Where a dangerous activity is carried out near a highway it may amount to a public nuisance (bcd). As, for example, where a piece of equipment projected over the highway and caused injury to a person walking along the pavement the court found for the pedestrian against the owner. If however the projection over the highway is the branch of a tree that fell onto a pedestrian this does not constitute a public nuisance unless the owner should have known or knew the branch to be rotten.

If the architect is asked to survey property that the client intends to buy, he should take note of any dangerous or overhanging projections onto the highway, and tell the client.
Case law; the tort of Public Nuisance

Quasi-easements

Quasi-easements cover the right of an owner over part of his own land which would be an easement (qv) if the land were divided and in different ownership. This situation often arises where there is a large garden with a coach house at the end in which the owner keeps his car, and drives across his own land to get to the road. If the coach house is subsequently sold off, the new owner takes on the quasi-easement of the original owner and this will then become a full easement, and should be registered as a land charge (qv).

Conversely, easements are extinguished where two plots of land are acquired by one owner-occupier.
Law of Property Act 1925

Rats and Mice

The Local Authority have a duty to keep their area free from rats and mice, so if the client's historic building which is being restored, or the agri-businessman's barn which is being converted, is inhabited by a "substantial number" of these rodents, the the Local Authority must be informed. Agricultural and horticultural buildings are exempt since they are presumably expected to contain rats and mice.

The Local Authority will issue an order requiring the destruction of the pests, and they may give instructions as to the methods and poisons to be used for extermination. If the Local Authority require structural work to be carried out to make the extermination possible or to prevent re-infestation, it is permissible to appeal to a magistrate against the notice, but otherwise the owner must comply.

If the occupier or owner does not comply within the specified time, the Local Authority can carry out the extermination themselves and recover the cost of the work from them. In the case of food premises which suffer from food infestation (qv), the Ministry of Agriculture, Fisheries and Food have powers similar to those of the local authority. This covers buildings used for food storage, processing, and preparation as well as restaurants and food shops, and also buildings where food containers are handled. The MAFF normally uses poison control for extermination, and it is important to ensure that local wildlife and domestic animals are not put at risk.

Although mice and rats usually leave the premises as soon as building work begins (even if the building is not sinking) it would be sensible to inform the local authority, in order to avoid complaints and possible claims for damage from adjoining owners. If the building workforce leaves waste food about, vermin will soon infest the site, and the contractor should make proper arrangements for waste food disposal.
Prevention of Damage by Pests Act 1949

Restrictive Covenants

These normally go with the land, and restrict the owner in the use and enjoyment of his land; they can, for instance, limit the density of housing or the height of a building. These covenants may also require plans of proposed developments to be submitted to the ground landlord or other covenantee. If a restrictive covenant (bcd) is breached, the court may grant an injunction requiring demolition of the offending building; neglect to check the covenants could be disastrous. These covenants should have been entered as a charge on the land in the Land Charges Register (qv) or the Local Land Charges Register (qv) and they should also have been included in the title deeds to the property, though none of these sources is totally reliable. The client's lawyer should be asked to provide all the relevant information on restrictive covenants as early as possible, as they may be so restrictive as to make the project impracticable or uneconomic.

Mostly case law

Right of Light

Since 1959 it has been possible for an owner of property to register a notice prohibiting the adjoining owners the right of access and use of light. The notices are lodged in the local Land Charges Register (qv). This system saves the owner erecting a screen in order to exercise his rights, and has the added advantage of preventing a local eye-sore.

If no such notice has been lodged, the owner of an adjoining building has the right to a general amount of light necessary for normal purposes, this does not include the extra lighting requirements for, for example a studio or drawing office. The architect should remember that the local planning authority has no duty to check on right of light (bcd), and that they could pass plans that contravene those rights, so a search of the Land Charges Register is advisable.

Rights of Light Act 1959

Right of Support

This right is usually established as an easement (qv) and entitles an owner to have his building supported by the property of the adjoining owner. Should the adjoining owner remove his building, he must continue to support the owner's building, although he is not required to waterproof the dividing wall or to keep it in good repair. However there are regulations governing the demolition (qv) of buildings, and the local authority can compel the adjoining owner to waterproof and support the dividing wall. The authority also has powers to deal with dangerous buildings (qv) and to serve repairs notices on premises, so that the owner is not likely to be left out in the cold. Before relying on the adjoining owner's property for support, the architect must check the legal position with his client's lawyer and, if necessary, ask him to obtain an easement for right of support.

Law of Property Act 1925

Right of Way

If the site to be developed is "land locked", it will be necessary to check if an easement (qv) is required. The architect should satisfy himself that the terms of any existing right of way (bcd) allow his client and his successors to have right of access at all times, and that any details such as maintenance and security are compatible with the proposed development. If it is intended to change the use (see Use Classes) over the land from - for example - domestic traffic to heavy commercial traffic, the easement may well not be valid.

The Local Land Charges (qv) register should provide the client with most of the details, although it is not infallible.

Land Registration Act 1925 and Land Charges Act 1972

Tree Roots and Buildings

Any of the following trees are liable to cause damage to adjoining buildings. Studies have shown that damage is likely to be caused where the soil contains shrinkable clay and buildings are placed closer than:

— poplar, elm, oak, willow: min. distance 20 m
— horse-chestnut, ash, sycamore, maple: 15 m
— beech, lime, plane, robinia: 11 m
— birch, hawthorn, rowan: 10 m

Before the architect decides that the best policy would be to remove any offending trees, he should remember two things;

— firstly, that the tree may have a tree preservation order (qv) on it;

— secondly, that the removal of the tree could cause clay heave and resultant cracking of adjoining buildings. This is because the water that would have been taken up by the tree stays in the ground.

The blame for damage to the client's existing property or that of the adjoining owners could well rest with the architect.

Wildlife Protection

The Wildlife and Countryside Act lists 39 species of animals and insects which are protected, and the list can be varied from time to time. (See also protected plants, badgers, bats.) The species are not necessarily in remote country areas, but may be found in suburban or new town districts. In most cases it is the habitat of the creature which requires protection, so that the destruction of scrub, ponds, ditches and meadowland may have serious consequences. Wildlife conservation is an emotive subject, and the architect would be well advised to check with the local Natural History Society or the Nature Conservancy Council if there is any reason to suspect that the site may contain rare species. Substantial fines are imposed for destroying the habitat of a protected species, and the court is entitled to confiscate any car, boat or other equipment used in the process of destruction.

Wildlife and Countyside Act 1981

Public Health

Introduction

A picture of frock-coated officials inspecting model lodging houses in glazed brown brick crosses the architect's mind when he sees the words "Public Health". The law covered in this chapter is nevertheless one of the most important sections of public legislation, since it deals with all aspects of water supply, sewerage, drains, effluent, and waste disposal. The original Victorian regulations on basic sanitation have been supplemented by the major 1936 Public Health Act which extends the scope of health control into most fields of local authority activity, while later laws deal more fully with particular aspects of public health. Amongst other matters, the Control of Pollution Act 1974 deals with noise and water pollution, the Clean Air Act 1956 deals with air pollution and smoke emission, the Water Act 1973 transferred the control of water and sewerage to a single authority, the Water Authority, and the Building Act 1984 provides for further control over health requirements in buildings and dangerous buildings.

Most of the architect's responsibilities for designing safe and sanitary buildings are set out in the Building Regulations, but other legislation cannot be ignored just because it may seem repetitive and the public health requirements contained in different statutes and regulations are of equal importance and must be complied with.

Cesspools and Septic Tanks

The water authority may compel an owner to repair a leaking cesspool. If this is not possible the authority may at their own expense divert a public sewer so as to serve the premises. The Building Act gives the local authorities

parallel powers to compel owners to repair defective
cesspools or septic tanks. (See also Drains).
Public Health Act 1936 and Building Act 1984

Compensation for Damage by Local Authorities

All authorities carrying out work under the Public Health
Acts are liable to pay compensation for damage caused by
that work, although claims cannot be accepted unless the
authority would have been liable without their statutory
powers; in other words they are treated in the same way as
private citizens in dealing with claims. This also applies to
claims for negligence, and the architect should be aware of
the authorities' obligations in this respect.
Public Health Act 1936 and subsequent legislation

Culverts

If the architect is dealing with a site transversed by ditches,
the water authority may direct that they shall be culverted.
On the other hand it is not permissible to culvert a water
course without the permission of the authority. If this work
is done the architect would be well advised to produce his
own plan showing for record purposes their position on the
site.
Public Health Act 1936

Drains

The local authority has powers to require drains, private
sewers, waste pipes, water-closets and soil pipes which have
become blocked up or defective to be cleared or repaired.
Defective services are liable to a seven day notice from the
authority, whilst stopped-up services, for obvious reasons,
are under a 48 hour notice. Notices can also be sent to the
owner or occupier whose premises are served by a blocked
sewer. The architect may be faced with this situation when
working on existing property connected to a public sewer.
Public Health Act 1961 and subsequent statutes

Drains and Sanitary Fittings

The Building Act 1984 gives the local authority powers to
enforce repairs to any part of a defective drainage system,
or to a drainage system in an existing building if it does not

comply with the Building Regulations. The drainage system includes:

— cesspools (qv);
— private sewer;
— drain;
— soilpipe;
— rainwater pipe, or spout;
— sink or other necessary appliance.

Disused drains must be properly stopped off. 24 hour's notice must be given to the local authority before starting work on drains or cesspools, except in an emergency; in the case of drains being stopped off 48 hours' notice is required. The local authority can also demand that extra WCs should be installed in a building if they consider that the existing ones are inadequate or defective.
Building Act 1984

Food Infestation

If any building which is used for food storage is found to be infested with pests (rats and mice (qv) are different) then the owner or his agent must give notice to the Ministry of Agriculture, Food and Fisheries. When it is proposed to employ a firm to de-infest the area, their name and the intended methods of de-infestation must be given. The chemicals used for this work are fairly powerful, so the architect should assure himself that all precautions against injury to people and wildlife have been taken. (See also Wildlife Protection).
Prevention of Damage by Pests (Infestation of Food) Regulations 1950

Fumigation of Buildings

If a building has to be fumigated, the architect should satisfy himself that the contractor follows the procedure laid down and takes all due precautions to ensure that people or animals are not inadvertently exterminated. The fumigator must give notice to the local authority medical officer and to the police; the building must be completely sealed, all fires, naked lights and electricity shut down and large notices posted. Special fire precautions are required and dwelling houses must be ventilated for at least 24 hours after fumigation. A clearance certificate must be given by the fumigator to the occupier after fumigation. If foodstuffs are to be fumigated a special foodstuffs fumigation certificate is required.

Remember that bats (qv) are protected animals, and if they are present in the building special precautions will have to be taken. The Health and Safety Executive have taken over the powers of the Secretary of State with regard to the regulations. The responsibility for the fumigation of buildings in London lies with the London Boroughs.

Hydrogen Cyanide (Fumigation of Buildings) Regulations 1951

Hazardous Substances

Certain substances are defined as being hazardous, and architects concerned with buildings where these products are held should bear in mind that the Health and Safety Executive must be notified if any amount above the stated minimum is on the premises. The Health and Safety Executive will make conditions as to their handling, storage and transport. The substances most likely to be met in the building industry are bottled gas and large quantities of flammable liquids.

If in doubt consult the local Health and Safety Executive office and discuss the type and amount of hazardous substances which the client expects to hold on the premises. (See also Flammable Liquids and Flammable Gases).

The Housing and Planning Act 1986 contains 41 pages of conditions and procedures for dealing with large quantities of hazardous substances which are stored on open land. It lists the maximum quantities to be stored and the authorities who are regarded as Hazardous Substances Authorities. If the architect has or is likely to have hazardous substances on his client's site, he should leave the management of this strictly alone and refer the client to the relevant Hazardous Substances Authority.

Notification of Installations Handling Hazardous Substances Regulations 1982 and Housing and Planning Act 1986

Petrol Tanks

The disposal of derelict petrol tanks is the responsibility of the owner, and the local authority can compel him to deal with them in order to protect the public. They will also advise on specialist tank removers who will supply a gas free certificate once removal is completed.

Public Health Act 1961

Refuse Collection from Houses

The local authority collecting house refuse may, by making byelaws, require an owner or occupier to provide dustbins of an approved type, and they may prescribe where they are to be put for collection. There have been many disputes over what is house refuse and what is trade waste (qv), the latter can be construed to include large quantities of waste paper, so architects beware! They get more free advertising literature through their letterboxes than any other profession and much of it swells the house refuse collection. The local authority have the right to charge for any refuse other than agreed household refuse. The courts have found that the refuse from holiday sites with chalets and caravans and hostels is not considered to be house refuse. The local authority has a duty to remove house refuse in any manner they think fit, unless the dwelling is too isolated or inaccessible.

Public Health Act 1936 and case law

Sewers

In the Building Act 1984, the term sewer covers drains and sewers serving more than one building and their yards; however, in the Public Health Act the term sewer covers all sewers and drains used for the drainage of buildings and yards; they may be either a public or a private responsibility. The following substances may not be discharged into a sewer:

— those injurious to health;
— those likely to damage the sewers or upset the treatment plant;
— chemical refuse;
— calcium carbide;
— petroleum spirit;
— waste steam;
— liquids over 110 degrees F which are injurious when hot.

The architect should confirm that discharges into sewers are not liable to cause damage.
Public Health Act 1936 and Building Act 1984

Sewers: Private

The owner or occupier has a right to have drains or private sewers connected to the public sewer except where the discharge is considered to be trade effluent (qv).
If a developer provides a private sewerage system the water authority may require it to fit into their general sewerage system and the authority will pay any additional costs incurred by compliance with their requirements. When doing large drainage layouts, it is sensible to discuss the system with the water authority at an early stage.
Public Health Act 1936

Sewers: Public

The water authority has the power to construct public sewers on any land without exercising compulsory purchase (qv) powers. There is no right of appeal against entry, though compensation may be payable. This then has the effect of an easement over the land.
The water authority has a duty to provide public sewers for domestic premises if their conditions are met.
The water authority has a duty to keep maps of their sewers and the architect should check the maps and ensure that he has full information on all buried services, as any maintenance on them will obviously involve disruption of the overlying land. These maps are the basis on which permission for building over sewers (qv) is decided.
If the water authority provides a public sewer which is used by the owners fronting onto the road in which the sewer is laid, they are then entitled to claim a proportion of the cost of construction or maintenance from the owners in certain circumstances. The amount will depend on the additional value conferred on the properties by the construction or maintenance of the sewer.
Public Health Act 1936

Statutory Nuisances

A local authority is obliged to abate a statutory nuisance by serving an abatement notice or a prohibition notice.

Statutory nuisances include; premises in such a state as to be prejudicial to health or a nuisance (bcd);

— an animal kept in such a place or manner as to be prejudicial to health or a nuisance;
— an accumulation or deposit which is prejudicial to health or a nuisance;
— dust or effluvia caused by any trade, business, manufacture or process and injurious, or likely to cause injury to the public health, or a nuisance;
— a workplace, which is not provided with sufficient means of ventilation, or in which sufficient ventilation is not maintained, or which is not kept clean, or not kept free from noxious effluvia, or which is so overcrowded while work is carried on as to be prejudicial to the health of those employed therein;
— domestic water storage tanks constructed or kept in such a way that the water can become contaminated;
— a foul, choked or silted watercourse which is prejudicial to health or a nuisance;
— a tent, van, shed etc. used for habitation which is overcrowded or has insufficient sanitary accommodation so as to be a nuisance or prejudicial to health;
— open quarries or shafts that could be dangerous to the public, particularly children;
— smoke causing a nuisance.

A statutory nuisance has been defined in law as being a threat to health or a private or public nuisance as understood by common law. An individual may use the courts if he considers that the local authority or any other person is causing a statutory nuisance.

The client whose site adjoins a derelict or insanitary site may wish to invoke these powers.

Public Health Act 1936

Trade Effluent

Consent must be obtained from the water authority, before any "trade effluent" is discharged into a public sewer. Where trade effluent is to be discharged, notice must be given to the water authority giving details of:

— the place;
— nature of discharge;

— maximum temperature;
— maximum quantity discharged daily, and maximum rate.

The authority will then give its consent with or without conditions. If the water authority intend to charge for the effluent, they are also entitled to meter the discharge. Trade effluent is defined as a liquid with or without particles of matter in suspension produced in the course of trade or industry. This includes farms and horticultural premises and any premises used for scientific research; it does not include domestic sewage.

It is advisable to check with the local authority before discharging waste from any building other than a dwelling This would include such building types as health centres and laundrettes.

Control of Pollution (Discharge into Sewers) Regulations 1976

Trade Waste

The architect should check with the local authority what arrangements, if any, they have for collecting trade waste; if they do provide such a service they may make a charge and state the conditions under which the refuse will be collected. This could have a significant effect on the layout of service areas, as the authority may require waste to be separated. If they require bulk refuse collectors such as Paladins, these are large, need good ventilation, and the refuse vehicles need room to manoeuvre.

Public Health Act 1936

Unoccupied Buildings

Unoccupied buildings and sites are always at risk from vandalism and from fly-tipping of refuse. The local authority has powers to protect such sites against unauthorised entry and risks to public health; they can take immediate action if they think the premises are dangerous, and recover the costs from the owner.

If the architect has a project on a site adjoining unoccupied property, he should ask the local authority to take steps to protect that property.

Local Government (Miscellaneous Provisions) Act 1982

Waste

The definitions of waste vary according to the governing legislation; these definitions are taken from the Control of Pollution Act 1974:

— household waste is from dwellings, residential homes, universities and schools;
— industrial waste is from factories coming under the Factories Act 1961 and the Nationalised Industries;
— commercial waste is from premises used for trade or occupation; sport, recreation and entertainment.

The architect should enquire of the local authority their classification of the waste arising from his client's project, since the type of waste will affect the storage method and cost of disposal (see also Trade Waste and Waste from Construction Sites).
Control of Pollution Act 1974

Water Authorities

Under the Water Act of 1973 water authorities are responsible for:

— water supply and fittings (qv);
— sewers (qv) and sewerage;
— sewage treatment and disposal;
— land drainage;
— pollution of rivers and streams (qv), prevention and monitoring;
— recreation on inland waterways except canals which are dealt with by the British Waterways Board;
— reservoirs.

Under the Building Act 1984, the local authority can enforce the provision of a wholesome water supply.
Water Act 1973

Water Supply and Fittings

Water authorities have the power to lay their water mains in, on, or over any land after giving reasonable notice to all the owners and occupiers of the land. Water authorities are obliged to provide water to new domestic buildings, but in some cases part of the cost may be charged to the building owner. In the case of non-domestic buildings there is no duty to provide a supply if this would endanger other supplies; and it is advisable to confirm that the supply is available and adequate before detailed schemes are produced.

Under the Building Act 1984, the local authority can enforce the provision of a wholesome water supply. If a common water pipe serves two or more houses, single pipes serving each dwelling cannot be demanded unless:

— the supply pipe becomes defective or inadequate;
— the water rates are not paid;
— houses are converted to produce more dwellings;
— the supply is interfered with.

Area water authorities can, and often do make their own byelaws for preventing waste, contamination or misuse of their supply. These bye-laws may include the design, size and materials used in fittings and connections. This may cause problems: when, for example, a doctor requires the handbasin in his consulting room to have taps with a good flow of water for hand-washing, but does not want the outlet designed to take a plug. The designer is then left with the problem of equating the water authority's requirement for a handbasin outlet with a plug to prevent undue water consumption and the doctor's requirement for a plugless fitting on hygienic grounds.

Water authorities may also have strict byelaws on connections to hoses and outside taps generally, and there may be restrictions or extra charges for water used for car-washing, horses, horticulture or similar water uses.

Water Acts 1945 and 1973, Building Act 1984, and other legislation

Wells and Boreholes

If the client wishes to obtain his own water supply by drilling for it on his site, there are certain requirements which must be complied with. Any well or borehole more than 50 ft below ground made in search of water must be notified to the Natural Environment Research Council. A journal of the work must be kept.

Although there is no legal requirement to test the water before tapping an underground water supply, it must be tested by a qualified analyst before it can be used. The architect would be wise to persuade his client to employ a hydrologist to analyse the quality and flow of water. It is illegal to let underground water run to waste, or even to draw off more than is actually required for the project, unless, like the waters at Bath, it cannot be dealt with in any other way.

Water Act 1945 and Science and Technology Act 1965

Building Control

Introduction

Introduction

Building regulations in England and Wales have a long history going back in London at least to the time of Richard I, when in 1189 Henry Fitzalwyne was Mayor of the city. He did a great deal for the city and decreed that "all men in this city should build their houses of stone up to a certain height, and cover them with slate or baked tile". In this way Fitzalwyne improved the fire resisting properties of housing which hitherto was made mainly of timber and thatched with straw or reed.

Since then building regulations have flourished, from the inclusion of minimum distances between the overhanging storeys of buildings over a narrow street, and the need to collect "night soil" from privies (still a duty of the local authority); to the highly sophisticated requirements of the current Building Regulations of 1985. The architect now has the choice of either quietly going along with the conditions set out in the Approved Documents, or of providing unusual design solutions; the latter option does however require a detailed knowledge of building materials and construction, as well as structural and environmental requirements. The building control officer will undoubtedly call for detailed drawings and calculations to support the design.

Before getting involved with any design work, the architect should check whether there are any local requirements over and above the national regulations. The obvious case is that of Inner London, where parts of the London Building Acts 1930 to 1978 still apply, as for example, regulations dealing with party walls.

Less obvious are the County and City Acts listed in this section, all of which have some sections relating to building control. So the reminder here is to check all these points with the local authority before embarking on a project. If the architect proposes a way-out design solution, it is well worth checking the building control officer's reaction to the design, and assessing with him how much additional information his department is likely to require. Where the architect is upgrading a building and has done his best to comply with the few specific requirements for means of escape, resistance to the passage of heat, and access for the disabled, and still finds it impossible to comply, he can apply to the local authority for a relaxation and if this is refused he can then appeal to the Secretary of State.

The Building Regulations themselves are not the only legislation governing building construction; there are other regulations dealing with such matters as retaining walls, projections over highways and industrial chimneys which can trip-up the unwary architect.

Building Control: Definitions

Building
The Building Act 1984 defines a building as "any permanent or temporary building, and........any other structure or erection of whatever kind or nature (whether permanent or temporary)"

Structure
And a structure or erection "includes a vehicle, vessel, hovercraft, aircraft or other movable object of any kind in such circumstances ....that in the opinion of the Secretary of State justify treating it ....as a building". This does make it difficult for the even the most imaginative architect to design a building which can legally escape the requirements of building control.

Construct or Erect
Construct or erect means "the carrying out of such operations (whether for the reconstruction of a building, the roofing over of an open space between walls or buildings, or otherwise) as may be designated in building regulations as operations falling to be treated for those purposes as the construction or erection of a building and the conversion of a moveable object into...... a building".

Erection
Erection includes: "the re-erection of a building or part of a building when an outer wall...... has been pulled down, or

burnt down, to within 10 ft of the surface of the ground adjoining the lowest storey of the building.....''. It also covers the re-erection of a framed building.

House
A house ''means a dwelling house, whether a private dwelling house or not''.

Workplace
A workplace ''does not include a factory, but otherwise it includes any place in which persons are employed otherwise than in domestic service''.
Building Act 1984

Alterations to Deposited Plans

Once plans have been passed by the local authority, any alterations to those plans which affect building control matters must be shown on revised plans and a set deposited with the the local authority before building operations on those alterations are carried out.
Try not to let this happen as it can cause delays.
Building Act 1984

Approved Inspectors

There is provision in the Building Act 1984 for the private client as well as for public bodies to have their work supervised on site by an ''approved inspector''.
Approved inspectors will normally have to apply for registration every five years and they must not have any professional or financial interest in any major project that they supervise; this does not apply to minor works such as dwelling houses. The Secretary of State holds the registers of both approved inspectors and of public bodies who have opted to use self-certification. Local authorities hold copies of these registers.
This subject has been discussed at length in the technical press, and there are as yet very few approved inspectors, as one of the big problems is the insurance that they have to carry.
Building Act 1984 and Building (Approved Inspectors Etc) Regulations 1985

Building Act 1984

This is a consolidating Act and it is the main Act that gives the Secretary of State power to make regulations relating to buildings and the space around them, and to provide practical guidance on the provisions within any building regulations; currently known as the Approved Documents. Failure to comply with the Approved Documents is not an offence, but failure to comply with the Building Regulations is. In other words it gives the Secretary of State power to make building regulations (as future Statutory Instruments) for the purposes of "Securing the health, safety, welfare and convenience of persons in and/or about buildings, or matters connected with buildings. Furthering the conservation of fuel and power. Preventing waste, undue consumption, nuisance or contamination of water in respect of the design and construction of buildings and the provision of services, fittings and equipment in or in connection with buildings". It also gives local authorities in England and Wales, including Inner London, power to pass or reject plans. The Secretary of State has the power to resolve disagreements as to whether plans or proposed works comply with building regulations. The local authority and, on appeal, the Secretary of State have powers to give relaxations (qv) of the regulations in certain cases.

The Act also covers sections dealing with:

— supervision of building work by local authorities;
— supervision of their own work by public bodies;
— provision of drainage, sanitary conveniences, water supply;
— means of escape from fire;
— raising of chimneys;
— cellars and rooms below water level;
— defective premises;
— dangerous buildings;
— paving and drainage of yards and passages;
— maintenance of entrance courtyards;
— demolition;
— power to order testing of materials etc. (qv);
— special provision for Inner London Boroughs, the City and the Temples.

There are seven Schedules including:

— Schedule 1 Building Regulations;

— Schedule 2 Relaxation of Building Regulations;
— Schedule 3 Inner London;
— Schedule 4 Provisions consequential upon a public body's notice.

Regulations apply to new work and any other work that constitutes a material change in buildings. Work approved by the local authority must be commenced within three years, otherwise the approval is void.
Building Act 1984

Building Control Exemptions

Some buildings are exempt from building control: these include:

— some educational buildings (not Inner London) (qv);
— buildings of statutory undertakings (qv);
— United Kingdom Atomic Energy Authority (UKAEA);
— British Airports Authority and Civil Avation Authority.

Houses, hotels and offices, and showrooms belonging to the above, which are not part of their buildings, usually come under the Building Act.
The Act may also exempt local authorities and county councils, or any other bodies that act under an enactment for public purposes. The exact demarcation between construction subject to control and that exempted is a fine one, and the architect should make sure that he knows which is which. The building control department of the local authority should be able to advise on the distinction, but if not, the Department of the Environment may be able to give a ruling.
Building Act 1984

Building Control Fees

Fees are required for the submission of work to the building control section of the local authority.
There are four categories of fees:

— plan fee is payable for passing or rejecting plans deposited with the local authority;
— inspection fee, for inspection of work, with regard to the principal regulations, for which plans have been deposited;

— building notice fee, for inspection of work with regard to the principal regulations, for which a building notice (qv) has been given to the local authority;

— reversion fee, for consideration of plans and inspection of work reverting to local authority control.

It is advisable to check the current scale of fees with the local authority, and explain the situation to the client well in advance of depositing plans.

Building (Prescribed Fees etc) Regulations 1985 and 1987

Building Notice

A building notice is served on the local authority by the person intending to build as an alternative to depositing "full plans". If the building owner opts to have the work supervised by the local authority, he can choose whether to serve a building notice or to submit full plans.

When a building notice is served the work must be supervised (as opposed to inspected) by the local authority or an approved inspector (qv). The statutory contents of a building notice are set out in the Building Regulations 1985, and the local authority can ask for further information, including calculations and specifications.

Where the work involves means of escape in case of fire, and where fire certificates will be required, full plans must be submitted, and must comply with the Mandatory Rules for Means of Escape in case of Fire.

Building Regulations 1985

Building over Sewers

Where the proposed development will be built over a sewer or drain which is shown on the statutory map of sewers held by the water authority, the building control authority must satisfy themselves that the construction is adequate and they may make conditions, including requiring the building owner to enter into an agreement. The local authority must notify the water authority of any proposed works of this type. It is essential to check the map of sewers before starting any major development scheme, since it has been known for the water authority to refuse permission to build over the sewer at all. This is particularly important if work is notified to the local authority by a building notice (qv) as they will then only have small scale plans of the proposal. The local

authority have the power to require alterations or even demolition of the works if they are not satisfied. Inner London procedures for building over sewers may differ.
Building Act 1984 and Building Regulations 1985

Chimneys: Industrial

There are regulations exempting industrial and boilerhouse chimneys from the height restrictions: these include temporary replacements while the existing chimney is being inspected, maintained, repaired or re-built. As some chimney replacements could take a long time, for example a large multi-flue boiler-house chimney built into the fabric of the main building, the architect should confirm that any temporary chimneys are acceptable to the local authority. (See also Furnace Chimneys).
Clean Air (Height of Chimneys)(Exemption) Regulations 1969

City of London and the Inner and Middle Temple

The City of London's earliest charter dates from William I. It contains 25 wards, and retains the right to exercise all the functions of a London Borough.
The Inner Temple and Middle Temple also have separate identities as local government areas, though they share some of these functions with the City of London.
Building control within the City is now in line with the rest of Inner London. The Temples also follow them with the exception of sections 59, 60, 61 which deal with drainage.
The City of London (Various Powers) Act 1987 allows the Corporation to make bye-laws covering both alterations and new work to drainage or connections to sewers, whether in the City or not. Plans and details of the work must be submitted and seven days notice given before work starts.
Building Act 1984, Building (Inner London) Regulations 1985 and City of London (Various Powers) Act 1987

Dangerous Buildings

If the local authority consider that a building, a structure, or part of either, to be in a dangerous condition or to be structurally overloaded, they may apply to a magistrate's court for an order requiring the owner:

— either to rectify the matter, or;
— to demolish the dangerous part of the building and clear away all demolition material.

If the building is overloaded, the local authority may obtain an order restricting the use of the building until the court is satisfied that all necessary work has been carried out. If neither of these orders are complied with the local authority may carry out the work themselves and recover the cost from the owner.

When the local authority consider the building to be in a dangerous condition and requiring immediate action, they have the power to carry out essential work immediately, although they do have to notify the owner or occupier, and they may recover the cost.
Building Act 1984

Defective Premises

If the local authority consider that any premises are in such a defective state as to be a health hazard or a nuisance, they may serve an abatement notice (qv) on the owner listing the defects that must be remedied. If after nine days no action has been taken the local authority may carry out the necessary work on the defective premises (bcd) and recover all reasonable expenses.

The local authority may not serve a notice or carry out any remedial work that contravenes a Building Preservation Order. There is no statutory definition of what constitutes a health hazard or nuisance; presumably the authority usually move on complaints from adjoining owners, and the procedure is most likely to be invoked by an architect dealing with rehabilitation in neglected terrace housing or blocks of flats.
Building Act 1984

Demolition

As a general rule, anyone wishing to demolish a building must notify the local authority. The notice must identify the building and the extent of the demolition work; copies of the notice must also be lodged with adjacent occupiers and the area offices of British Gas and the Electricity Board. Exceptions include: buildings with an overall cubic content of less than 1750 ft^3, or conservatories, greenhouses, sheds or prefabricated garages that form part of a larger building and some agricultural buildings.

Listed buildings which are in a dangerous or dilapidated condition come under the Town and Country Planning Act 1971. If preparations for or actual demolition of a building start without permission the local authority may serve a notice on the owner or other person in control.

A local authority notice may require the person receiving the notice:

— to shore-up, weatherproof, and make good any damage to adjacent buildings;

— to disconnect and seal, or remove a drain or sewer and make good;

— to arrange for the disconnection of gas, electricity and water;

— to remove all demolished material from the site and leave all in a clean and safe condition;

— to control burning on site.

(See also Waste from construction sites)

It is worth making sure that the contractor has sent in a demolition notice before starting work.

Building Act 1984

Demolition Under Streets

Any of the London Boroughs (qv) or the Common Council must give their consent before any work under a street can be carried out; this includes:

— demolishing any works, building, vault, arch or cellar;

— building a wall or preventing access to any existing vault or cellar;

— filling in any vault, cellar or underground room (qv).

The Building Act 1984 defines the meaning of street, which is very comprehensive and includes such areas as courts, alleys and passages, whether a thoroughfare or not. (See also Highways and their like.)

When carrying out surveys of old buildings fronting onto the street, special care should be taken when plotting the

underground boundaries: it has been known for one of the authors to get lost in the maze while searching for old wells.
Greater London Council (General Powers) Act 1986

Flood Defences

The Greater London Council had the power to incorporate any banks, walls and so forth as part of their flood defences within the London Excluded Area. This would now seem to be in the hands of the borough councils who must first serve a notice on the owner, lessee and occupier describing the steps they intend to take in respect of their particular property. (See also Retaining walls.)
Greater London Council (General Powers) Act 1986

Inner London Building Control

For the purposes of building control, Inner London comprises the Inner London Boroughs (qv), the City, the Inner Temple and the Middle Temple. Building Control within Inner London now conforms to the National Building Regulations. There is supplementary legislation covering means of escape, drainage etc. and the architect is advised to check these points with the relevant building control authority. As far as party walls (qv) are concerned, the provisions of Part VI of the London Building Acts (Amendment) Act 1939 still apply.
Building Act 1984, Building (Inner London) Regulations 1985 and 1987

Inner London Boroughs

These comprise the following boroughs listed here together with their main address:
Camden: Town Hall, Euston Road NWI
The City of Westminster: City Hall, Victoria Street SW1
Greenwich: Town Hall, Wellington Street, Woolwich SE18
Hackney: Town Hall, Mare Street, E8
Hammersmith & Fulham: Town Hall, King Street, W6
Islington: Town Hall Upper Street, N1
Kensington & Chelsea (Royal Borough): Town Hall, Hornton Street, W8
Lambeth: Town Hall, Brixton Hill SW2
Lewisham: Town Hall, Catford SE6

Southwark: Town Hall, Peckham Road, SE5
Tower Hamlets: Town Hall, Patriot Square, E2
Wandsworth: Town Hall, Wandsworth SW18
Information from DoE 10.86

Local Acts

The 1984 Building Act requires a copy of any local Act
controlling planning or building operations to be held at the
local authority's offices; these documents must be open for
inspection by the public. The 1984 Act does not impose a
duty on the local authority to ensure that the existence of
these acts is made known to those concerned.

The Berkshire Act has been chosen as a demonstration of
local building legislation additional to national building
control requirements, as it is recent and contains some
interesting clauses. There are many of these local acts; some
are county acts and some deal with specific areas or towns,
and the architect working in a new area should check
whether any of them apply to his project; it is also worth
while checking the local authority's actual requirements
under their act at an early stage.

Typical local Act clauses are:

Parking Places, Safety Requirements
Typical amendment by a local Act to increase the level of
fire precautions. ''Where plans are deposited with districts
for building regulation approval and these plans show that
the work involves the construction extension or alteration of
a building in order to provide parking places for more than
three motor vehicles at a level below 1.2 m below ground or
generally for more than 20 motor vehicles, the council will
reject the plans if after consultation with the fire authority,
and if applicable the licensing authority, they are not
satisfied with:

—   the construction of the vehicular approaches;
—   the means of access for the fire brigade;
—   means of ingress and egress (including the provision
of signs);
—   means of ventilation;
—   safety of electrical, mechanical and heating equipment;
—   the provision of emergency lighting;
—   fire protection, fire alarms, firefighting equipment and
appliances;

— the precautions taken to prevent flammable substances getting into the drains''.

Most of this is common sense and good practice, but the exact level of provision required should be checked with the authority at an early stage.

Chimneys
This is another clause which could affect architects:
''s.22 Power to order alterations to chimneys''. If the magistrate's court have had reported to them a complaint by the district council, and they are satisfied that any gas vapour or fumes from a chimney of a building is or is likely to be injurious to health or a nuisance, they may make an order requiring the owner to raise the chimney to a given height, or by any other means to abate the nuisance. However the remedial work required must not cost more than £600 for a single private dwelling house or £1,800 in any other case.

Local Acts and the Building Act 1984
This is a typical example of the modification of the Building Act by a Local Act, (Berkshire Act s.44): this section refers to an amendment to the Building Act 1984 s.72 (Means of Escape from Fire) in sub-section (6) which requires that district councils shall substitute:
''This section applies to any (Building Act states ''a'') building that exceeds one storey (Building Act states two storeys) in height and in which the floor of any upper storey is more than 4.5 m (the Building Act states 20 ft ie 6.1 m) above the surface of the street or ground on any side of the building and that -
a) is used in whole or in part as a flat or as a tenement dwelling.
b) and c) as Building Act.''

Access for Fire Brigade
''Except where buildings erected or extended were the subject of planning permission granted without a requirement to include such access, the district council will reject plans for buildings or extensions deposited for building control approval if the plans do not show adequate means of access to that building for the fire brigade or the plans disrupt the existing means of access to a neighbouring building.''

Although checking means of access with the fire authority is a normal part of the design process, this Act requires that the fire access should be clearly shown.

Dust on Building Sites
"Dust etc. from building operations. This applies to any building operation including demolition and cleaning works which is carried out in the open air, or which causes dust to be emitted into the open air. It applies to all building work except demolition under the Building Act 1984 s.81. The council may give notice to any person carrying out or controlling the operation, requiring them to take all reasonable steps (having regard to safe working conditions under the Health and Safety at Work Etc. 1974 s.16) to reduce the nuisance within a time specified in the notice".

Fire Precautions in Public or other Buildings
This example shows how a local Act can amend a national building control act. "Where the Building Act 1984 s.71 (Entrances, exits, etc to be required in certain cases) applies for the purposes of preventing injury or danger to persons resorting to any such building the council may after consultation with the fire authorities require the owner or occupier to:

— alter lighting or heating apparatus or fittings;
— alter the arrangement of chairs and seating;
— repair or renew fireplaces, flues, chimney vents etc."

This clause puts more onus on the architect to check the authority's extended requirements with regards to means of escape; it is probably intended to deal with conversions rather than new work, but in either case a written request to the authority for detailed information would be advisable. *Berkshire Act 1986.*

Local Acts Affecting Building Control

This is a list of the local Acts which contain clauses directly relevant to building control; other Acts and other clauses may have an indirect bearing on building design in such matters as refuse disposal, access to highways, or sewage disposal. Obviously, this cannot be a finite list, as new local Acts are made from time to time. Architects should check with their local authority if any local or county acts or byelaws exist.

West Glamorgan Act 1976
Cheshire Act 1980
Merseyside Act 1980
South Yorkshire Act 1980
West Midlands Act 1980
West Yorkshire Act 1980
Avon Act 1981
Derbyshire Act 1981
East Sussex Act 1981
Greater Manchester Act 1981
Isle of Wight Act 1981
Kent Act 1981
Cumbria Act 1982
Humberside Act 1982
Hampshire Act 1983
Staffordshire Act 1983
Lancashire Act 1984
Bournemouth Act 1985
Clywd Act 1985
Essex Act 1985
Leicestershire Act 1985
Poole Act 1985
Surrey Act 1985
Tyne and Wear Act 1985
West Glamorgan Act 1985
London Building Acts 1930 to 1978; although parts of these
acts have been repealed, many sections still apply to Inner
London (qv).
There are other local regulations within local authorities and
the London boroughs: for example, the London Borough of
Croydon has a byelaw dealing with underground rooms.

London Port Authority

Jurisdiction over the London Port Authority is now vested
in the Common Council of the City of London. The City
acts as a local authority for any buildings within the gates of
the Port of London; functions assigned to them include
drains, WCs, nuisances, water supply, defective premises,
handling and sale of food.
London Port Health Authority Order 1965

Means of Escape

In public buildings, the local authority can compel the owner to provide additional or modified entrances, exits and passages to form a satisfactory means of escape. The local authority must consult the fire authority, and they have power to apply to the courts for a closing order until the work has been done if they think that the public is in danger. In buildings over two storeys, where the upper storey floor is more than 20 ft above the ground, the local authority can require provisions for means of escape. The requirements must be within the Fire Precautions Act 1971 and apply to:

— flats and tenements (see also multiple occupancy);
— inns, hotels (qv), boarding-houses, hospitals (qv), nursing homes (qv), boarding-schools, children's homes, and similar institutions;
— restaurants, shops (qv), stores, warehouses; with sleeping accommodation on upper floors for employees.
(See also Fire Certificates under specific building types).
Building Act 1984

Outer London Boroughs

These comprise the following boroughs, here listed with thier main addresses:
Barking & Dagenham: Civic Offices, Dagenham, Essex
Barnet: Town Hall, The Burroughs, Hendon NW4.
Bexley: Civic Offices, Bexley Heath, Kent.
Brent: Town Hall, Forty Lane, Wembley.
Bromley: Town Hall, Bromley Kent.
Croydon: Taberner House, Park Lane, Croydon
Ealing: Town Hall, Ealing W5.
Enfield: Civic Offices, Enfield.
Haringey: Civic Centre, Wood Green, N22.
Havering: Town Hall, Romford, Essex.
Hillingdon: Civic Offices, Uxbridge.
Hounslow: Civic Offices, Lampton Road, Hounslow.
Kingston-upon-Thames(RoyalBorough):Guildhall,Kingston-upon-Thames.
Merton: Town Hall, Broadway, Wimbledon SW19.
Newham: Town Hall, East Ham Road, E6
Redbridge: Town Hall, High Road, Ilford.

Richmond-upon-Thames, Municipal Offices, Twickenham, Middx.
Sutton: Civic Offices, St. Nicholas Way, Sutton, Surrey.
Waltham Forest: Town Hall, Walthamstow, E17.
Information from the DoE Oct 1986

Passing Plans that do not Comply

A "section 36 notice" (qv) may not be given on the grounds that the plans contravene building regulations, if plans were deposited, and passed by the local authority, and the work has been carried out in accordance with those plans. In other words if the local authority failed to notice a contravention of the building regulations on the plans deposited, they cannot call for work to be pulled down or altered. This case also applies where notice of rejection was not given within the relevant period from their deposit.

This section does not affect the right of a local authority, the Attorney General or any other person to apply for an injunction for the removal or the alteration of any work on the ground that it contravenes any regulation or provision in the Building Act. The court then has power on granting an injunction to order the local authority to pay compensation to the owner.
Building Act 1984

Plans for Building Control

The local authority have a duty to pass plans submitted to building control (qv) unless they can be shown to contravene the building regulations; the local authority may then require the plans to be made conformable with the regulations. If the plans are inadequate, the authority may require the plans to be completed satisfactorily.

Where plans are referred to in the Building Act as for example in section 16, they include all drawings showing sections elevations details and so forth as well as specifications or "any other information in any form"; this would include calculations of structural members.

If in any doubt as to what constitutes adequate plans, the architect should consult the building control department; even if this results in too many drawings it is better than

having to revise drawings in a hurry with the risk of mistakes.
Building Act 1984

Rackrent

Refers to a rent that is not less than two-thirds of the rent that a property might reasonably be expected to be let for, from year to year; it allows for deductions for the probable average annual repairs, insurance and other expenses necessary to maintain the property in a state which enables it to be let at the assesed rent. The calculations do not include the tenant's usual rates and taxes.
Building Act 1984

Raising of Chimneys

If a neighbour erects or raises a building to a greater height than an existing adjoining building and:

— any chimney or flue of the existing building is on the party wall or;

— any chimney of the existing building is 6 ft or less from the nearest part of the higher building, then;

— the local authority may serve a notice on the owner of the existing lower property requiring him, if it is at all practicable, to build-up his chimney stalks or flues so that their tops will be the same height as the tops of the neighbouringing higher chimney stalks or the same height as the higher building, whichever is the taller.

The local authority authorises the owner of the heigher building to allow his neighbour to carry out the work.
Building Act 1984

Refuse Facilities

The local authority will reject plans of buildings that do not show satisfactory means of storing refuse (see also Waste) for removal and for satisfactory access from the building to the street for the removal of rubbish. It is an offence to close or obstruct the access from a building to the street for the removal of rubbish without the consent of the local authority. This consent may impose conditions for alternative means of access. The authority have power to say how the refuse (waste) is to be stored, and it is advisable to check the approved containers and storage places with the Cleaning Department. One local council now insists that wheeled bins are used for trade refuse instead of the former plastic sacks; this means that storage space has to be found in existing yards and stores.

Building Act 1984

Relaxations of Building Control

The power to give relaxations is held by the Secretary of State, but under the Building Regulations this power has been delegated to the local authority.

Relaxations may not be given by approved inspectors (qv). If a relaxation is refused, the local authority must notify the applicant that he has the right to appeal to the Secretary of State within one month. Relaxations are usually only granted for the following;

— means of escape in case of fire (which is mandatory and therefore allows the specific requirements to be changed);

— resistance to the passage of heat (again, because specific U-values are given an alternative may be accepted for certain types of building);

— access for the disabled (where specific requirements are indicated and alternatives are put forward).

The architect should consult the local authority at a very early stage if he is likely to require a relaxation, as it is a lengthy process and the outcome is uncertain, particularly where the local authority have to give public notice of the relaxation in the local press.

Building Act 1984 and Building Regulations 1985.

Retaining Walls: Greater London

Approval must be sought from the borough council if a retaining wall is to be constructed within four yards of a street and supports the carriageway or footway maintainable by the authority. Applications must include plans, and sections of the retaining wall together with a specification. The architect should check whether the borough council is the authority for the street or whether it is the highway authority; in the latter case the requirement comes under the

Highways Act 1980, and he should consult the highway authority. (See also Retaining walls.)
Greater London Council (General Powers) Act 1986

Section 36 Notice

Where any work, to which building regulations apply, contravenes any of the regulations, the local authority may serve a section 36 notice on the owner. This notice can also apply to work done without building control approval. The owner must comply with the notice within 28 days, and he may either pull down the offending work, or make such alterations to the building that will enable it to comply.

The notice cannot be served more than twelve months after the contravening work has been completed, and if the local authority have approved plans which contravene the regulations they cannot serve a notice if the work conforms to those plans. This is unlikely to happen to the architect, but he may be consulted on these matters in connection with work that he has not designed.

Building Act 1984

Short-Lived Materials

If plans show that it is proposed to construct, or place or assemble on site a building made of short lived materials, the council may reject the plans regardless of whether they conform to the building regulations or not; alternatively they may impose conditions as to the use of the building and fix a time limit after which it must be removed.

The local authority may not impose conditions that conflict with a grant of planning permission (qv). It is advisable to check the current list of short-lived materials with the building control department.

Building Act 1984

Testing of Soil, Building Materials etc.

The local authority have power to carry out tests on site material including:

— soil and subsoil tests on the site of the building;
— tests on materials and components;
— tests of any service, fitting or equipment that is being or it is proposed to use inconnection with the building.

The local authority may carry out any tests themselves, or have them carried out for them. In either case the developer or person who is required to have the test carried out normally pays; but an application may be made to the local authority requesting them to meet all or part of the cost.

A careful record should be kept on site of all materials taken for testing, as there could be later dissension as to the validity of the test.

Building Act 1984

Time Limit on Deposited Plans

If the local authority have passed plans for a proposed development, and the work has not been carried out within three years from the time they were deposited, the local authority may at any time before the work is commenced declare that the plans are no longer effective. This notice may be served on the original developer or his agent, or upon the current owner of the land.

It is not unknown for an architect to be asked by a developer to take over a project at very short notice; the imminent expiry of the consent may be the reason for haste.

Building Act 1984

Environmental Control

Introduction

A many-tentacled legal organism, environmental control legislation may catch the unwary architect in many unexpected places. It includes the design of fireplaces, reduction in noise levels, and preventing polluting matter from entering any watercourse; the subsequent alterations to buildings or services to meet the various requirements are invariably costly. Most of this legislation is designed to prevent damage to the environment or to the community and the requirements are usually sensible and practicable, but it is as well to be aware of the controls before the specification and design are finalised.

The Acts which most concern building work are the Clean Air Act 1956 and the Control of Pollution Act 1974 and their subsequent amendments and regulations; other controls on environmental damage related to sewers, drains, and water supplies are covered in the public health legislation.

Fireplaces: Approved Appliances

It is an offence to have a non-approved appliance fitted in a smoke control area (qv), but if a fireplace already exists, the local authority may repay the owner or occupier for part of the approved cost of adapting the fireplace to comply with the regulations.

There are thirty or so approved appliances which range from wood-chip fired air heaters to the more traditional enclosed stove. New appliances are added to the approved list from time to time and the architect should consult the Solid Fuel Advisory Service to check the current list.

Clean Air Act 1956 and subsequent orders

Fuel: Authorised Types

If a building is within a smoke control area (qv), it is an offence to emit smoke which is not from an authorised fuel. At present, there are nearly thirty authorised fuels, and the architect should satisfy himself that the fireplace that he is proposing to install is an approved appliance (qv) and that it can burn such fuels. Authorised fuels should be readily available for sale within smoke control areas.
Clean Air Act 1956 and subsequent regulations.

Furnace Chimneys

Furnaces over a certain size must have the height of their chimneys approved by the local authority to ensure that the smoke does not pollute the atmosphere or cause a nuisance. New or upgraded furnaces within this category includes those that burn 100 lbs or more solid fuel, or 1.25 million BTUs per hour liquid or gas or pulverised fuel. If plans and specifications of a new furnace are submitted to the local authority, and are approved by them, then the furnace is deemed to comply with the regulations.
Boiler house chimneys which are within the flight paths of aircraft and over a certain height have to be fitted with warning lights of a pattern approved by the Civil Aviation Authority. (See also Chimneys: Industrial).
Clean Air Acts 1956 and 1968

Intruder Alarms

There is a Code of Practice on Noise from Audible Intruder Alarms dated 1982 and published by HMSO, which sets out the amount of noise that may be emitted by noisy intruder alarms. If any such installation is part of the building work, it is advisable to check that the system complies.
Control of Noise (Code of Practice on Noise from Audible Intruder Alarms) Order 1981.

Noise Abatement Order

If any building within a noise abatement zone (qv) remits noise to a level exceeding those registered for that particular building, then the local authority may serve a "noise abatement order". They may order a reduction in noise from such premises, and it is an offence not to comply. If the

architect is involved with the design of a building housing
noisy processes which is within a noise abatement zone (qv)
he should check the registered noise levels.
Control of Pollution Act 1974

Noise Abatement Zones

The local authority may designate noise abatement zones,
in which certain specified buildings must comply with the
noise levels registered in the noise level register kept by the
local authority. In the case of new buildings within the zone
the local authority may decide an acceptable noise level for
them; noise emissions include that from audible intruder
alarms (qv). The type of premises most likely to be affected
are factories, and their extensions, which are near to
residential areas.
It is advisable to check whether the proposed building comes
within an abatement zone, as this will affect the amount of
sound insulation required and could well increase the cost
of the job.
Control of Pollution Act 1974

Pesticides

There are many regulations which are designed to protect
the environment and govern the use of pesticides; these
apply to watercourses, buildings and other structures. The
regulations cover chemicals used for treating timber against
insect or fungal attack such as dry rot or woodworm. The
architect should ensure that all timber specified has been
treated in accordance with the regulations, and in existing
buildings, that only approved chemicals are used to eradicate
rot or beetle. A timber treatment firm has been heavily fined
for using a chemical which damaged the habitat of a colony
of whiskered bats in a building. (See also Bats)
Food and Environment Protection Act 1985

Pollution of Rivers and Streams

If the client is a riparian owner and the water running
through his land is polluted by untreated sewage from
neighbouring land, he has the right to seek an injunction and
claim damages under the common law of trespass.
Conversely the architect should check any existing drainage
systems on his client's land to ensure that no faecal matter

is discharging into a stream or river. This law applies to local authorities as well as to individuals.

As the discharge will probably be illegal anyway, it would be simpler for a charge to be made under statute law. (See also Pollution of Waterways).

Control of Pollution Act 1974 and Common Law

Pollution of Waterways

Any person, and that includes the designer, contractor and engineer as well as the user, who allows noxious or polluting matter to be thrown into, run off or pour into waterways is liable to prosecution. Waterways in this context includes streams, rivers and coastal waters.

Should the site adjoin a stream or other watercourse the architect should check that none of his contractors use it as a convenient rubbish tip; as there could be charges not only for pollution, but also for the destruction of wild life habitat. (See also Wildlife Protection).

The object is to forestall the pollution of rivers and streams (qv), but if it is necessary to dispose of potentially polluting effluent, the Water Authorities must be approached for consent. The Water Authority also have a duty to keep and maintain registers of all applications.

Control of Pollution Act 1974

Radioactive Waste Pollution

Radioactive waste is dealt with by the Radioactive Substances Act of 1960. If such waste also contains polluting matter, it is also dealt with under the Control of Pollution Act 1974. If the architect has any reason to suppose that discharges from the building or the site have radioactive properties, he should seek advice from the Health and Safety Executive as to its safe disposal. In any case, he should not allow any polluting matter to be discharged in an uncontrolled manner.

Control of Pollution (Radioactive Waste) Regulations 1985

Refuse Collection and Disposal

The collection of house and trade waste is normally carried out by the local authority, and its disposal is either the function of the same authority or of the county council. In the case of ''hazardous waste'' disposal is normally the

function of the county councils: in the former GLC and Metropolitan County Councils areas there are seven special authorities charged with this duty.
Public Health Act 1936 and Local Government Act 1985 and subsequent orders

Smoke Control Areas

The local authority may declare smoke control areas, which have to be confirmed by the Secretary of State. All smoke control orders should be registered in the Land Charges Register (qv). "Authorised fuels" (qv) must be used in these areas, and it is illegal to buy or sell solid fuel of any other type in these areas.
Only authorised appliances (qv) may be used in smoke control areas. Where the architect is involved with buildings such as churches, chapels and charitable premises within designated areas, the local authority may provide a grant towards the cost of adapting existing appliances.
Clean Air Act 1956

Special Waste

The waste material from certain types of premises is regarded as "special waste" and there are strict regulations governing the disposal of such waste. The premises are scheduled in the regulations, and are mainly buildings such as veterinary surgeries, laboratories, and pharmaceutical premises where acids, alkalis, and other hazardous chemicals have to be dealt with; these are listed in Schedule 1.
Radioactive waste is included if it has properties other than radioactivity that make it dangerous. The local authority may require particular arrangements to be made for storing, transporting, and handling special waste pending its disposal; it is unlikely that the water authority will allow any such waste to be discharged directly into their sewers. It is worth checking if the waste from the premises is likely to contain any dangerous ingredients, as any necessary provision for storage or disposal may affect the design.
Control of Pollution (Special Waste) Regulations 1980 and Waste Regulations and Disposal (Authorities) Order 1985

Streams and Ponds: Cleaning

Pollution of waterways (qv) includes vegetable waste from cleaning out or cutting reeds and other riparian vegetation. In this context, "stream" includes a river, a water-course, or inland water except a lake or pond which does not discharge into a stream.

If the client is considering any large-scale cleaning out of a stream bed or clearing vegetation in a stream or pond which discharges into a stream, he must first obtain permission from the water authority (who are most unlikely to refuse their consent) and ensure that all cut vegetation is removed.

Controls of Pollution Act 1974 and subsequent regulations

Health and Safety

Introduction

The responsibilities of the employer for the safety of his staff are widespread and varied. Many of these are covered in the sections relating to the design of workplaces and to safety on construction sites. The general assumption must be that the average architects' office is as safe a working environment as any and that few special precautions are required. There are, however, certain general requirements.

Health and Safety at Work etc Act

The Health and Safety at Work etc. Act 1974 is an enabling act. This means that it provides a general framework for the direction of government policy and permits, within that framework, the introduction of an infinite amount of secondary legislation. This secondary legislation will establish specific requirements for different industries and processes.

The main Act establishes the basic responsibilities of the various participants within the working environment and, most unusually for legislation, spells them out in simple language.

Employer's responsibilities for his employees: ''It shall be the duty of every employer to ensure, so far as is reasonably practicable, the health, safety and welfare at work of all his employees.''

Employer's responsibilities to others: ''It shall be the duty of every employer to conduct his undertaking in such a way as to ensure, so far as is reasonably practicable, that persons not in his employment who may be affected thereby are not thereby exposed to risks to their health or safety.''

Employee's responsibilities: The employee has a general duty to take reasonable care for the health and safety of both himself and others who may be affected by his acts or omissions whilst at work. He must also cooperate with his employer or with anyone else who is empowered to take action over health and safety matters.

A series of free booklets is available from the Health and Safety Commission outlining the basis of the Act:

— Health and Safety at Work etc Act 1974: the Act outlined

— Health and Safety at Work etc Act 1974: advice to the self-employed

— Health and Safety at Work etc Act 1974: advice to employees

— Health and Safety at Work etc Act 1974: advice to employers

— Health and Safety at Work etc Act 1974: your obligations to non-employees.

For further advice on any aspect of health and safety law, contact the local office of the Health and Safety Executive.

Accidents

Any serious accident must be reported to the Health and Safety Executive as soon as possible after the event and a written report must be sent on an approved form within 7 days. A serious accident is one which:

— causes death, including a death resulting from an accident up to 12 months earlier;

— results in a broken bone, other than a foot or finger;

— requires immediate admission to a hospital for more than 24 hours;

— causes incapacity to work for 3 days, excluding the day of the accident but including non-working days.

The report must be made by the employer or, in the case of some one undergoing training including those on YTS etc, by the employer at the organisation offering the training. Any accident affecting any person at the workplace must be reported if it is covered by one of the above. Also covered are road accidents occurring during road maintenance or during construction work on buildings adjacent to or over a road.

Reporting of Injuries, Diseases and Dangerous Occurrences Regulations 1985

Dangerous Occurrences

A number of dangerous occurrences have been specified which, whilst not having to cause injury, must be reported in the same way as injuries. Those most likely to affect architects and architectural practices are:

— collapse of lifting equipment, hoists, cradles etc
— an explosion in a pressure vessel;
— a major electrical short circuit;
— an explosion or fire leading to a stoppage of work for more than 24 hours and caused by the ignition of process materials, process waste products or finished products;
— an escape of a flammable material;
— collapse of scaffolding more than 5 m high;
— accidental collapse of any building or structure undergoing construction, maintenance or demolition and involving the fall of more than 5 tonnes of material;
— collapse of a floor or wall in any workplace;
— accidental contact with an overhead power line.

A number of other occurrences are also specified.
Reporting of Injuries, Diseases and Dangerous Occurrences Regulations 1985.

Diseases

A long list of notifiable diseases is given. It seems unlikely that any of these would result directly from work in an architectural office. Asbestos-related diseases are included.
Reporting of Injuries, Diseases and Dangerous Occurrences Regulations 1985

First Aid

Every employer has a statutory requirement to provide adequate provision for first aid for all staff. This includes the provision of an adequate number of suitably trained first-aid officers. If the trained first-aid officer is absent in exceptional circumstances, the employer must ensure that there is another person available to coordinate actions in the event of an accident etc. If there are only a few employees, the requirement may only be to provide a staff member able to maintain the first-aid equipment and to coordinate first-aid care. There is even a requirement for the self-employed to ensure that they have adequate first-aid provisions.

The Health and Safety (First-Aid) Regulations 1981 are very general in their requirements. A more precise definition of what the law considers to be "adequate" is given in the official Code of Practice by the Health and Safety Executive. Lists of an adequate contents for as first-aid box are given in a priced Health and Safety Executive publication "First aid at work". HS (R) 11, available from Her Majesty's Stationery Office.

Flammable Gas

Any supplier of flammable gas by a fixed line (mainly the Gas Boards) who thinks that death or injury has been caused by a faulty fitting, including flues etc, must send a report to the Health and Safety Executive within 14 days.
Reporting of Injuries, Diseases and Dangerous Occurrences Regulations 1985

Flammable Liquids

Highly flammable liquids, other than petrol or similar substances, must be kept in covered containers in fire resisting rooms or structures or buildings in a safe position - ie some way away from other buildings. A highly flammable liquid is defined as any liquid which has a flashpoint of under 32 deg C. Unless it is not practical, the tanks or containers must be marked "Highly flammable" or with some other sign giving note of the danger. If it is not possible to mark the container, itself, a sign must be placed near to it.
Liquefied petroleum gas must be specifically labelled and, if possible, be stored in the open air. No LPG may be stored in workplaces unless it is in use in the manufacturing process.
Highly Flammable Liquids and Liquefied Petroleum Gases Regulations 1982

Flammable Liquids: Fire Precautions

Suitable ventilation must be provided to prevent the escape of vapour from any flammable liquid into the general atmosphere of the workplace. All ducts, trunking etc used as part of this exhaust ventilation, must be fire resisting structures. Pressure relief must be provided in case of explosion.

Adequate means of escape must be provided in every room used for the handling of these substances. Suitable means of fire fighting must also be provided.

Highly Flammable Liquids and Liquefied Petroleum Gases Regulations 1982

Inspectors

Because so much of health and safety legislation is based on the concept of what is ''reasonably practicable'' there is a requirement for extensive inspection of workplaces. The inspectors have wide ranging powers to enter workplaces at any reasonable time or at other times if they believe that there is a specific and immediate danger, to collect samples, to take photographs and to inspect processes, equipment and documents. Notices requiring improvements to be made over a period of time may be issued and it is also possible that the immediate shutdown of a factory, machine or process may be ordered until specified improvements have been made. It is unlikely that this would apply to an architect's office -assuming that the office is not a fire risk etc - but it might happen on a construction site for which the architect was responsible in some way. (See also On the site).

Health and Safety at Work etc. Act 1974

Safety Policy Statements

All employers, except for those who employ fewer than 5 people at any one time, must have a written statement of health and safety policy. This essentially states who is responsible for health and safety matters. This document must be regularly updated in order to allow for changing circumstances and the employees must be made aware of its contents.

The policy statement will differ greatly from one company to another but the Health and Safety Executive has produced a free guidance booklet on the subject: ''Writing a safety policy statement: advice to employers''. This is available from area offices of the Health and Safety Executive.

Health and Safety at Work etc. Act 1974 and Employers' Health and Safety Policy Statements (Exception) Regulations 1975

Safety Representatives and Safety Committees

Recognised trades unions have the right to appoint safety representatives in any company. If possible, these representatives must have been employed by the company for a minimum of 2 years or must have 2 years experience in similar employment. The employer must take all reasonable steps to keep the representatives informed and must show them all relevant documents. The representatives must be allowed reasonable time off work for training and to perform their duties. (See Payment and benefits: time off for official and other duties).

At the request of two or more safety representatives, the employer must establish a safety committee within 3 months. This must represent the interests of both employees and management and should consider all matters relevant to health and safety.

Health and Safety at Work etc. Act 1974 and Safety Representatives and Safety Committees Regulations 1977

Housing

Introduction

This subject has been separated from other building types because it has much legislation of its own; the law relating to "dwellings", as houses are called by the law, is not only wider in scope but more stringent than most other construction and planning regulations.

Housing legislation over the years has developed from basic requirements for housing provision to a body of Acts and regulations dealing largely with tenants rights and the role and duties of housing authorities. The main Act at present is the 1985 Housing Act which embodies most of the earlier legislation, and includes the powers of local housing authorities, a range of procedures for improving housing stock, and eligibility for grants.

The private architect designing one-off houses is not usually involved with public housing legislation, but the firms dealing with rehabilitation, conservation, and housing association work are more likely to be asked by their clients what grants are available to them. Large private houses which are to be turned into flats come within stringent regulations on means of escape, fire resistance and compartmentation; the architect should be well aware of these so that he may advise his client at an early stage in the project of the extra work and expense involved.

Local authorities have power to serve notices on the persons in control of housing which is unfit for habitation or which lacks the standard amenities. Other housing defects may also warrant the serving of notices. In most cases, there is a right of appeal to the courts and as there is a time limit set for appeals, the architect should ensure that action is taken without delay.

Assured Tenancies

Assured tenancies are held in a similar manner to secure tenancies (qv). The term "assured tenancy" refers to tenants of bodies approved by the Secretary of State, such as housing associations. Lists of these approved bodies are published in Government orders from time to time.

The difference between assured and secure tenants is unlikely to be of great significance to the work of the architect.

Housing Act 1980 and subsequent Government orders

Clearance Areas

A clearance area is the most drastic way of dealing with unfit housing. Usually called slum clearance, it involves clearing all the buildings in the area if the houses are unfit, badly arranged (such as back-to-back housing), or injurious to health. The local housing authority who declare a clearance area must provide definitive maps and notify the public of their intention. The land in the clearance area itself and — here's the rub — any other land required to make the area viable, may be compulsorily purchased; they must clear it as soon as possible except that houses which have been served with demolition orders (qv) may be used for temporary housing.

If a building becomes listed after compulsory purchase (qv) the Secretary of State is required to give permission for its demolition.

Housing Act 1985

Closing Order

A closing order can be made by the local housing authority on a house which is unfit for human habitation (qv) and which cannot be repaired at reasonable expense. This means that the owner can only use the house for an "approved purpose" which does not include any kind of living accommodation; this situation often occurs where flats over shops are well below standard, and the means of escape from fire is inadequate or non-existent.

If the architect is asked to prepare a scheme for rehabilitating such property he would be well advised to check with the local authority whether a closing order has been served; and in any case it is essential to carry out a thorough structural

survey, since closing orders are not usually made on sound property. Housing grants (qv) may be available for essential works.
Housing Act 1985

Common Parts Grants

There is a new grant within the Housing and Planning Act 1986 which covers the improvement or repair of "common parts" of a building containing one or more flats. There is a number of qualifying conditions which must be met before the grant will be made. These include the nature of the tenancies and the requirement that the local authority must be satisfied that the grant-aided work will put common parts of the building into reasonable repair. Future Government orders will determine the rateable value ceiling above which a grant will not be available. Further orders will set the level of eligible expenses. The common parts grant may cover work which will make the common parts of the building more suitable for any disabled persons living there.
Housing and Planning Act 1986

Compulsory Purchase

The local housing authority has compulsory purchase powers to acquire land for housing, and for other amenities beneficial to housing such as shops, recreation, and similar facilities. They may also provide streets and open spaces and the London borough councils may compulsorily purchase land and provide commercial buildings in connection with housing. These compulsory purchases may be made only ten years ahead of development.
The architect is advised to check with the local authority whether they intend to exercise these powers on or adjoining his client's proposed development, as the threat of compulsory purchase can reduce the value of such property.
Housing Act 1985

Covenants on Conversions

Where the client has gained planning consent to convert a large house or several houses into flats, and there is a restrictive covenant (qv) preventing him from carrying out the conversion, the local housing authority may obtain a court order to override any such restricting covenants. This

is most likely to happen where local housing authorities have a policy of increasing the housing stock by converting large single houses into flats, The architect should check if any such covenants exist, and if they do, whether the local housing authority is prepared to apply for an order.
Housing Act 1985

Defective Dwellings

Houses which are defective because of their original design or construction may be designated by the Secretary of State or the local authority as ''defective dwellings''. These houses include numerous system-built houses, most of them in pre-cast concrete and some in steel; all these houses have suffered through major design faults which have rendered them either structurally or environmentally unsound.

Once designated, owners of these houses who have purchased them from a public authority may be given a ''reinstatement grant''. The house must have a working life of 30 years after reinstatement and the owner must be able to get a mortgage from a building society. If these conditions are satisfied the reinstatement grant will cover 90% of the cost with a maximum limit set by the Secretary of State. If reinstatement is not possible at a reasonable cost then the Housing Authority must re-purchase the dwelling at 95% of its defect-free value, giving the owner a secure tenancy (qv). There are detailed conditions attached to these grants and they are varied from time to time by Government order. Though most of the reinstatement work is carried out by housing authorities, the architect involved in housing association work may find that some projects include designated defective dwellings.
Housing Act 1985 and Housing Defects (Expenditure Limits) Order 1986

Defective Premises

In spite of its title, the Defective Premises Act deals only with dwellings, but it is important as it imposes a duty on all those who take on work in connection with the provision of a dwelling. This includes the construction, conversion, or alteration of a dwelling and any building turned into a dwelling.

Those who owe a duty to the owner under the Act are:

— the builder;
— the architect;
— specialist sub-contractors;
— manufacturers of specially ordered equipment.

The obligation is not only to the building owner, but to any other person who acquires an interest in the property. The Act calls for the work to be done in a workmanlike or professional manner and with proper materials; the completed dwelling must be fit for habitation (qv) and comply with habitation standards.

The Act may be enforced independently of any contract that may exist, since purchasers rights cannot be excluded by contract. The Act allows for "approved schemes" which give the owner rights in respect of defects; the National House Building Council (bcd) scheme is an approved scheme and is probably the best known one. The NHBC Scheme applies where any NHBC builder makes a special contract with the building owner on a form approved by the NHBC. This contract imposes extra contractual obligations on the builder and in return the NHBC provides insurance cover against any default by the builder. It also has the advantage that if the builder becomes bankrupt the NHBC will compensate the owner for damages. The requirements for design and construction if a dwelling is constructed under an approved scheme are discussed in the House Building Standards (Approved Scheme etc) Order 1979.

Defective Premises Act 1972

Demolition Order

This is one of the options for dealing with unfit houses which cannot be repaired at reasonable expense. A demolition order is usually served by the local authority on the owner of unfit housing unless:

— it is a listed building (qv);
— it is supporting adjacent buildings.

A time limit is given for demolition and if it is not met the local authority must demolish the house and recover costs. However the Act seems to imply that anyone capable of bringing the house up to human habitation standards can apply for permission to do so. Any building which has had a demolition order served on it is likely to be in a bad structural condition, and a thorough survey is advisable before accepting any commission to reconstruct such a building.

Housing Act 1985

Earth Closets

Earth closets are defined as ''a closet with a movable receptacle for the reception of faecal matter and its deodorisation by the use of earth, ashes, or chemicals, or by other methods''. If the client has an earth closet (regardless of whether it is in good working order, or does not constitute a health hazard or a nuisance) a local authority can order it to be replaced by a water closet if there is a sufficient water supply and sewerage available.

If the service pipes are more than 100 ft away from the building, the local authority may agree to pay part of the expenses.

Building Act 1984

Fitness for Habitation

The 1985 Housing Act contains a nine point standard that is the basis for deciding whether a house is fit for human habitation or not. These standards cover the following;

— repairs;
— stability;
— freedom from damp;
— internal arrangement;
— natural lighting;
— ventilation;
— water supply;
— drainage and sanitary conveniences;
— facilities for the preparation and cooking of food;
— the disposal of waste water.

Even if one of these standards is sadly lacking to an extent which makes the house unhabitable, the house must be declared unfit. If the house cannot be put in order at ''reasonable expense'' either by the owner or by the local authority (who will recover the cost), the house will be subject to one of the four following procedures:

—   an undertaking to make the house fit (qv);
—   a clearance area (qv) order;
—   a closing order (qv);
—   a demolition order (qv).

On starting a commission to rehabilitate unfit housing, it is important to check which of these orders, if any, are in force and what time limits are set for compliance with them. It may be possible to get a change of order; for example a closing order may be withdrawn if an undertaking to repair is given.

Appeals against some orders may be made to the courts but, as there are time limits for these appeals, the architect is advised to ensure that prompt action is taken.

Housing Act 1985

General Improvement Areas

This is a less rigid designation than a Housing Action Area (qv); it has no fixed time limit for completing work in the area and the local authority does not have such far reaching powers, but they can still compel owners to provide standard amenities. A General Improvement Area is declared in the same way as a Housing Action Area, but it must not include a Clearance Area (qv) or Housing Action Area. It is mainly intended to improve the environment and owner-occupiers are encouraged (with luck grants will be available) to improve their property.

Under the Housing Act the local housing authority is empowered to provide any amenities beneficial to housing, and in a General Improvement Area they can pedestrianise streets; the object is to up-grade the whole area to give the inhabitants a more pleasant place to live in.

Housing Act 1985

Housing Action Areas

Now that most of the major slum clearance areas have been dealt with, reconstruction of an area of bad housing is likely to be initiated by declaring it a Housing Action Area. The local housing authority, or any other qualified person (this would most probably be one of the pressure groups such as Help the Aged, Shelter, or any local group with sufficient status) can report that an area is unsatisfactory in terms of physical housing and social conditions. If the report states that the area can be brought up to standard within five years, then the local housing authority may declare it a Housing Action Area. This decision must be reported to the Secretary of State, definitive maps made and the public and in particular the residents of the area must be notified.

Within the Housing Action Area the local housing authority can:

— compulsorily purchase land;
— convert, improve, repair and manage houses;
— carry out environmental works and give grants for these purposes.
— compel owners to carry out "standard amenity" improvements.

Some local housing authorities carry out "enveloping" projects; which means doing street scale environmental improvements, commonly known to architects as "face-lifts".

Housing Act 1985

Housing Associations

The Housing Corporation holds a register of Housing Associations. Registered housing associations are restricted as to their activities:

— they must let houses or have them occupied by members;
— they may build, improve, repair or convert houses for sale or lease;
— they may dispose of surplus land as they see fit with the consent of the Housing Corporation or the Charity Commissioners.

There are grants available for all the above purposes, including sales and repairs or improvements to dwellings whose tenants are exercising the right to buy (qv). The local authority may give housing grants (qv) or loans, and the Public Works Loan Commissioners may give loans, to registered housing associations. The architect working with a housing association will often find that the local housing authority are helpful in the matter of loans or grants, but in return may expect to have some rights to nominate tenants from their own housing waiting list. Housing Associations are required to keep very detailed accounts in a prescribed

manner with strict auditing; the architect must therefore ensure that he submits invoices that conform to the procedures laid down.
Housing Associations Act 1985

Housing Corporation

This is an increasingly powerful body charged with the supervision of all registered housing associations (qv). For most purposes the Housing Corporation has similar powers to those of local housing authorities; the Corporation may:

— make roads or streets;
— create open spaces;
— provide services;
— build commercial, recreational, or other non-housing projects as part of a housing development.

It is advisable to make sure that any housing association which commissions an architect is registered, and has discussed its proposals with the Housing Corporation. If housing corporation approval is not forthcoming, it is unlikely that the scheme will go ahead. Only a limited amount of money is budgeted at any one time for housing association projects, so that the starting date of the contract may be considerably later than expected, and any cost estimates should take this into account.
Housing Associations Act 1985

Housing Grants

There are four types of grant available through the local authority for houses which are not up to current standards. In addition, there are also thermal insulation grants (qv) and common parts grants (qv) for flats. The object of these grants is to improve the standard of the housing stock to an acceptable level.

— Improvement grants (qv). These are discretionary grants given to certain categories of dwellings in order to bring them up to the required standard.
— Intermediate grants (qv). These are normally mandatory if the ''standard amenities'' (qv) are missing.
— Special grants (qv). These are available where a house is in multiple occupation (qv) and apply to ''standard amenities'', means of escape, and repairs and replacements.

— Repairs grants (qv). These are for substantial and structural repairs only.

If a particular grant has once been given to a property, further grants for the same purpose will not normally be given. It is important to reach an agreement with the grant-making authority as to what work is eligible and what the cost limits are before starting work; also when payment of the grant will be made. The property is usually inspected before and after the grant-aided work is carried out. Some authorities may be unable to pay grants when payment falls due, and the client may have to wait some time before receiving payment.

The grants may be given regardless of the age of the property; one of the authors encountered a kind-hearted new town authority who gave grants for installing sanitary fittings in a sixteenth century castle, on the grounds that the existing ruinous garde-robe hole was not quite up to acceptable standards.

Housing Acts 1980 and 1985 and various Government orders.
Housing and Planning Act 1986

Improvement Grants

These are discretionary grants given to houses built before 2 October 1961 and are given in order to create more dwellings by conversion or similar means. Grants are available to owners or tenants, but the property must be brought up to the required standard and have a set period of useful life as a dwelling, usually thirty years. There are ''eligible expense'' limits set from time to time which govern the amount of the grant, but these do not normally affect housing action areas (qv) or housing for the disabled. (See Housing Grants).

Housing Acts 1980 and 1985 and various Government orders

Improvement Notice

This notice is served on the ''person having control'' of the house in order to compel him to provide any one or more of the ''standard amenities'' (qv) which may be deficient, and to bring the house up to standard or reduced standard. The full standard for improvement comprises:

— all standard amenities (qv);
— a state of reasonable repair;
— thermal insulation (qv) to current standards;
— availability as a dwelling for fifteen years;
and it must be in all respects fit for human habitation (qv).

The local housing authority may serve an improvement notice if four conditions are met:

— The house is in a housing action area (qv), a general improvement area (qv), or the tenant requests the local housing authority to take action.
— The house has not got the exclusive use of any one or more of the standard amenities.
— The house is capable of improvement to full standard or reduced standard.
— The house was constructed or converted before 3 October 1961.

Provisional improvement notices may be served which allow for negotiation on the full or reduced standard between the owner and the local housing authority, but if a compulsory improvement notice is served, the local housing authority must offer a loan for the purpose.

The standard of work required to provide satisfactory amenities is well established, but each local authority may have slightly different requirements; for example, one authority will accept internal bathrooms where another will not; it is advisable to check such details with the local authority before starting work, as any departure from approved standards may result in the grant being disallowed. *Housing Act 1985*

Intermediate Grants

These grants are for providing "standard amenities" (qv) or special amenities for the disabled and must be given if the conditions are met. They are subject to eligible expense limits which allocate a set amount of money to each amenity and also give a ceiling figure, which is higher in special cases. Standard amenities are:

— fixed bath or shower;
— hot and cold water to bath or shower.
— wash-hand basin;

— hot and cold water to wash-hand basin in Greater London;
— sink;
— hot and cold water to sink;
— WC.

The actual amounts available for standard and special amenities are varied by Government order from time to time, and this information is obtainable from the local authority. (See also Housing Grants.)
Housing Act 1985

Multiple Occupancy: Management of Dwellings

When the local authority thinks that a house in multiple occupancy is not being properly cared for, they may make a "management order". This means that the manager of the house must follow a "management code", that is, he may have to repair the house and then keep it clean and in good order. He is also responsible for cleaning the common areas, the gas and electricity supplies, water, drainage and waste disposal,as well as the ventilation, lighting and heating to these areas. Means of escape from fire are also his responsibilty and he must ensure that all escape routes are kept clear.

If the architect is called in to upgrade such premises, he should check the requirements set out in any relevant multiple occupancy management, control (qv), defects (qv), or means of escape (qv) orders which have been served. Grants (qv) may well be available for much of this work.
Housing Act 1985

Multiple Occupancy of Dwellings: Control

Houses can be in "multiple occupancy" if they are occupied by people who do not form a single household, thus it could include any dwelling from a single sub-letting to a purpose-designed hostel. The local authority may operate a registration scheme and thereafter attach "control provisions" preventing multiple occupancy of an unregistered house or one where the number of households or occupiers exceeds the registered number. They may also serve an overcrowding notice, giving the maximum number of people who

should to occupy each room. (See also Overcrowding of Dwellings and Sleeping Space Standards).
Housing Act 1985

Multiple Occupancy of Dwellings: Defects

Where the local authority finds that a house in multiple occupancy is defective for the number of people living in it they can require work on any of the following to be carried out to housing standards including:

— natural and artificial lighting;
— ventilation;
— water supply;
— personal washing facilities;
— drainage and sanitary conveniences;
— food storage, preparation area and cooking facilities;
— proper means for disposing of waste water;
— space heating or satisfactory provision for people to use space heating appliances.

The detailed standards for these facilities are not laid down in the Act, and it is advisable to ensure that the defects notice and any information given by the local authority sets out exactly what is required.
Housing Act 1985

Multiple Occupancy of Dwellings: Fire Precautions

Where the local authority finds that a house in multiple occupancy has inadequate means of escape for the number of occupiers they are obliged to require all necessary work to be done to provide an efficient means of escape from fire to the housing standards. This requirement is mandatory where:

— a house has at least three floors excluding the basement and
— where the combined area including the staircases and the basements exceeds 500 m².

It will probably be necessary to consult the fire authority as well in order to agree details of stair construction, fire doors, notices, fire alarms, fire-fighting equipment etc. and it is important to get agreement between the local authority and the fire authority as to the work to be done. Remember that

student hostels, staff quarters and similar group living accommodation come under this classification.
Housing (Means of Escape from Fire in Houses in Multiple Occupation) Order 1981

Obstructive Building Order

A property may be in such a condition that its nearness to other buildings makes it dangerous or injurious to health. In this case the local housing authority may serve an obstructive building order on the property requiring the owner to demolish it; and if necessary they may "occupy the building and demolish it".
Housing Act 1985

Overcrowding of Dwellings

The local authority is obliged to check that the number of people sleeping in a given size of room does not exceed the statutory standards. The space standards are:

No of rooms	No of people	Floor area of room	No of people
1	2	110 sq ft or more	2
2	3	90 sq ft or more but under 110 sq ft	1.5
3	5	70 sq ft or more but under 90 sq ft	1
4	7.5	50 sq ft or more but under 70 sq ft	0.5
5 or more	2 per room	less than 50 sq ft not allowed	

This means for example that a house with three rooms all over 110 ft^2 could sleep five people, two in each bedroom and one in the living room, but if the rooms were all less than 90 ft^2, only three people could sleep in the house.
These figures are used mainly for calculating overcrowding where the authority wishes to bring a prosecution for private lettings, but they do apply to all housing, and the architect involved in the field of holiday apartments and hostels should bear them in mind.
Housing Act 1985

Repair Notice

The local authority must serve a repair notice on "the person having control of the house" if it is unfit for human habitation (qv) or not up to a reasonable standard. This notice must specify the work to be done, and the time within which it must be done; failure to do the repairs allows the local authority to carry out the work itself and to recover the cost. If the house cannot be repaired at "reasonable cost" the authority can purchase the property.

These provisions come under Part VI of the 1985 Act and also apply to huts, tents and caravans which have been on the same site for two years. This could affect self-build groups living temporarily in caravans or huts while building their own houses, a process which frequently takes more than two years.

Housing Act 1985

Repairs Grants

Repairs grants are for substantial and structural repairs only. If the local authority has served a repair notice (qv) on the property, the grant must be given; otherwise it is discretionary. There are "eligible expenses" limits governing the amount which can be spent on repairs; these are varied from time to time. Usually only owner-occupiers get the grant, and higher eligible expenses limits apply to repairs when the house is adapted for disabled people.

Time limits are set for carrying out the repairs, and there may be conditions as to future occupancy. It is worth checking with the client and the local authority if a grant has already been given, in which case no further money will be available; or if a the property is eligible for a repairs grant, exactly what work is covered.

Housing Act 1980, Grants by Local Authorities (Eligible Expenses Limits)(Amendment) Order 1981 and subsequent orders. Grants by Local Authorities (Repair) Order 1982 and Housing Act 1985

Right to Buy

A secure tenant (qv) under a scheduled public landlord has the right to buy his dwelling if he has been a tenant for the prescribed number of years. If the landlord holds the freehold the tenant has the right to acquire that freehold; if however the landlord is a leaseholder, the tenant has the right to buy the lease. Certain classes of public landlords are exempted from these obligations, such as "tied houses". Housing which has been specially adapted for the disabled or sheltered housing for the elderly is exempted from the right to buy. Also exempt is housing which is particularly suitable for the elderly by reason of its location, layout or facilities.

Housing Act 1985. Housing (Right to Buy) Regulations and Orders 1980 onwards. Housing and Planning Act 1986

Right to Buy: Designated Areas

If public housing has been sold under the right-to-buy (qv) schemes and it is within a National Park (qv) or in a "designated region" or "designated area", the conveyance or lease may contain certain covenants or restrictions, including the option to re-purchase the property, binding on the purchaser and on subsequent purchasers.

Designated areas include Areas of Outstanding Natural Beauty (qv), large tracts of the Norfolk coast, and the county of Devon. New areas are added to the list from time to time, and deeds and leases should be carefully checked before any work is started.

This applies particularly to alterations which affect the character of the property, and there are also restrictions on permitted development (qv) in National Parks and AONBs.

Housing (Right to Buy)(Designated Regions) Regulations 1980 and subsequent orders

Right to Repair in Secure Tenancies

There is a statutory scheme by which a secure tenant (qv) is entitled to carry out covenanted repairs to his dwelling and recover the cost from his landlord. Standard forms are available for claiming payment from the landlord; as well as forms which enable the landlord to repudiate payment.

Secure Tenancies (Right to Repair Scheme) Regulations 1985

Rooms Below Water Table

It is an offence to build a room or cellar below the ordinary level of the subsoil water on or near the site of the building, without obtaining permission from the Local Authority. In general this applies to:

— a house;
— a shop;
— an inn;
— an hotel;
— an office.

If the room already exists the local authority may serve a notice requiring the owner to carry out remedial works such as tanking or pumping, alternatively he may choose to fill it in or block it up. Special regulations apply to cellars under streets.
Building Act 1984

Secure Tenancies

There are three qualifying factors which define a secure tenancy under a public landlord. These are:

— that the property is let as a separate dwelling;
— that the landlord is a listed public landlord, and
— that the dwelling is the tenants only or principal home.

There are a number of exceptions scheduled in the 1985 Housing Act, mainly public employment categories of tenants. Secure tenants enjoy certain rights (subject to qualifications), including the right to buy (qv) the freehold or lease, and the right to carry out repairs (qv) at the landlord's cost.

The architect is most likely to be involved in the rights appertaining to secure tenants when he is dealing with a housing association, or rehabilitation project; since the status of the tenants affects many kinds of financial aid for repairs, reinstatement, and improvements, it is advisable to establish the rights of the tenants at an early stage.

If certain conditions are met, secure tenants may be dispossessed if the landlord has put forward a redevelopment scheme for the area which has been approved by the Secretary of State or, in the case of a housing association, by the Housing Corporation.
Housing Act 1985 and Housing and Planning Act 1986

Sleeping Space Standards

An early regulation defined how a room should be measured for calculating sleeping accommodation and this is stated as "the area of any part of the floor space over which the

vertical height of the room is, by reason of a sloping roof or ceiling, reduced to less than 5 ft shall be excluded from the computation of the floor area of that room''. Bay windows may be included if they are more than 5 ft high as can cupboards and projecting chimney-breasts. Measurements are made at floor level to the back of any projecting skirtings. (See also Overcrowding of Dwellings)
Housing Act (Overcrowding and Miscellaneous Forms) Regulations 1937

Special Grants

These are only available for houses in multiple occupation. If the local authority serve a notice requiring standard amenities (qv) or means of escape to be provided in a multiple occupancy house, they must give an appropriate grant, otherwise these grants are discretionary. The special grant has three components:

— standard amenities, similar to the intermediate grant (qv);
— means of escape;
— repairs and replacements, similar to a repairs grant (qv).

Each component is subject to a maximum grant, the amount of which can be varied by government order; the current figures should be available from the local authority. These grants are most likely to be required for upgrading older property used for hostels or lodging houses. (See also Housing Grants.)
Housing Act 1985 and various government orders and regulations

Standard Amenities

This expression refers to the amenities considered to provide the basic minimum level of sanitation and water supply for dwellings. The standard amenities may be installed in sub-standard housing with the aid of an intermediate grant (qv).
Standard amenities are:

— fixed bath or shower;
— hot and cold water to above;
— wash-hand basin;

— hot and cold water to above;
— sink;
— hot and cold water to above;
— WC.

There are standard grants available for each item, though these change from time to time and at present houses in Greater London are allowed extra money for these standard amenities.
Housing Act 1985.

Thermal Insulation Grants

These grants are designed to improve the thermal insulation of houses with little or no insulation at present. This is part of the Government's energy saving programme. Applicants with special needs, usually the elderly with small incomes, the disabled, and similar categories, will normally get 90% of the cost, while all others get 66%; there is a maximum payment in each case. The local authority must be advised before work is commenced and only approved materials on the authority's list are accepted as eligible for grant. The grant is a once only payment. The categories of "special needs" people who are eligible for the higher rates of grant; the list of approved materials; and the rates of payment; are varied from time to time. The local authority will be able to give up to date information. (See also Housing Grants.)
Homes Insulation Grants Order 1984

Time and Place Notice

When the local housing authority has declared a house unfit for human habitation (qv) and it cannot be repaired at reasonable expense, they must serve a time and place notice on the owner, the mortgagees, and the "person having control". This notice makes arrangements for a meeting between all the interested parties to discuss the future of the premises. The person in control may then give an undertaking that the house will be made fit and that it will not be lived in until the work has been carried out. If the local authority is not satisfied that the undertaking is being kept, they may make a closing order (qv) or demolition order (qv) on the property; alternatively they may purchase the house and use it for temporary housing.

The architect should be aware of these options so that he may give his client sound advice; whichever option is taken, it is important to get agreement with the local authority as to the exact procedure to be followed, and if the house is to be made fit for habitation, the full extent of the work required. Housing grants (qv) may be available for some rehabilitation work.
Housing Act 1985

Underground Rooms

These are defined in the Housing Act 1985 as; rooms in dwellings which are 3 ft below the street:

—   when the surface of the ground is within 9 ft of the room.

Where these rooms occur the local housing authority can require special provision for lighting and ventilation.
Housing Act 1985

Undertaking to Make Fit

Houses that have been declared unfit for human habitation (qv) by the local authority can be salvaged by the owner giving an ''undertaking to make fit'' the property. This is an alternative to the other procedures which apply to houses unfit for human habitation. The situation is most likely to occur where a group of decayed houses is not interesting enough to be scheduled as listed buildings (qv), but which nevertheless has some architectural merit and is worth bringing up to habitable standard. This happens quite often in older towns where housing which was originally of good quality has gone through a slum phase and is now being revitalised.
Check the range of housing grants (qv) which may be available for rehabilitation.
Housing Act 1985

Well Maintained Houses

When the local authority acquires an unfit house, either by agreement or by compulsory purchase, the value paid is usually that of the cleared site. However, if the property has been carefully looked after, the owner may be entitled to an additional ''well-maintained payment'' under certain conditions. There may also be allowances for disturbance to a business which is run from the dwelling. If the architect is involved in work with such property, he may suggest to the owners that an effort to secure these additional payments is worth while.

Housing (Payments for Well-Maintained Houses) Order 1982

Building Types

Introduction

The Building Act 1984 and the Building Regulations 1985, which are empowered by it, cover virtually all building types and should be studied before starting any design work. There are, however, many regulations which apply to certain buildings only and the designer should make certain that he is aware of these. It is not possible in a general document such as this to cover all of the possibilities and we have concentrated upon those buildings most commonly encountered.

Most of the building types with special requirements will be work places of one sort or another so that the Factory Inspectorate will be the best source of information. There will, however, be many other sources and we have attempted to list these in the appropriate sections.

The building types are arranged alphabetically within this section, with reminders on general items such as access for the disabled.

Housing, being such a large subject, with vast quantities of its own legislation, has been covered in a separate chapter.

Access for the Disabled

It is now mandatory for all public buildings to which the public have access to be provided with properly designed entrances and internal access for disabled people. The Act also requires the architect to make provision for car parking suitable for disabled people and to provide clear signposting of the route from the car park to the disabled persons entrance. Toilet facilities for the the disabled must be also be provided and signposted.

If the local authority provides public toilets, they must also provide similar facilites for the disabled and must signpost them clearly. The local authority may serve a notice on any place of entertainment requiring the owner to provide toilet facilities and other arrangements for the disabled if similar provisions are provided for the general public.

The main Act requires access and sanitary facilities for the disabled to be provided at universities, school buildings, teacher training colleges and other further education establishments.

New "places of employment" must provide access, internal access, sanitary facilities and parking for the disabled as far as is practicable and reasonable. The premises designated are those covered by the Factories Act 1961 and the Offices, Shops and Railway Premises Act 1963 (see also Factories and Offices). These two Acts cover almost all types of commercial and industrial premises. Parts of other premises which are used for manufacturing or service trades may be treated as factories.

The planning authority is obliged to point out to those planning applicants who are required to provide facilities for the disabled the need to comply with the Chronically Sick and Disabled Persons Acts, BS 5810: 1979 "Code of practice for access for the disabled to buildings" and Dept of Education and Science Design Note 18 "Access for disabled people to educational buildings". There is, as yet, no power to enforce compliance with these documents but it is advisable to comply as new legislation is under consideration and later alterations to the buildings could be expensive. As the designated building classes may change, the architect should consider making such provision in any type of building unless it is obviously unsuitable.

The situation will become clearer now that the new Section M of the Building Regulations has been published. This comes into force at the end of 1987 and will provide teeth to the legislation which has been discussed above. Much will depend upon the new Approved Document, which will provide guidance as to acceptable standards of provision. This has been promised but has not yet appeared.

Chronically Sick and Disabled Persons Act 1970, Chronically Sick and Disabled Persons Act 1976, Local Government (Miscellaneous Provisions) Act 1976, Disabled Persons Act 1981 and Building (Disabled People) Regulations 1987

Cinemas and Film Exhibitions

Cinemas and other premises used for showing films require a licence from the local authority. Architects are advised to check the licensing requirements, which may include fire precautions, safety, the storage of cinematographic film and the safety, health and welfare of children in attendance.

It should be noted that these requirements are over and above the normal fire precautions and building regulations which must also be complied with.

Cinemas Act 1985

Commercial Developments

English Industrial Estates Corporation may now provide an advisory service to help a developer find a suitable location for his proposed commercial development. The Corporation may also provide certain services if the site chosen is managed by them and this also applies to premises that the client may wish to take up. Architects working with commercial development promoters may find this assistance useful.

Industrial Development Act 1985

Crematoria

In addition to the normal development controls, there are special requirements governing the sites for crematoria:

— they must at least 200 yds from a dwelling house unless the owner, the lessee, if any, and the occupier agree in writing

— they must be at least 50 yds from a public highway

— they must not be erected in a consecrated part of a burial ground.

Once a crematorium is built, the architect must ensure that a certificate showing that it is properly equipped for cremating human remains is sent to the Secretary of State.

Cremation Act 1902 and Cremation Act 1952

Dogs and Cats

If it is proposed to run an establishment for boarding dogs and cats or for breeding dogs, whether as new build or part of an extension or conversion to a private house, a licence

must be obtained from the local authority. This will include conditions for the construction and services requirements. The owner must also be aware of possible offences under the Control of Pollution Act 1974, including noise pollution, as well as the possibility of committing a statutory nuisance by annoying the neighbours with smell, noise or pollution. It is an offence to discharge any material into a stream or watercourse.
Animal Boarding Establishments Act 1963 and Breeding of Dogs Act 1973

Factories

A factory is any premises used for the manufacture, alteration, repair or breaking up of any article. There are many types of operation covered by this definition which might easily be overlooked. These include:

— Laundries;
— Printing and publishing;
— Film set manufacture and repair;
— Gas storage plants holding more than 5,000 ft^3

Open air operations are covered by the Act provided that the other criteria apply. Construction sites are not covered.
Factories Act 1961

Factories: Access for the Disabled

The law in this area is in a state of confusion, pending the arrival of a new Approved Document to support the Building Regulations 1985. There is a requirement for provision, so far as is practicable and reasonable, to be made for disabled people using the premises, mentioning access, car parking and sanitary conveniences in particular. There is as yet, however, no clearer definition of the designer's responsibilities in this area, with the section of the Disabled Persons Act 1981, requiring that BS 5810: 1979 Code of practice for access for the disabled to buildings, not yet having been brought into force. There are, however, two relevant sections of this legislation currently in force.

— Section 3 amends the Town and Country Planning Act 1971 so that planning authorities are required to draw to the attention of applicants for all factory premises the relevant provisions of the Chronically Sick and Disabled Persons Act 1970 and of BS 5810: 1979.

— Section 5 requires that where provision has been made for the disabled at any premises, signs must be erected both inside and outside the building. Where car parking has been provided, an appropriate route into the building must be indicated.

Chronically Sick and Disabled Persons Act 1970, Chronically Sick and Disabled Persons (Amendment) Act 1976, Disabled Persons Act 1981 and Building (Disabled People) Regulations 1987

Factories: Construction

Doors: In factories not requiring a fire certificate - see section on fire certificates - all doors leading from rooms where more than 10 people are employed and onto stairs or corridors forming means of escape must open outwards. The fire authority can grant exemption from this requirement. All doors or windows to be used as a means of escape must be suitable marked.

Fire Precautions (Non-Certificated Factory, Office, Shop and Railway Premises) Regulations 1976

Floors: Where any wet process is involved, adequate drainage must be provided in the floor to remove all excess water. All floors must be sound and sufficient to withstand all normal stresses. The surfaces must be kept free of any substances likely to cause slipping. All floor openings must be fenced.

Factories Act 1961

Stairs: All stairs, both internal and external, must have handrails, on the open side where there is one, or on both sides if both are open or if the stairs are particularly hazardous. On the open sides, there must be further protection from falling in the form of lower rails or similar.

Factories Act 1961

Wall and ceiling finishes: with the exception of certain types of factory, all walls and ceilings must have painted or similar finishes which permit cleaning by means of washing with soap and water or detergents etc. This effectively bars the

use of many rough textured finishes, such as fair-faced concrete or brickwork.
Factories (Cleanliness of Walls and Ceilings) Order 1960

Factories: Fire Certificates

Fire certificates are required:

— where more than 20 people are employed at any one time or where more than 10 are employed other than on the ground floor;

— where any manufacturing process involves the use of liquefied petroleum gas, pressurised flammable liquids, expanded plastics and other specified substances.
Fire Certificates (Special Premises) Regulations 1976.

Applications for certificates must include details of the building's use and a set of plans. The final certificate will include details of the use, means of escape, fire fighting equipment and fire alarms. The fire authority may specify details of works required before the certificate will be granted.

If changes to the structure or interior of a building requiring a certificate are planned, notice must be given to the fire authority. If the authority believes that the proposed changes will adversely affect the means of escape and the provisions for fire fighting and fire alarms, it can order the occupier to take appropriate action.
Fire Precautions Act 1971

Factories: Hoists and Lifts

In factories not requiring a fire certificate (see also Factories: fire certificates) - hoists or lifts must be built in an enclosure and with access doors providing at least 30 minute fire resistance. The top of the shaft must either be vented or covered in a material easily broken by fire. The fire authority can grant exemption from this requirement.
Fire Precautions (Non-Certificated Factory, Office, Shop and Railway Premises) Regulations 1976

Any hoist or lift in other factories must have a substantial enclosure with gates, which must not open except when the lift or hoist is at a landing. Similarly, the lift or hoist must not move if the gate is open. The gates must prevent any person or part thereof - arms and legs etc - from being trapped between the moving parts of the lift and the enclosure. There is an exemption granted permitting the use of lattice doors.

Factories Act 1961 as amended by the Hoists Exemption Order 1962

Factories: Welfare Facilities

Eating facilities: Where dangerous substances are involved, there is a requirement for separate areas to be provided for the staff to eat and drink. There are additional requirements for certain industries, lead being a recent example.

Factories Act 1961 and Control of Lead at Work Regulations 1980.

Sanitary accommodation: there are strict regulations governing the number of sanitary conveniences required in all factories.

— at least one for every 25 women employed
— at least one for every 25 men employed, up to the first 100 (this number does not include urinals). For numbers above 100, one to be provided for every additional 40 men.

There are more lenient requirements for factories built or converted before 1938, provided that the local authority is consulted.

All sanitary facilities must have adequate ventilation and lighting. Conviences, other than urinals, must be under cover and suitably enclosed with a "proper door and fastenings". Where both men and women are employed, the interiors of the conveniences must be screened from view even when the door is open. The entrances must be separate and adequate signs are required.

Sanitary Accommodation Regulations 1938 as amended by the Sanitary Accommodation (Amendment) Regulations 1974.

Washing facilities: Adequate washing facilities must be provided in a convenient location, with hot and cold running water. The inspector can give exemption from this requirement if there are suitable facilities conveniently available elsewhere.

Factories Act 1961

Factories: Working Conditions

Overcrowding: A minimum of 11m^3 per person, measuring only the lower 4.2 m in height of the work room.

Temperature: In any work area where most of the work performed does not involve major physical labour, a temperature of at least 16 degrees C must be achieved after the first hour of work.

Ventilation: The law requires that reasonable ventilation is provided and that fumes are removed as far as is possible. If the fumes are considered to be dangerous, they must be removed. All stationary internal combustion engines must be partitioned off from the main work area, except for maintenance, and vented to the outside.

Factories Act 1961 as amended by Factories Act 1961 etc. (Metrication) Regulations 1983

Fire Certificates: New Legislation

A wide range of changes to the legislation relating to fire certificates is to be introduced in the Fire Safety and Safety of Places of Sport Act 1987. This Act has received the Royal Assent but, at the time of going to press, had not been brought into force. The main changes will be:

— Much greater powers for the fire authorities to exempt particular premises from the need to have a fire certificate. This exemption may then be withdrawn should the authority believe that circumstances have changed in any way: e.g. structural alterations or the use of the building to store explosive or flammable substances.

— Greater attention to be paid to the provision of means of escape and fire fighting facilities. The Secretary of State will be able to produce Codes of Practice covering these subjects. Failure to comply with these may be ''tending to establish liability.''

— The Fire Authorities will be able to issue Improvement Notices requiring improvements to be made to means of escape etc.

Food Premises

A food business is any trade or business in which a person handles food and a food premise is any building or part of a building in which a food business is carried out. The only exception to this is certain agricultural buildings, ie those where vegetables etc are handled after harvesting. Food is defined as all the ingredients of food and drink except for water and live birds and animals.

Food Hygiene (General) Regulations 1970 and Food Act 1984.

Many food premises will be classified as public buildings and will, therefore, have a requirement to provide special facilities for the disabled (see also Access for the disabled).

Food Premises: Hygiene

The main requirements for the construction of food premises are all set out in the Food Hygiene (General) Regulations 1970. It may be assumed that all food processing plants, cafes, restaurants, kitchens and food shops will be covered by these regulations. The local authority does, however, have the power to grant exemptions if it thinks fit.

Clothing stores: Storage must be provided for all outdoor clothing and footwear not worn during working hours. This must be be in the form of either special cupboards or lockers.

Lighting and ventilation: Adequate lighting and ventilation must be provided.

Sanitary conveniences: Must be positioned so that no odours enter the food handling area. No convenience must be placed in a room where any food is handled nor must one open directly onto a room where open (ie unwrapped) food is handled. Adequate ventilation and lighting must be provided and notices must be fixed near to each convenience requesting users to wash their hands.

The local authority has the power to require the owners or occupiers of certain designated premises to provide and maintain whatever sanitary facilities it thinks fit. Those premises supplying food to be eaten on the premises are specifically designated, as are all ''places of entertainment''. Facilities must also be provided for the disabled.

Local Government (Miscellaneous Provisions) Act 1976 as amended by Disabled Persons Act 1981

Sleeping accommodation: Any room used for handling open food must not communicate directly with sleeping accommodation.

Soil drainage: No fresh air intake for a soil system should be placed in a food room.

Wash basins: Sufficient wash basins must be provided for the use of all those engaged in food handling. Hot and cold water or controlled temperature hot water must be provided for all basins. Special basins must be provided for washing both food and food handling equipment. These must be kept separate from those used by the staff for washing. Hot and cold water or controlled temperature hot water should normally be provided. Where the sink is used for washing fish or vegetables etc or where a bactericidal agent is used for washing glasses or ice cream equipment, cold water only may be provided.

Water supply: An adequate water supply must be provided to service the sanitary conveniences. No water cistern must supply a sanitary convenience unless it has an efficient flushing cistern or similar device designed to prevent contamination of the water supply.

Food Hygiene (General) Regulations 1970

Food Premises: Maintenance

All walls, floors, doors, windows, ceilings, woodwork and the remainder of the building's structure must be kept clean and well maintained in order to reduce the risk of infestation.

Food Hygiene (General) Regulations 1970

Health Buildings on Crown Land

If an architect is asked to design a private hospital or nursing home on land where the Crown has an interest, his client is not exempt from the requirement to notify the Secretary of State of the intention to build a private hospital (see also Hospitals — private). These regulations do not apply if the hospital is to be built for or on behalf of the Crown.

Health Services Act 1976

Horses

Riding establishments, defined as those premises which hire out horses or teach riding, must have a licence from the local authority. This applies both when the establishment is an individual unit and when it is part of a country activity centre. The conditions attached to the licence cover most aspects of construction and design and it is advisable to ascertain these conditions at an early stage in the design process. They deal with stabling accommodation, shelter, food and forage storage, water supply, bedding storage, exercise areas, precautions against disease and fires, safe storage of medicines, first aid equipment and storage for stable equipment and saddlery. The conditions are not set out in the Act so that requirements may vary from one local authority to another.

Riding Establishments Act 1964

Hospitals: Private

Application must be made to the Secretary of State for Social Services for authorisation to design private hospitals with acute treatment facilities. The facilities requiring this authorisation include extending or converting any private hospital premises containing surgical procedures under general anaesthesia, obstetrics, radiotherapy, haemodialysis, peritonal dialysis, pathology and diagnostic radiology. Unless there are special circumstances, eg the Secretary of State considers that the development could interfere with National Health Service facilities, he has to grant this authorisation.

Health Services Act 1976, Health Services Act 1980 and Health Services (Authorisation) Regulations 1980

Hotels

The legislation, itself, does not define hotels specifically. The Home Office "Guide to the fire precautions act 1971: 1 Hotels and boarding houses" does, however, provide a list of buildings which may be covered by the Act. These include public residential accommodation, eg hotels, motels, inns, boarding schools, boarding houses, hostels etc. It also covers institutional type buildings which provide sleeping accommodation, such as welfare homes of various types.

Hotels will, of course, be covered by the requirements for food premises and places of public entertainment (see also Food premises).

Hotels: Fire Certificates

The legislation on hotels is mainly concerned with fire precautions. A certificate is required if sleeping accommodation is provided for more than 6 people, counting both guests and staff, or where there is any sleeping accommodation above the first or below the ground floors. The legislation is identical to that for offices etc (see also Offices: fire certificates)

Fire Precautions Act 1971 and Fire Precautions (Hotels and Boarding Houses) Order 1972

Industrial Developments

The English Industrial Estates Corporation may now provide an advisory service to help the developer find a suitable location for his proposed industry. The Corporation may also provide certain services if the site chosen is managed by them. This also applies to premises that the client may wish to take up. There is also a Welsh Development Agency with similar functions. The architect who is involved in feasibility studies for a developer should ascertain the full extent of the help which is available.
Industrial Development Act 1985

Nursing and Residential Homes

The regulations are similar for all nursing homes, mental nursing homes, residential care homes, community homes and voluntary homes. The regulations do not go into great detail and it is advisable to contact the District Health Authority before embarking upon any detailed design work. In general, the requirements cover:

— space requirements for each patient, with regard to their age, sex and level of disability;
— sanitary and washing facilities;
— lighting, heating and ventilation;
— kitchen facilities, bearing in mind the requirements of the type of patients to be cared for;
— facilities for laundering linen and clothing
— secure storage of drugs;
— facilities for safe keeping of patients' valuables;
— fire precautions and means of escape.

A fire certificate will be required (see also Offices: fire certificates). The architect would be well advised to consult the fire authority at an early stage of the design as it will be able to give information on the materials for partitions and furnishings as well as on escape routes. Many patients are in wheel chairs or bed-bound and fire precautions are of great importance.

The success of a comfortable and well managed home relies upon the effective design of the service areas and the circulation system. The Health Authority will provide both advice and guidance.

In long-stay nursing homes, the need for privacy is greater, and the Health Authority may state what provisions should be and what type of furniture is required.

The Secretary of State for Health requires an initial and annual registration fee for nursing homes, mental nursing homes and residential care homes.

Nursing Homes Act 1963, Child Care Act 1980, Registered Homes Act 1984 and subsequent regulations

Nursing Homes and Hospitals: Private

If an architect is commissioned to design a large new nursing home or private hospital, extend an existing one or even convert a building into one, the Secretary of State for Social Services must be notified before planning permission is sought. If the hospital or home contains facilities for "acute" treatment, authorisation must be sought (see also Hospitals -private)

"Notifiable" changes consist of such items as a change in facilities or the number of beds provided. These become "controlled premises" when they have a total of more than 120 patient beds.

A fire certificate will be required for these premises (see also Offices: fire certificates).

The Secretary of State for Health requires and initial and an annual registration fee for nursing homes.

Health Services Act 1976, Health Services Act 1980 and Health Services (Notification) Regulations 1980

Offices

An office is a building or a part of a building used for administration, handling money, the operation of telephones and all clerical work. The requirements of the act do not apply if the only employees are close relatives of the employer. A dwelling is not covered if it is only used as an office by the person who normally lives there.

Offices, Shops and Railway Premises Act 1963

Offices: Access for the Disabled

The law in this area is in a state of confusion, pending the arrival of a new Approved Document to support the Building Regulations 1985. There is a requirement for provision, so far as is practicable and reasonable, to be made for disabled people using the premises, mentioning access, car parking and sanitary conveniences in particular. There is as yet, however, no clearer definition of the designer's responsibilities in this area, with the section of the Disabled Persons Act 1981 requiring that BS 5810: 1979 Code of practice for access for the disabled to buildings, not yet having been brought into force. There are, however, two relevant sections of this legislation currently in force.

— Section 3 amends the Town and Country Planning Act 1971 so that planning authorities are required to draw to the attention of applicants for all office, shop and railway premises the relevant provisions of the Chronically Sick and Disabled Persons Act 1970 and of BS 5810: 1979.

— Section 5 requires that where provision has been made for the disabled at any premises, signs must be erected both inside and outside the building. Where car parking has been provided, an appropriate route into the building must be indicated (see also Access for the disabled).

Chronically Sick and Disabled Persons Act 1970, the Chronically Sick and Disabled Persons (Amendment) Act 1976, Disabled Persons Act 1981 and Building (Disabled People) Regulations 1987

Offices: Fire Certificates

Fire certificates are required:

— where more than 20 people are employed at any one time or where more than 10 are employed other than on the ground floor.

— where any manufacturing process involves the use of liquefied petroleum gas, pressurised flammable liquids, expanded plastics and other substances specified in the Fire Certificates (Special Premises) Regulations 1976.

Applications for certificates must include details of the building's use and a set of plans. The final certificate will include details of the use, means of escape, fire fighting equipment and fire alarms. The fire authority may specify details of works required before the certificate will be granted.

If changes to the structure or interior of a building requiring a certificate are planned, notice must be given to the fire authority. If the authority believes that the proposed changes will adversely affect the means of escape and the provisions

for fire fighting and fire alarms, it can order the occupier to take appropriate action.
Fire Precautions Act 1971

Offices: Hoists, Lifts and Stairs

Any hoist or lift must have a substantial enclosure with gates, which must not open except when the lift or hoist is at a landing. Similarly, the lift or hoist must not move if the gate is open. Continuous lifts, paternosters, are excluded from this part of the regulation. The gates must prevent any person or part thereof - arms and legs etc - from being trapped between the moving parts of the lift and the enclosure. There is an exemption granted permitting the use of lattice doors.
Offices, Shops and Railway Premises Act 1963 as amended by the Offices, Shops and Railway Premises (Hoists and Lifts) Regulations 1968

All stairs, both internal and external, must have handrails, on the open side where there is one, or on both sides if both are open or if the stairs are particularly hazardous. On the open sides, there must be further protection from falling in the form of lower rails or similar.
Offices, Shops and Railway Premises Act 1963

Offices: Welfare

Clothing stores: Space must be provided for storing and, where necessary, drying, both working and non- working clothes.
Offices, Shops and Railway Premises Act 1963.

Drinking water: An adequate supply of potable water must be supplied in a place convenient for the work rooms. It must be dispensed by:

— a jet or fountain;
— disposable cups;
— ordinary cups, provided that there is a facility for rinsing them in clean water.

If no piped water is available, suitable water storage vessels must be installed.
Offices, Shops and Railway Premises Act 1963

Overcrowding: Any measurement of overcrowding must take furniture and equipment into consideration. A minimum of 3.7 m² floor space or 11 m³ air space must be allowed for each person normally employed there.

Offices, Shops and Railway Premises Act 1963 as amended by Offices, Shops and Railway Premises Act 1963 etc. (Metrication) Regulations 1982.

Temperature: An office must be capable of being heated to a minimum of 16 deg C. after the first hour of work, except where that temperature would cause deterioration of goods or where constant public access would make that temperature unreasonable.

Offices, Shops and Railway Premises Act 1963 as amended by Offices, Shops and Railway Premises Act 1963 etc. (Metrication) Regulations 1982.

Lighting: All glazed windows and skylights must be kept clean, as far as is practicable. They may still be whitewashed or shaded to prevent glare.

Offices, Shops and Railway Premises Act 1963.

Sanitary facilities: The regulations governing the provision of sanitary facilities are both detailed and complex.

Where there are suitable supplies of running water, the following number of sanitary of conveniences must be provided:

Numbers of staff	Numbers of WCs
a) Where there are less than 5 staff in total or where no one works more than 2 hours a day	1
b) Mixed staff but where no urinals are provided.	
Numbers of each sex	
1 - 15	1
16 - 30	2
31 - 50	3
51 - 75	4
76 -100	5

Where there are more than 100 staff an additional wc must be provided for each 25 extra staff.

c) Mixed staff where urinals are provided

	Numbers of WCs	Urinals
Numbers of male staff	1	-
1 - 15		
16 - 20	1	1
21 - 30	2	1
31 - 45	2	2
46 - 60	3	2
61 - 75	3	3
76 - 90	4	3
91 - 100	4	4

Where there are more than 100 staff an additional appliance for each extra 25 staff must be provided. Of these, 75% must be WCs.

Where trough type urinals are provided, 600 mm space per person should be allowed.

Where suitable running water is not available, chemical closets may be provided.

	Numbers of chemical closets
a) Where there are 5 or fewer members of staff or where no one works more than 2 hours per week	1
b) Numbers of each sex	
1 - 15	1
16 - 30	2
31 - 50	3
51 - 75	4
76 - 100	5

Where there are more than 100 staff an additional closet for each extra 25 staff must be provided.

Where more than 10 female staff are employed suitable disposal facilities must be provided for sanitary dressings.

If members of the public use the facilities, and where more than 10 people are regularly employed, an additional WC for each sex must be provided.

Unless it is impracticable, no sanitary convenience should be sited in a room where anyone, other than a lavatory attendant, works. If this has to be done, a mechanical ventilation system must be installed to discharge to the open air. The system must be kept in operation when someone is employed in the room. Any enclosed space between a room where a sanitary facility is provided and a work room must be ventilated.

All sanitary facilities must have effective weather protection and suitable doors with fastenings. Urinals must be effectively screened from view. Where there is separate accommodation for each sex, adequate signs must be installed. *Offices, Shops and Railway Premises Act 1963 and Sanitary Conveniences Regulations 1964.*

Washing facilities: Hot and cold running water must be provided, except where it is not reasonably practicable or in offices adjacent to construction sites - site offices etc. *Offices, Shops and Railway Premises Act 1963 (Exemption No 1) Order 1964.*

If running water is available, the following numbers of basins, troughs or washing fountains must be provided.

Numbers of staff	Numbers of basins etc
a) Where there are less than 5 staff in total or where 1 no one works more than 2 hours a day	1
b) Mixed staff	
Numbers of each sex	
1 - 15	1
16 - 30	2
31 - 50	3
51 - 75	4
76 - 100	5

Where there are more than 100 staff an additional facility must be provided for each 25 extra staff.

If members of the public use the facilities, and where more than 10 people are regularly employed, an additional basin for each sex must be provided.

If there is no running water, fixed or portable wash bowls must be provided.

a) Where 5 or less are employed 1 basin or bowl required

b) 1 basin or bowl for each additional 5 employees of each sex.

All facilities must be protected from the weather and have adequate ventilation. Where there are separate facilities for each sex, signs must be installed.

Offices, Shops and Railway Premises Act 1963 and Washing Facilities Regulations 1964

Schools: Access for the Disabled

Schools are specifically designated as building types requiring requiring facilities for the disabled (see also Access for the disabled)

The planning authority is obliged to point out the need to comply with the Chronically Sick and Disabled Persons Acts, BS 5810: 1979 "Code of practice for access for the disabled to buildings" and Dept of Education and Science Design Note 18 "Access for disabled people to educational buildings". There is, as yet, no power to enforce compliance with these documents but it is advisable as new legislation is under consideration and later alterations to the buildings could be expensive.

The new Section M of the Building Regulations provides some teeth to this legislation but, until the promised Approved Document has appeared, the standards of access required will remain uncertain.

Chronically Sick and Disabled Persons Act 1970, Chronically Sick and Disabled Persons Act 1976, Local Government (Miscellaneous Provisions) Act 1976, Disabled Persons Act 1981 and Building (Disabled People) Regulations 1987

Schools: Construction

School premises are governed by many items of legislation, most of which relate to inspection and licensing. This is aimed at the managing body, be it local education authority or private company rather than at the designer. There is one statutory instrument which provides detailed design parameters for the school architect, the Education (School Premises) Regulations 1981. The following sections relate entirely to this regulation.

The land must be adequate for the buildings, recreation areas and playing fields. In addition, allowance must be made for car parks, delivery bays and service roads.

The buildings must be sufficient to allow for the following activities:

—   teaching;

—   access and circulation of people and goods;

— storage of equipment, materials and food;
— cloakroom accommodation;
— food preparation.

Specific standards are set out for the provision of sanitary facilities.
Education (School Premises) Regulations 1981

Schools: Playing Fields

There is an extensive schedule of requirements for playing fields, covering both the minimum areas and the performance requirements. These apply to schools where the pupils are aged 8 years or over. All grass areas must be capable of withstanding 7 hours per week use. Artificial surfaces can reduce the required areas by as much as a half and the presence of swimming pools, sports halls etc which are not included as part of the teaching facilities can also affect the requirements. Sixth form colleges and special schools have special requirements.
Education (School Premises) Regulations 1981

Schools: Teaching Facilities

The requirements for teaching facilities include playrooms for nursery schools but not any space required for access, circulation, storage etc. An extensive table is given, with different requirements for pupils in the age ranges under 9; 9 — 11; 11 — 13; 13 — 15; 15 + . There is also a requirement for nursery schools.
In schools where there are pupils over 16 years of age, private study or social areas must be provided.
Education (School Premises) Regulations 1981

Schools: Playgrounds

Playgrounds must consist of a mixture of paved and hard porous areas. "Paved" is defined as concrete, tarmac etc. "Hard porous" is a loosely compacted water-bound surface, such as crushed brick, or a bitumen-bound surface allowing drainage. Different ratios of each are required for nursery schools, for schools for those under 8 years of age and for all others. In nursery schools, the playground area must be separated from other areas by a wall, fence, hedge or similar.

In sixth form colleges, a sports hall or similar facility may remove the requirements, provided that adequate provision is made.

Education (School Premises) Regulations 1981

Shops

A shop is any premise used primarily for retail selling. This also includes buildings used for the storage of goods in connection with the retail trade, other than warehouses etc, buildings to which the public deliver goods for repair and premises used for the storage and sale of solid fuels.

Offices, Shops and Railway Premises Act 1963

Shops: General Requirements

Most of the requirements for shops are the same as those for offices, with the Offices, Shops and Railway Premises Act 1963 and its various amending regulations providing the basic legislative framework. Special requirements for shop premises tend to be related to the nature of the product sold. Additional information on shops may, therefore, be found in the sections on Food etc.

Sanitary accommodation: The basic requirements are identical to those for offices. There are, however, exemptions for retail sales kiosks in public parks, places of entertainment, historic buildings etc. In order to qualify for this status the buildings must have one room only, a floor area of less than 9 m^2 and must not be connected to any other building. The public must not be allowed entry into the kiosk itself and must not be charged for using the kiosk. Suitable public or other facilities must be available for the use of the employees.

Offices, Shops and Railway Premises Act 1963 (Exemption No 7) Order 1968

Sports Grounds

Following recent disasters, there is now a stringent system of certification for all sports grounds "designated" by the Secretary of State. This certification is currently restricted to those grounds which it is anticipated will hold more than 10 000 spectators and which have been listed in one of the designation orders which are issued at regular intervals. These orders are subject to regular change and consist of lists of those grounds added to the list of those designated.

Safety at Sports Grounds Act 1976 and the Safety at Sports Grounds Regulations 1976. Those grounds designated are listed in a series of Safety at Sports Grounds (Designation) Orders

Changes to the legislation are proposed which will extend the coverage to any sports grounds which the Secretary of State may choose. This legislation had not been brought into force at the time of publication.
Fire Safety and Safety of Places of Sport Act 1987

Sports Grounds: Certificates

The certificate may be:

— general, ie issued for all activities in a stadium for an indefinite period;
— special, ie issued for specified activities on a specific occasion.

The certificate may specify:

— the maximum number of spectators;
— the number of spectators accommodated in any particular area;
— the number, size and situation of all entrances and exits;
— the requirement that all entrances, exits and circulation areas should be kept well maintained and free from obstruction.

Records must be kept of the numbers attending and the safety record of the stadium. The certificate will include a full plan of the stadium.
Applications: The local authority must be certain that the applicant for a certificate is in a position to ensure that the conditions in the certificate will be complied with. If an application is rejected, the applicant may appeal to the Secretary of State.
Alterations and inspection: If any alterations to the stadium are proposed which might have an effect upon the safety standards, the certificate holder must give full notice of the proposals to the local authority. The authority, the police, the building inspectors etc may all inspect the stadium at any reasonable time and may all demand access to the attendance records etc. Spectators must not be allowed into the stadium until a certificate has been issued and must not be admitted for purposes other than those specified in the certificate.

Safety at Sports Grounds Act 1976 and the Safety at Sports Grounds Regulations 1976. Those grounds designated are listed in a series of Safety at Sports Grounds (Designation) Orders

Sports Grounds: Covered Stands

Legislation is proposed which will result in covered stands holding more than 500 spectators requiring a certificate, even though the ground as a whole is not designated. The requirements will be similar to those for the certification of complete grounds. This legislation had not been brought into force at the time of publication.

Fire Safety and Safety of Places of Sport Act 1987

Wild Animals as Pets

Anyone wishing to keep a wild animal, such as a chimpanzee, exotic deer, baboon, giraffe, racoon or snake as a pet, will have to obtain a licence from the local authority and comply with the conditions imposed. Licences are required for both large and small species, with the original Act listing 25 of them, although this number may be varied by future legislation. The conditions cover the provision of escapeproof enclosures, lighting, ventilation, drainage, fire precautions, exercise areas and prevention of disease, all of which may involve considerable capital and maintenance costs. Conditions are strictly enforced and regular inspections are performed.

Wild Animals Act 1976

On the Site

Introduction

This chapter deals with the many places where the contractor is likely to be committing some offence against safety or environmental control regulations. While these offences are not properly the architect's affair, he still has a duty to point out to the contractor (preferably in writing) any breaches of regulations which he has observed.

The two areas of legislation where the contractor is most at risk are the Health and Safety Regulations and the Environmental Pollution Controls. There are regulations or Codes of Practice governing practically every type of site operation from tower cranes to hammers; and too much noise, smoke, or oily water emanating from the site will attract repressive notices from various authorities, with possible delays and extra costs to the contract while matters are put right.

The architect should also concern himself with his own safety and that of his staff during site visits, particularly when using scaffolding and access ladders. On most sites safety foot and headgear is provided under the contract for regular supervisory staff, but any architect making an occasional visit is advised to bring his own safety gear particularly if, like one of the authors, the boots happen to be size three; it is conducive neither to safety nor comfort to walk a muddy site in a pair of borrowed size tens.

Asbestos

These regulations prohibit the sale or use or importation of products containing asbestos (crocidolite and amosite). A licence is required from the Health and Safety Executive before an employer or a self-employed person can work with asbestos insulation or asbestos coatings. Removal of asbes-

tos, especially in the form of lagging and insulation, requires the workforce to wear special safety equipment; it is usually advisable to have the removal carried out by specialist firms. Disposal of asbestos in the London area is now dealt with by a waste authority covering the whole of London, and in Merseyside and Manchester by the new authorities set up to replace Merseyside and Greater Manchester.
Asbestos (Prohibitions) Regulations 1985 and Asbestos (Licensing) Regulations 1983

Controlled Waste

If the building site contains waste classified as "controlled waste", it must be tipped on a licensed waste site, that is on a site that holds a disposal licence from the relevant authority. Controlled waste comprises household, commercial and industrial waste, but not special waste (qv).
Control of Pollution (Licensing of Waste Disposal) Regulations 1976

Damages: Joint Liability

Anyone liable for damages suffered by another person may get back part of the costs from third parties who can be held jointly liable for that damage. Unless a period of limitation applies to that particular kind of damage the persons concerned continue to be liable.
Architects working with other professionals should make every effort to limit their share of any joint responsibilities. (See bcd Civil Liability and Joint Liability.)
Civil Liability (Contributions) Act 1978

Flammable Liquids and LPG

There are strict requirements for the storage and labelling of these materials, as well as instructions on the precautions to be taken to prevent fire and explosions.
Highly Flammable Liquids and Liquid Petroleum Gases Regulations 1972

Guard Dogs

Should the contractor decide to employ the services of a guard dog it is required to be under the control of its handler at all times, unless the dog is secured so that it cannot roam the premises. It is obligatory to post a notice saying that

guard dogs are employed at all entrances to the building or site.
Guard Dogs Act 1975

Improvement Notices

A Health and Safety Executive inspector can serve an improvement notice on any person who is contravening the Health and Safety regulations. The notice must set out the contraventions and the inspector's reasons for serving the notice, and the requirements for remedial action. A time limit is set for compliance with the notice.

When an improvement notice has to do with a matter subject to building control or similar controls (such as fire precautions) the inspector cannot enforce more stringent remedial works than are required by those regulations.

Although the contractor is responsible for his workforce, any contravention of these regulations should be brought to his attention.

Health and Safety at Work Etc Act 1974, Codes of Practice, and regulations

Noise Control

Before work on the site begins, an application may be made to the local authority giving details of proposed noise control measures. If noise control measures are agreed with the local authority, the site is deemed to comply with noise control regulations, although this does not prevent the authority from taking action if the agreed noise loadings are exceeded. The architect is advised to ensure that the builder, contractor, or demolition contractor on his building site complies with BS 5228:Pt 1:1984 Code of Practice for Basic Information and Procedures for Noise Control, relating to the control of noise on construction and demolition sites. This British Standard recommends methods of noise control relating to construction sites and other open sites, and gives guidance concerning: methods of predicting and measuring noise; the minimizing of the impact of site noise upon people in the vicinity of site operations, relevant legislation; liaison procedures for those concerned with construction and open site processes.

Should the architect be drawn into a dispute between the contractor and the local authority on the question of satisfactory noise control, he would be advised to consult BS 5228:Pt 2:1984 The Guide to Noise Control Legislation for construction and demolition including road construction and maintainance.

Control of Noise (Codes of Practice for Construction and Open Sites) Order 1984

Notification of Works

Certain types of building operations come under the Factory Act 1961: these are defined as:

— the construction, structural alteration, repair or maintenance of a building (including re-pointing, re-decoration and external cleaning of the structure);
— the demolition of a building;
— the preparation for and laying the foundation of an intended building.

It does not include an operation which is a work of engineering construction within the meaning of the act.

The contractor must notify the Health and Safety Executive district inspector 7 days before starting work. Additional information required includes:

— a statement as to whether the building work is to be carried out by a main or sub-contractor;
— the trade of the contractors;
— their full name and registered address;
— site phone number if any;
— number of workers expected to be employed;
— starting and completion dates.

Although this is not the direct responsibility of the architect, it is as well to check that the contractors have sent in the correct notices in order to avoid friction with the Health and Safety Executive.

Construction (Notice of Operations and Works) Order 1965

Prohibition Notices: Health and Safety

A Health and Safety Executive inspector can serve a prohibition notice on any person who contravenes the Health and Safety Regulations where there is a risk of serious personal injury. This type of notice is only served where the inspector has reason to believe that the work in hand will give rise to a risk, and if the operations appear to be likely to cause immediate serious personal injury he can order it to cease forthwith. When a prohibition notice is served, no further operations can be carried on by the person on whom the notice has been served until remedial action has been taken.

Although these matters are under the control of the building contractor, the architect has a duty to bring any contraventions to his notice.

Health and Safety at Work Etc Act 1974, Codes of Practice and Regulations

Reporting Injuries and Dangerous Occurances

It is now mandatory to notify the Health and Safety Executive of such occurences as a major collapse of scaffolding or building, and injuries caused whilst using equipment or machinery. The Health and Safety Executive produce guidance on this subject in their publication HS(R)23; it contains a list of Health and Safety Executive offices and their inspectorates, together with sample forms and a copy of the regulations.

Although the notification of such accidents (bcd) is unlikely to be the direct responsibility of the architect, he has a duty to inform the contractor if he has observed any event which should be reported.

Reporting of Injuries, Diseases and Dangerous Occurences Regulations 1985

Safety: Constrution Regulations

These Regulations apply to all building operations including those undertaken for or on behalf of the Crown, municipal and other public authorities. They set out the duties of the employer to provide safety measures and of the employee to comply. Subjects covered include:

— excavations;
— shafts and tunnels and the safe egress from them in case of flooding as well as fencing them, and safeguarding their edges;
— dangerous or unhealthy atmospheres;
— safe demolition practices;
— work on or adjacent to water;
— fencing of machinery;

— the safe use of electric power;
— prohibiting the throwing or tipping of tools from scaffolds;
— the use of head and eye protection.

Compliance with regulations and codes of practice are the contractor's responsibility, but it is sensible to check that the safety requirements are being met, and the contractor should be notified of any breaches.

Construction (General Provisions) Regulations 1961

Safety on Site

The Health and Safety at Work Act consolidates most of the previous legislation, and it has the aim of preventing accident and illness amongst the workforce as well as paying compensation for industrial injuries. There are, however, some regulations still in force which come under the Factory Acts 1937 and 1961 as well as the Offices, Shops and Railway Premises Act 1963. Enforcement of Health and Safety legislation is in the hands of the Health and Safety Executive through their inspectors. The Health and Safety Commission can order investigations or inquiries into accidents. Codes of Practice published or approved by the Health and Safety Executive have a legal standing and non-compliance affects the findings of any court. It is vitally important that those persons in charge of sites are aware of the requirements and check that they and their employees understand their responsibilities. A comprehensive coverage of the subject is given in the Construction Safety Manual published by the Building Employers' Federation.

The inspectors have wide powers, including access to premises, taking measurements or samples, and removing materials from the site. They may also inspect documents and collect evidence.

The Act provides for safe handling, storage, transport and use of materials. Any materials supplied or stored on site must not present a health or safety hazard, nor must any site procedure cause the emission of noxious fumes or smoke into the atmosphere. Remember also that safety includes protection against eye damage, noise, vibration, dangerous chemicals and dust, as well as the more obvious risks of slipping off buildings, stepping on nails, or standing under falling objects.

Although safety on the site is the contractor's responsibility, the architect has a duty to point out (preferably in writing) any breaches of the Safety Codes that he observes; above all, the architect should check that his design and maintenance manuals procedures comply with health and safety requirements, both for new and alteration work (see also bcd Statutory Duty).

Health and Safety at Work Etc Act 1974, Codes of Practice, and Regulations

Safety: Working Conditions

There are many regulations that deal with safety on the site. They specify safety requirements for scaffolding including putlogs and ledgers, access lifting gear, trestles, slung and suspended scaffolds, boatswain's chairs etc. These regulations state the plank sizes widths of working platforms, guard rails and toe boards. Records of scaffold operations must be kept on the prescribed forms and available for inspection. Regulation 23 of the Construction (Working Places) Regulations 1966 states that the employer of any workmen, not employed by the contractor that had the scaffold erected, is responsible for checking the scaffolding and satisfying himself that the regulations have been complied with. The architect must satisfy himself that all the regulations are complied with before carrying out any inspection which requires him to use any of the specified structures. He also has a duty to notify the contractor if he observes any breach of the regulations.

Other regulations govern the use of site machinery, especially wood-working machines (see also Reporting Injuries and Dangerous Occurences).

Construction (Working Places) Regulations 1966 and Woodworking Machines Regulations 1974

Site Fires

There are strict regulations controlling the emission of "dark smoke" from fires. Where a building is being demolished or a site cleared in connection with building operations, it is permissible to burn timber or any other material except natural or synthetic rubber, flock or feathers. But even this permission is subject to there being no reasonably safe or practicable alternative method of disposal; in any case the

burning must be carried out in such a way as to minimize the emission of smoke and it must be under the direct and continuous supervision of the occupier or his agent. The bonfire must only consist of site material, and not include rubbish from other sites (see also Demolition and Fires near Highways).
Clean Air (Emission of Dark Smoke) (Exemption) Regulations 1969

Site Lifting Gear

There are regulations which apply to all building sites and govern:

— the safe use of hoists;
— lifting gear and its safe anchorage;
— fixing and erection;
— cranes and their cabs;
— pulley blocks and gin wheels.

The failure of lifting gear can have disastrous effects both on the structure and on the workmen (see also Safety on the Site).
Construction (Lifting Operations) Regulations 1961

Vehicles on Footpaths

If a vehicle serving the site has to travel over a footpath, footway or bridle path (qqv), the Gas Board must be informed. A vehicle which is a ''restricted use appliance or vehicle'' has limitations as to weight transmission, and in all cases the speed is limited to five miles per hour. The regulations mainly affect vehicles over one ton weight.
Vehicles (Conditions of Use on Footpaths) Regulations 1963

Waste from Construction Sites

Waste from building sites, whether from demolition work, new work, repairs or alterations to existing work, is classed as industrial waste; and should be tipped on a site licensed for controlled waste (qv). However, it may be deposited on unlicensed sites as long as it is tipped with the owners approval, and it does not contain liquid or solid poisonous, noxious or polluting substances.

As provision for the proper disposal of waste is always priced in the bill of quantities, there is no possible excuse for fly-tipping to the detriment of the environment.

Control of Pollution (Licensing of Waste Disposal) Regulations 1976

Welfare on Building Sites

The regulations governing the welfare of the workforce apply to all building sites including those under contracts by or on behalf of the Crown. They deal with:

— shelters;
— accommodation for eating;
— protective clothing and its storage;
— drinking water;
— washing facilities and sanitary accommodation related to the number of employees.

The contractor must also provide protective clothing for visitors to the site.

These requirements are in addition to those concerning safety on the site (qv) and altogether they represent a considerable responsibility for the contractor. The architect is bound to point out to the contractor any breaches of the welfare regulations that come to his notice.

Construction (Health and Welfare) Regulations 1966

In the Office

Introduction

This chapter sets out the laws governing the conduct of businesses and partnerships as well as reminders on such subjects as copyright and data protection. The Codes of Conduct are not included in this chapter as, unlike the duty of care, professional liability and negligence, they are not legislation but agreed professional principles. Most of the courts' decisions on partnership matters are based on case law rather than statute law. The conditions relating to staff and their employment are dealt with under Employment.

Advice to the Client

Over and above his normal professional duties, an architect is expected to have enough knowledge of the law to enable him to advise his client on the legal rights affecting the use of land. This would include a working knowledge of planning and building law together with a cognisance of covenants (qv), easements (qv), and other land charges (qv). He is not expected to understand the finer points of law in the way that a solicitor or barrister would do, but he should know when to advise his client to employ expert legal skills. If the client obtains legal advice from a lawyer the architect can accept this information with confidence.

The architect should be able to appreciate the legal effect of any interference with any rights of light (qv) or air, or easements; he should then inform his client of these matters. It is not the architect's duty to advise his client on legal matters.

Mainly case law

Arbitration

If the parties to a contract agree to have their disputes settled by arbitration (bcd), this agreement must be made in writing. Most contracts in the construction industry incorporate an arbitration clause, but the agreement to submit to arbitration can be a separate document. Both parties to the contract must concur in referring a disagreement to an arbitrator. The arbitrator cannot compel evidence to be given, but he can apply to the courts for power to call witnesses, and the courts can set aside his decision if he commits a legal error.

It is accepted that the arbitrator must:

— have no connection with the parties to the disagreement;
— be technically competent to assess the evidence;
— understand the principles of giving judgement.

Services rendered by an arbitrator are exempt from the Supply of Goods and Services Act 1982. Any obligations will be covered by common law. (See also bcd Discovery/inspection of Documents and Scott Schedule).

Arbitration Acts 1950 and 1979, Supply of Goods and Services Act 1982 and Supply of Services (Exclusion of Implied Terms) Order 1985

Architects' Registration

The term "architect" is confined by law to people whose names are on the Statutory Register of Architects, held by the Architects Registration Council of the United Kingdom (bcd). It is a contravention of the Act to use the designation "architect" or to incorporate the word in any business name unless the architectural work of the firm is controlled by a registered architect. The Registrar of Companies informs ARCUK of any new company names containing the words "architect" or "architectural" so that the company Articles of Association can be checked.

Unfortunately there is considerable abuse of the word "architectural" by unregistered people, since this term is not barred under the Acts, and the public are frequently deceived into thinking that they are employing registered architects.

Architects coming across such instances should report them

to ARCUK so that legal action can be taken and the good name of the profession upheld.

Architects (Registration) Acts 1931 and 1938 and Architects (Registration) (Amendment) Act 1969

Breach of Contract

A contract (qv) is breached when any of its conditions or warranties are broken, but the breach is not necessarily a positive action. A breach of contract (bcd) may arise where a breach of duty is the result of negligence of any of the duties set out in the contract. As an example an architect may be negligent over his site supervision, and issue a certificate for faulty work.

If a contract is breached the client or the contractor may sue for damages or determine the contract, and the remedy is sought under common law (See also bcd Remoteness of Damage).

Contract law is based on case law.

Business Names

It is no longer permissible for a business or professional firm to use a name for the firm that suggests a connection with the Government, local authorities etc. In other words it will not be well seen if an architectural practice decide to call themselves NHS Hospital Consultants, DoE Environmental Consultants or even DES Schools Designers.

The names of all partners in a business including the professions must now have their names printed on all business letters, written orders or receipts for goods or services.

If there are more than 20 partners in an architectural practice, the list of partners can be kept at head office instead of being printed on business stationery.

Business Names Act 1985

Changes in Partnership

Unless a specific arrangement is made in the partnership deed, the Partnership Act says that a partnership is automatically dissolved on the death or bankruptcy of any partner. Legally a partnership ceases to exist if anything happens to make the activities of that partnership illegal; such as partners being struck off their professional register.

Other legal grounds for dissolving a partnership are insanity, permanent incapacity, prejudicial conduct damaging to the business, persistent breaking of the partnership agreement, carrying on the business at a loss, and continual in-fighting between the partners which makes it impossible to carry on the business. In these cases the courts will uphold a partner's application to have the partnership dissolved. Like any other contract, if one party has deliberately misled the others about the practice, the partnership can be rescinded.

New partners joining a firm are not responsible for existing liabilities unless they accept that responsibility.

A retiring partner is responsible for liabilities incurred during his partnership, and may be held responsible for liabilities incurred after he retired.

The best method of dealing with changes in a partnership is by a "contract of novation" which includes all parties to any contracts current at the date of the change. This contract sets out the liabilities of the new, existing, and retiring partners towards all other parties with whom they have a business relationship; it has the effect of preventing delayed action claims catching up with a former senior partner. It is advisable to advertise changes of partnership in the professional journals and in the London or Edinburgh Gazettes and to make sure that all obsolete headed paper etc. is destroyed.

Partnership Act 1890 and Misrepresentation Act 1967

Contract

A contract (bcd) is a bargain between two parties; each side agrees to do something for the other. Any contract is made by one party proffering terms, and the other party accepting them after the necessary bargaining. The terms of the contract are agreed between the parties, and any conditions may be incorporated, with the exception that contracts leading to illegal activities are void. Usually the courts rely on the written conditions of the contract, but sometimes unforeseen factors occur, and the courts then have to adjudicate. There is an enormous amount of literature on the subject of contracts, and much of it deals with the various forms of building contract, but in essence the contract remains a simple bargain and the architect should remember that a single sentence agreed by both parties is as valid as the most impressive legal document.

This implies that any correspondence between the architect and his client could form a contract, and the architect should check the wording in his letters carefully or he may find that he has contracted to do much more than he bargained for (see also bcd Unfair Contract Terms Act).

Copyright

Copyright law covers all types of "artistic work" regardless of its artistic quality, and includes paintings, drawings, engravings, photographs and works of architecture being either buildings or models of buildings. Even the most hideous building is protected from imitation by undiscriminating building owners; an argument which could be used more often by architects who are asked to "do one like I saw in California".

The copyright (bcd) is vested in the owner of the work, except where the work is carried out as part of a contract of service or is specially commissioned and paid for, when the copyright rests with the person who commissioned the work. Employees who prepare designs in their own time hold the copyright but if they are specifically instructed to do so by their employer, the copyright is the employer's. The courts recognise that a proper remuneration should be paid for valuable original work, and works of genius paid for at bargain prices may be restored to their creator.

However, the copyright of a work of architecture is not infringed by taking photographs, or making drawings or engravings of the building. If the building is reconstructed at a later date, that reconstruction is not an infringement of copyright, provided that the original building was built with the permission of the copyright holder.

Copyright Act 1956 and Copyright (Amendment) Act 1983

Corporate Partnerships

It is legally permissible for a group of companies to form a partnership, or for a company and a group of professionals to form a partnership. A company is limited as to its liability to the companies assets only, and not to those of its members; this provides some protection against the statutory liability of general partners. The service company which is formed by many architectural practices to take care of their premises and administration is a typical example of this kind of partnership.

Companies, unlike partnerships, are limited as to the activities they can carry out, so that they cannot be used as a substitute for a partnership.

Partnership Act 1890

Cost Limits: Preparing Plans

The architect's design must be based on sound building principles, and be in accordance with his employer's instructions. In preparing his plans and specification to comply with the overall cost limit given him by his client, the architect is warranting that he can work within that limit. If however his client insists on having a "Rolls Royce" job for the price of a "Granada", the architect is within his rights to accept a lower standard of work on the finishes etc. of the building.

In order to prevent any argument, the architect is well advised to explain the problem to his client at an early stage, and either reduce the cubic capacity of the building, or persuade his client to increase the cost limit if he requires a good class job.

Case law

Data Protection: Coverage

Data users who hold or have control of computer based records on living individuals who can be identified from the information have to register. This information may be held on their own computer or in common with other persons (computer bureaux, the firm's accountant or other advisers). If the data is held by a bureau, they must inform the architect of the need to register. Information held and maintained clerically on index cards etc is outwith the scope of the Act, but information held in a form which enables it to be processed on a computer at a later date may need to be registered. Registration is required if a data user allows other persons to process personal data on a computer in his possession.

Architectural firms who keep staff records on computer should check their liability under the Act.
Data Protection Act 1984

Data Protection: Exempted Data

There are many types of exempted data in this section that are unlikely to concern an architect, namely for reasons of national security, however if the data is held in a payroll system for the purposes of calculating pay etc the user may be exempt if the information is not disclosed for any reason other than obtaining actuarial advice, for the purposes of audit or for medical statistics relating to the work place.
Data Protection Act 1984

Data Protection: Principles

The act requires data users to adhere to seven principles including the following:

— Personal data shall be obtained and processed fairly, and held only for one or more specified and lawful purposes. Personal data is defined as including an expression of opinion about an individual: but excludes any indication of intentions of the data user in respect of the individual ie his intention to promote or move to another department a member of staff.

— Personal data shall not be used or disclosed in any manner incompatible with that purpose.

— Personal data shall be accurate and where necessary kept up to date. Information relevant for the registered purpose shall be adequate but not excessive.

— Personal data shall not be kept for longer than is necessary for that purpose.

— Data subjects are entitled at reasonable intervals and without due expense to be informed by the data user if he holds personal information about him, and he may have access to that data and if necessary have the information corrected or erased.

— Appropriate security measures must be taken against unauthorised access to, or alteration, disclosure, or destruction of personal data, and against accidental loss or destruction of personal data.

If an architect's firm registers as a computer bureau they

may not disclose registered data without the prior authority of the person for whom the service is provided.

It is an offence under the Act to fail to register (see Data Protection: registration).

Data Protection Act 1984

Data Protection: Registration

All existing data users and computer bureaux were given six months from 11 November in which to register. This made 11 May 1986 the final day for registration. Registration Packs are available from the Post Office: these contain application forms, a guidance booklet to help applicants complete the forms, address labels for the return of completed forms and registration fee of £22.00 for each application to the Registrar. Registration has to be renewed every three years.

Copies of the Register will be locally available; probably at the public reference library.

Further reading
Data Protection Act 1984 c35 HMSO £4.00
Tolley's Data Protection Kit: £16.50
Also available with the Act: £20.50
Data Protection Act 1984: Guideline No 1. Office of the Data Protection Registrar, Springfield House, Water Lane, Wilmslow, Cheshire SK9 5AX.
Data Protection: the Data Protection Act, how does it affect you? Free from: Ernst & Whinney, Becket House, 1 Lambeth Palace Road, London SE1 7EU.
Data Protection Act 1984 and subsequent regulations

Deed of Partnership

There is no statutory prescribed form for a deed of partnership, (though standard forms are available). A deed of partnership is an ordinary contract and subject to the law of contract; and all the conditions of the partnership with a few constraints (qv) may be decided by the partners themselves. When a partnership is formed or where the partnership changes, it is advisable for each party to seek independent legal advice. The partnership contract cannot bind a third party, and any conditions the partners make for themselves are not binding on third parties who have not been notified of their existence. A partnership deed usually contains a starting date and some procedure for terminating the partnership. The Partnership Act recognises partnerships as being either for a fixed period or terminable by the agreement of the partners ("at will"). If the partnership is for a fixed term it can only be ended in accordance with the terms of the deed, or by the courts. If the partnership is terminable at will, then any partner can give notice to the others that he is dissolving the partnership. Partnerships on the point of dissolution may become acrimonious, and it is advisable to ensure that the formula for disolving them is very carefully worked out in the deed.

The courts may adjudicate in this matter, but the assets -which were probably the original cause of the disagreement are likely to disappear in the process.

If a partnership continues to function after the date of termination in the partnership deed the assumption is that the conditions are the same as they were when the partnership was in force.

Partnership Act 1890

Employing Experts

If an architect feels that he is not competent enough to deal with a specific technical problem he can either ask the client to employ a professional expert, or obtain advice or assistance from an expert himself. In the first case the architect cannot be held negligent for any professional failures in that specialised field. In the second case, as the architect is responsible for the selection of the expert, he may not be able to pass the liability (qv) on to a third party and could therefore be held to be negligent.

If the architect obtains expert advice from a manufacturer who warranted that the material would work and solve all his problems, then both could be held jointly liable, as they both owed a duty to the client to consider the suitability of the material specified.

Mostly based on case law

Employment Agencies

There are two distinct types of employment organisations who supply extra labour for those who do not wish to take on extra permanent staff:

— employment agencies supply workers who are paid by the customer;
— employment businesses supply workers who are paid by that business, but who work under the control of the customer.

Both these types of organisation must be licensed, and the condition of the licence are strict. There are regulations on employing under-eighteens or those in full-time education. The agencies may not normally demand a fee from the people seeking employment; their income is derived from the hiring organisation. The current licence and a copy of any regulations must be displayed on the premises.

Any architect either looking for staff or seeking employment should check these points to ensure that he is dealing with a reputable agency.

Employment Agencies Act 1973

Group Partnership

Although originally, partnerships were limited to twenty members, most professions including that of ''building designer'' are exempt from this rule. An attractive method of organising large numbers of partners efficiently is to form a ''group partnership''. Each branch of the firm becomes a separate partnership, but subservient to a partnership agreement between the groups, usually with head office as the ''senior partner''.

Partnership Act 1890

Income Tax: Cars

There are various regulations which prevent a business man from getting too many tax-free benefits from his office; amongst these are regulations which treat company cars and fuel allowances as part of his income. At present the rules only apply to directors and employees earning over £8,500 per year, but the limits change from time to time, and the architect should keep himself informed.

Finance Act 1986

Latent Damage

There are now limitations on the time during which actions for latent damage to property can be brought, as long as the damage does not include personal injury.

The time limit for an action for negligence is either:

— six years from the date of the damage, or;
— three years from the date when the plaintiff or his predecessors had knowledge of the damage;

and in either case he was entitled to bring an action.

The plaintiff must know:

— the material facts about the damage;
— that the damage was attributed to negligence;
— the identity of the person responsible for the negligence or any others responsible.

There is an over-riding time limit for actions of 15 years from the date of the negligent act or ommission. If the plaintiff was disabled at the time when the action accrued, he can still bring an action up to three years after he gets fit or dies; but the fifteen year limit still applies.

Any successive owner who acquires the property after the damage occured but before anyone knew about it; can bring an action which will be dated from the time that he acquired an interest in the property. The date of the original damage remains unchanged.

The plaintiff can either ascertain the facts about the damage from his own knowledge or by asking expert advice.

This is a complex subject, and not one that the architect should try to deal with on his own; as soon as he suspects that their may be a cause for an action for latent damage he should seek expert legal advice.

Limitation Act 1980 and Latent Damage Act 1986

Liability

As a general rule liability does not lie between an employer and someone providing a contract for services; in this case the latter is termed an independent contractor. However liability does fall on the employer if someone provides a contract of service; in this case he is the servant of the employer and has agreed to supply his work skill for a remuneration.

As an example, an architect can be held liable for the
negligence of his staff, and he can also be held liable for the
negligence of his partners, but not for an outside consultant
who has provided services in which the architect has no part,
such as a contract for services to carry out an aerial survey
paid for by the client.
Mostly case law

Liability of a Principal for his Assistant

An architect who has his own practice, or is a partner in a
firm is liable for any act that he has deputed to his assistant.
This is based on the principle that in case law, a master has
a vicarious liability (bcd) for the acts of his servant.
The definition of "vicarious" is given as deputed or
delegated.
Case law

Limitations of Liability

For a simple contract, any action for liability must be
brought within six years. Where a contract is under seal the
time limit is extended to twelve years.
For actions founded on tort, such as negligence, the time
limit is six years. In cases of damages for personal injuries it
is three years.
In all these cases the cause of action accrues from the date
of the breach of contract, or when the damage occurred.
This is not a simple matter, and the latest well-known
decision was given in the Pirelli General Cable Works
Limited v Oscar Faber and Partners 1983, where it was
established that the liability for negligence should be dated
from the actual date when the damage occurred, and not
from the date when it was discovered. There are exceptions
to this ruling, notably when the building was "doomed from
the start" by reason of professional or technical incompe-
tence.
The 1986 Latent Damage Act amends the time limit set in
the 1980 Limitation Act for negligent actions not involving
personal injury to 15 years but this is not necessarily the limit
of the architect's liability. Under certain circumstances, it
also allows an action for negligent damage to be brought by
someone acquiring an interest in a property after that
damage is said to have occurred.

This is an extremely complex subject and any architect unfortunate enough to find himself with an action on his hands will require specialist legal advice.

(See also bcd Latent Defect, Liability and Limitation of Actions)

Limitations Act 1980

Limited Partnerships

This type of partnership must be registered with the Registrar of Companies. There must be a minimum of one general partner and one "limited partner". In practice a limited partner usually puts a capital sum into the business, and his liability is limited in respect of that investment, but the Act does not limit his liability to bear the losses of the whole firm out of his share of the profits. A limited partner can sell his interest with the consent of the general partners, but he cannot take his money out of the firm without the general partners consent. Should the limited partner take part in the management of the firm he will find himself being treated in law as a general partner, and he will then have to shoulder their burdens.

Since there is no tax advantage in forming a limited partnership, this type of association is seldom promoted.

Limited Partnerships Act 1907

Measurement: Metric Units

The Weights and Measures Act 1985 sets out certain units which may not now be used for trade; these include:

— a furlong = 220 yards
— a chain = 22 yards
— a square mile = 640 acres
— a rood = 1210 square yards
— a square inch = 1/144 of a square foot
— a cubic yard = a cube one yard on all sides
— a cubic foot = 1/27 of a cubic yard
— a cubic inch = 1/1728 of a cubic foot
— a ton = 2240 lbs
— a metric ton = 1000 kgs (now to be known as a tonne)
— a hundredweight = 112 lbs
— a quarter = 28 lbs
— a stone = 14 lbs

There some controls on the units in which building materials may be sold. Except for quantities under one tonne or under one m^3, building aggregates, hardcore and ballast must be sold in multiples of 0.2 m^3, or by weight. Demolition material is exempted. Ready mixed mortar and concrete must only be sold in multiples of 0.1 m^3 except under 1.0 m^3. Pre-packed Portland cement must be marked with the weight.

There are strict controls on bulk ballast vehicles. Many of the old Imperial units have now gone by the board, but they have now been given definite metric equivalents. The latest version is of particular interest to those involved in estate work as it gives metric equivalents for:

— a chain = 20.12 m
— a furlong = 201.20 m
— a rood = 1012.00 m^2

Incidentally, a UK nautical mile equals 1853 m, a foot-candle equals 10.76 lux, a hand equals 0.1016 m high, and a bushel equals 36 x 37 x 10^{-3} m^3.

Weights and Measures Act 1985 and Units of Measurement Regulations 1986

Music while you Work

If the architect or his staff play recorded music during working hours he should, by rights, obtain a licence from the Performing Rights Society. If he is unlucky enough to be caught without a licence, he could be made to pay half as much again on top of the set fee.

The architect may prefer to allow his staff to perform their own traditional music on the plumbing samples, parallel motion strings, or even a comb. If however he should wish to obtain a licence, he should apply to the Performing Rights Society in London.

Negligence: Shared Responsibility

Where an architect designed inadequate foundations for a block of flats, and the building inspector passed them as satisfactory, the courts found both parties negligent and

apportioned the damages at 75% to the architect, and 25% to the local authority.
Case law

Office Equipment

Considerable responsibility is laid at the door of those selling goods to provide only those items that are safe and fit for their purpose. It is an offence to supply consumer goods which fail to comply with general safety regulations or to agree to supply such goods.

Although the architect will be mainly concerned with furniture and equipment used in his office, these rules will also apply to an architect who designs and supplies specific furniture or fittings for his client. He should, therefore, take care that his designs are tested for fitness of purpose and safety in use before they are installed.
Consumer Protection Act 1987

Partner to Partner

Partners have certain duties toward each other. Each has a duty of good faith towards his partners; he must give true accounts and full information on all subjects affecting the partnership. Negligence of one partner towards the others can also be a breach of this duty. He must account to his partners for all monies or other benefit he receives whileacting as a member of the firm. This is strictly interpreted; if he obtains information in the course of business which results in a profit to him, this advantage must be shared with the other partners.

He must not engage in any activity which results in a conflict of interest with the firm or with his other partners.

The Act provides that day to day decisions may be taken by a majority of the partners, but major decisions concerning the policies or constitution of the partnership must be taken by all the partners. A partner cannot be expelled by a majority decision unless there is a clause permitting this in the partnership deed. However partners are not normally expelled unless their actions bring the firm into disrepute; the courts may set aside an expulsion made for personal reasons.

Skill in a partnership has a value as well as capital

investment, so that the distribution of profits should take account of this factor.

Partnership Act 1890

Partners' Liabilities

Each partner is legally the agent of the others, so that as long as the partners act within the terms of their partnership contract they are liable for each other's misdeeds.

If a partner acts beyond his authority whilst pretending that such authority exists, then the firm is still liable for his actions. If however such an action is not connected with the business of the firm, then the firm is not liable. In other words obtaining a discount on a case of wine by pretending to be a partner doesn't involve other partners, but the same action over buying drawing materials does.

Where a partner exceeds his authority in dealing with another party, and that party is aware that the authority is being exceeded and still goes ahead with the transaction then the firm is not liable. Conversely if the other party acts in good faith the firm is liable. The same principles apply to a situation where an architect pretends to be in business on his own. The law on this point is confusing, contradictory, and the decision of the courts depend on the circumstances.

Partners who commit crimes or other misdeeds in the course of the business may bring their fellow partners into the courts; wrongdoing committed outside the practice is a personal matter. Partners may have a civil liability for another partner's offences. They are not liable for another partner's criminal offences unless they connive at the crime. So fiddling VAT returns comes into the first category, and smuggling brandy on a yacht (not belonging to the firm) comes into the second.

Unlike companies, which have a legal identity, a partnership consists of individuals. Thus all partners are party to a crime committed in the course of the business, and they can all be prosecuted as a firm and as individuals; in theory all the partners including sleeping partners, could find themselves ''inside''.

Partnership Act 1890 and Civil Liability (Contribution) Act 1978

Partnership Bankruptcy

Since a partnership has no separate identity, a state of insolvency (bcd) means that all the partners are insolvent. Both the firm's, and the partners' personal assets are liable to be taken and this property will be invested in a trustee. All creditors can claim equally against all partners and the firm, but the Inland Revenue and persons holding security (mortgagees) have first call on the assets.
Insolvency Act 1985

Partnership by Association

A deed of partnership is not necessary to establish the existence of a partnership. A partnership may be established by association; there are complex court cases bearing on this point, and the decision as to whether or not a partnership exists usually depends on the original intention of the partners in forming an association and their subsequent actions. A willingness to share losses as well as profits (''risk factor'') is a strong presumption that a partnership exists, and any one who involves himself in the management of a partnership and claims a share of the profits is likely to be treated as a full partner unless there is evidence to the contrary.
Partnerships Act 1890

Partnership by Representation

Should an architect pretend that he is a partner, or allows any one else to pretend that he is a partner, then he will become liable for his actions as though he were a partner. If the partners in a firm pretend that another person is a partner when he is not, they become liable for his actions as though he were a real partner.
Partnership Act 1890

Partnerships

Most of the rules governing the operation of partnerships are derived from case law, since the Partnership Act of 1890 only lays down the basic principles. A partnership (bcd) is a formal relationship between people and not a separate legal entity which can function regardless of its membership, though in practice the "firm" is charged tax, VAT, and NI contributions as though it were a single body.

There are a number of points to remember about the nature of partnerships:

— First, it is essential that a partnership; must be a business, must be carried on in common, and must be intended to make a profit.

— Second, a partnership is a contract between parties and may be altered or terminated under the terms of that contract.

— Third, each partner stands in the relationship of agent and principal to his fellow partners.

— Fourth, each partner has a general liability for the actions of his fellow partners, although this does not apply to criminal actions.

— Fifth, each partner has obligations to his fellow partners akin to those of trustee; thus he must make decisions investments and so forth for the common good.

—· Sixth, partners are usually self-employed but the distinction between partners and employees is not always seen as clear-cut by the courts. An architect may, therefore, receive a salary as an employee, yet also share in profits and losses. A good partnership agreement should, therefore, clearly define his status as partner or employee. Associate partners who are employees of the firm do not normally have a legal status as partners, as they rarely share in the losses of the frim.

— Seventh, in order to be treated as a partnership, the profits or losses and not the gross income must be shared between partners.

— Eighth, the Companies Act requires that the names of all the partners must be printed on all business correspondence, but if there are more than 20 partners their names and addresses may be held at head office for inspection.
Partnerships Act 1890 and Companies Act 1985

Partnerships: Constraints

The courts only become involved with partnerships when the partners are in dispute with each other or someone else, and the argument cannot be solved by arbitration. If arbitration is chosen as a method of settling a dispute, then the provisions of the Arbitration Act of 1979 will apply. Any partnership agreement which is contrary to the public interest, may be set aside by the courts.

The Sex Discrimination Act of 1975 says that any partnership with more than six partners must not discriminate against applicants for partnership on grounds of sex; this also includes marital status. The provisions of the Race Relations Act of 1976 also apply to partnerships (see also Employment).

Anyone under 18 can become a partner, but he cannot be held personally liable, although his partners are liable for him; following in father's footsteps could be rough on father's partners. Partnership agreements which restrict the competition of partners who leave the firm may be set aside by the courts if they consider that such a restriction is against the public interest.

The Companies Act of 1985 deals with the proportion of qualified partners who must be included in any partnership. *Partnership Act 1890, Arbitration Act 1979, Companies Act 1985.*

Professional Negligence: Duty of Care

As a professional person, the architect owes his client a duty of care (bcd), and this has been defined as: undertaking to bring a fair, reasonable and competent degree of skill to the work. It is sufficient if he exercises the ordinary skill of an ordinary competent man exercising his particular art. This implies that an architect should not take on work unless he has complete confidence in his skills to handle it successfully. Even if an architect purports to have skills over and above the ordinary practitioner, he cannot be held to be more negligent than an ordinary competent architect. But if an architect holds himself out as being extra skilled and puts this claim in a contract, then he is bound by the terms of that contract. It should also be added that an architect setting himself up as a specialist in a particular field will have his competence judged on that basis.

The architect is deemed, by virtue of his training, to have certain responsibilities towards his client, and failure to discharge them in a proper manner may lay him open to charges of negligence (bcd). The case law on the duty of care has, of late, been bearing more heavily on the architect. (See also bcd Supply of Goods and Services).

Supply of Goods and Services Act 1982. Most decisions on this subject are based on case law

Property of a Partnership

The property of a partnership comprises all capital invest-ment, and property acquired during and for the partnership which is supplied for its use. Building leases or freeholds may be held in co-ownership rather than being the property of the partnership, or they may be vested in a service company. Goodwill is an asset in partnership property terms and must be valued at any change in the partnership.
Partnership Act 1890

Rateable Value

Rateable value is assessed by the Inland Revenue's Valu-ation Office and is calculated as follows; the rent at which the hereditament (that is, the property) might reasonably be expected to be let from year to year if the tenant undertook to pay all usual rates and taxes and, the landlord undertook to bear the cost of repairs and insurance and other expenses, if any, necessary to maintain the property in a state to command that rent.

Revaluation is supposed to take place every five years, but the last assessment was in 1973. The actual rate paid is based on a rate poundage fixed by the local authority every year, and this is based upon the amount of capital it needs to run its area.

Obviously the local authority's needs increase from year to year and the rates burden on occupiers of business premises can be a significant part of the running costs.

The New Valuation Lists Order 1987 specifies 1 April 1990 as the date on which the new valuation lists will come into force. Future orders will give the Secretary of State power to specify certain classes of hereditaments to be re-valued for the purpose of the new valuation lists.
Local Government Act 1948, General Rate Act 1967 and New Valuation Lists Order 1987

Salaried Partner

Salaried partner is not a legal term but such a person is normally an architect who is regarded as a partner both by the general partners and by everyone else, but who is limited

as to his powers under the partnership agreement. His partners are liable for his actions as though he were a general partner. He gets a fixed salary paid out of nett profits, but usually has little or no capital investment in the practice. The rights and duties of a salaried partner should be clearly defined in the partnership agreement.
Partnership Act 1890 and case law

Sleeping Partner

An architectural practice may borrow money from a person who agrees to get his repayments from the profits of the practice. If such a lender takes any part in the management of the firm as well, he could find that he is a ''sleeping partner'' and he may be roughly awakened by claims for liabilities on the practice: under these conditions a sleeping partner enjoys the status of a general partner.
Partnership Act 1890

Sub-Partnerships

Any partner can form a sub-partnership with other people, provided that this this new group follows the principles of a partnership. He will divide his share of the main partnership profits (or losses) with his fellow sub-partners. The sub-partners' liabilities are limited by the terms of the sub-partnership agreement, and they are not responsible for the affairs of the main partnership.
But should the sub-partners involve themselves in the management affairs of the main partnership they could well find themselves liable for losses or plaints against it.
Partnership Act 1890

Supervision on Site

When supervising work on site, and before issuing a certificate, the architect is expected to check that the work has been done in accordance with the contract. If he fails to do this and the work is not in accordance with the contract, he is liable to his employer for the faulty work, and may have to pay damages.
An architect is not expected to be on site all the time, once a week is the accepted norm; however if an important piece of construction is to be covered up it is advisable for him to inspect it, and satisfy himself that it has been constructed in

accordance with the contract drawings and specification, and that it has been inspected for building control approval.
Case law

Employment Law: an Introduction

The world of employment law is strewn with pitfalls for both employer and employee and is the subject of constant judicial action. It must also be remembered that many areas of employment law are subject to constant change so that any published source such as this will be out of date by the time that it reaches the bookseller. The advice given below is, therefore, general in its tone. Under no circumstances should this section of the book be seen as the answer to all of the problems which are likely to arise, merely as a guide to the areas in which problems are most likely to occur. Should you have difficulties in any of the situations outlined below, you should seek expert advice from one of the many sources available. The trades unions and the employers' organisations are obvious sources and the Department of Employment produces a large number of free pamphlets offering guidance which can be obtained from any Job Centre.

Above all, remember that employment is concerned with people rather than with the law. As a result, a correct legal judgement may not solve the problem if the conflicting parties have to continue working together after the case has been decided. It will normally be better to follow the dictates of common sense and diplomacy rather than the letter of the law. The decisions of case law suggest that this is the attitude that the judge will adopt and it makes sense to avoid the expense and inconvenience of the courts if at all possible.

One last factor to remember is that employment law is, effectively, an overlay to normal contract law. Between every employer and employee there is a contract that work will be performed in return for certain remuneration and other benefits. It is always possible for either side to sue the other for a breach of this contract. This is most likely to come into effect when the written contract contains benefits greater than those required by the relevant legislation. It is also the means by which an employer could seek to prevent an employee from leaving without providing the required period of notice. This is, however, a dangerous course of action. Recourse to the civil law is a risky and expensive business. It would be necessary for the employer to show not just that the contract had been broken but also that he had suffered damage as a result. This is not as easy or as cheap as it might appear!

The basis for all employment law is contained in three acts: Employment Protection (Consolidation) Act 1978, as amended by Employment Act 1980 and the Employment Act 1982. The periods of continuous employment required to qualify for many of the rights discussed below have been amended by the Unfair Dismissal (Variation of Qualifying Period) Order 1985.

Employment law tends not to lend itself to short definitions as these will often confuse by failing to indicate the essential relationships between the different aspects of the law. The chapters on employment law will, therefore, resemble short essays rather than dictionary definitions.

Employment: Staff and their Conditions of Employment

Continuous Employment

Many of the rights granted under employment protection law are conditional upon a certain period of continuous employment having been completed. There are a number of factors which govern the way in which the period of employment is calculated and the exact definition of continuity.

The first day of the period of employment should be included in the statement of conditions of employment. The period of employment will then run until the contract of employment is terminated. This period will include any notice which has to be served whether or not payment in lieu is made. If no notice is given, the minimum allowed by law (see also Dismissal: notice) will be assumed to have been given.

Essentially, the period of employment will include any weeks in which more than 16 hours are worked. When an employee normally works more than 16 hours but then has the contract hours reduced to 8 or more, the period of employment will still be considered continuous.

There are several factors which may result in an employee not working the above hours but which do not affect the period of employment:

— sickness, injury etc;
— lay off due to shortage of work;
— pregnancy;
— other reasons arranged with the employer or by custom which do not affect the contract of employment.

If the ownership of the company changes hands or if the employee is transferred within the company, the period of employment is still continuous. This also applies if promotion or similar results in a new contract being signed.

This whole area of the law is extremely complex and is subject to regular interpretation by the courts. If there is any doubt about an employee's continuity of employment, expert advice should be sought.

Guidance on this concept is given in "Rules governing continuous employment and a week's pay" by the Department of Employment.

Contract of Employment

A contract of employment can be either written or verbal and is not the subject of any particular legislation. It is merely an agreement that one person will perform certain tasks for another in return for payment. The main problem is to decide exactly how this differs from a contract for services. This hinges on the definition of what exactly is an employee. As with all other contracts, it is unwise to depend upon a verbal agreement.

On the assumption that it has been accepted that a new member of staff is actually an employee, it is a legal requirement that they should be given a written statement of the conditions of employment within 13 weeks of starting work. This statement must contain the following information:

— names of employer and employee;
— date of commencement of employment;
— dates of any previous employment if this will be taken into consideration when calculating rights and entitlements in the new job and the date when this period of continuous employment is considered to have commenced.

The employee must also be given written details of the following, either in the statement or in the form of a general statement of conditions of employment applying to all employees. This document must be either given to the employee or must be made easily accessible.

— if the contract is for a fixed term, the date of expiry;
— rate of pay or the method of calculating the rate, together with the frequency of payment, weekly, monthly etc, including fringe benefits;
— working hours and any special conditions relating to them;
— holiday entitlement, including public holidays, holiday

pay and the method of calculating holiday pay owing at the termination of employment;

— sick pay entitlement;

— pension scheme, including whether or not the employee is contracted out of the state scheme;

— length of notice to be given by both employer and employee;

— job title;

— disciplinary procedures and the name of the person to whom the employee should report if there is a grievance.

If there is no pension scheme, holiday entitlement etc the document should say so.

If the terms of employment change in any way, a written notice of this change must be provided within 4 weeks.

There is no legal requirement to provide a statement of conditions for any employee normally working less than 16 hours per week, although one must be provided if an employee has worked 8 hours per week for 5 years or more. Crown employees and those normally working abroad are also excluded, although the Crown treats its employees as if they were covered. It is, however, good practice to provide a statement as this can reduce misunderstandings. If the employer does not provide a statement there is no threat of prosecution, the employee merely having the right to ask an industrial tribunal to establish the conditions of employment. Similarly, the employee does not actually have to sign this statement as it is merely a listing of the conditions implicit in the actual employment contract.

The Department of Employment has issued a document outlining good practice in this area: "Written statement of main terms and conditions of employment". This includes a sample contract.

Employer and Employee

The status of both employee and employer entails specific rights and duties for both parties. Unfortunately, statute law is extremely imprecise about when someone actually becomes either. The definitions available describe an employer as "the person by whom the employee is or was employed." An employee is "an individual who has entered into or works under a contract of employment".

This, of course, fails to say who should have a contract of employment and what actually constitutes such a contract.

There is an obvious difference between someone who has a contractual agreement to provide a specific service; the contract between a window cleaner and his or her client may well include details of payment and the frequency with which the service should be provided. This relationship, however, would not normally be considered to be one of employer and employee. One of the crucial considerations is taken to be who has actual control over the way in which the worker performs the task. Under normal circumstances the window cleaner would be entirely responsible for deciding how the job should be done, the client merely having the power to judge the quality of the completed work and, perhaps, the way in which the process interfered with the normal operation of the client's home or business. Whilst this case may seem to be an obvious one, there will be times when this is not clear, the whole problem of "the lump" coming into this category. It has been declared in a court that a master bricklayer, operating quite legitimately, so far as the Inland Revenue were concerned, as a sub-contractor, was actually an employee when it came to the requirements of the Factories Act. The judge stated that "Many different tests or criteria have been suggested in many authorities. Any one test may, in my view, be substantially relevant in one case but largely irrelevant in another." Graham v Brunswick 1974. His conclusion centered around the fact that whilst the bricklayer and his mate provided their own tools, their work was effectively controlled by the main contractors on the site.

What all this goes to prove is that there may well be a problem in deciding exactly who is an employee. The frequent use of agency staff, "lump labour" and staff on Youth Opportunities and similar Government backed schemes, makes this difficulty an ever present one. Do not assume that because these staff have not signed contracts of employment they do not have have the same rights as those members of staff who have. When there is any doubt, consult an expert!

Probationary Period

The law allows a period of 2 years before the employee can take action against the employer for unfair dismissal. There is one exception to this:

— dismissal on the grounds of race or sex.

Discrimination on grounds of trades union membership is barred at all times

It is also quite normal for an employment contract to include a trial period of, for instance, 3 months, during which either employer or employee can withdraw from the contract with the minimum period of notice. It is important to include details of this period in the statement of conditions.

Conditions of Employment: Selecting Staff

The law is not interested in ensuring that the right person is selected for any particular job, that is the responsibility of the individuals involved. The law merely seeks to ensure that the selection takes place without discrimination on the grounds of race or sex. The various types of discrimination, which affect both advertising for staff and the treatment of staff after they have been appointed, are covered in the relevant sections (see also Discrimination).

Employment: Payment and Benefits

Introduction

The law is not concerned with the amount that the employer pays the employee or with holidays or with most other benefits. What is important is that there is a clear understanding about these payments and benefits once their levels have been negotiated. The main interest of Government is with the various payments made to those unable to work due to ill health or pregnancy. The law in this area has been the subject of much recent change, which has major affects upon the running of a business.

The basis for all employment law is contained in three Acts. Employment Protection (Consolidation) Act 1978, as amended by Employment Act 1980 and the Employment Act 1982. The periods of continuous employment required to qualify for many of the rights discussed below have been amended by the Unfair Dismissal (Variation of Qualifying Period) Order 1985.

Certification of Sickness

An employer is permitted to withhold payment of Statutory Sick Pay if it is believed that the employee is not actually ill. This is an exceedingly risky exercise and should only be done if the employer is absolutely certain. The example for this given in the DHSS guidance document is of an employee said to be unfit to work because of a sprained ankle but then seen playing football. (Make sure that the employee does not have a twin!)

The law does not specify what arrangement the employer should make with employees over the notification of absence due to illness, it merely provides some restrictions over what can be negotiated:

— notification cannot be required before the first qualifying day. If the employee sends notification of illness by post, the notification will be considered to have been made on the day of posting;

— notification must not be required on a printed form;

— the employer must have informed the employee of the rules.

Self certification will normally be adequate for the first 7 days of absence, although medical certificates may still be obtained from a doctor. The employer is free to make his own certification arrangements although a doctor's medical certificate must not be required for the first 7 days, including weekends. A medical certificate does not have to come from a registered medical practitioner. Osteopaths, herbalists, acupuncturists etc may all issue certificates and it is up to the employer to consider each certificate on its own merits. Whatever the source, it is unwise to question any certificate without very strong evidence.

Social Security and Housing Benefits Act 1982 as amended by the Statutory Sick Pay (General) Regulations 1982, the Social Security Act 1985, the Statutory Sick Pay (General Amendment) Regulations 1985, the Statutory Sick Pay (Additional Compensation of Employers and Consequential Amendments) Regulations 1985 and the Statutory Sick Pay (Medical Evidence) Regulations 1985.

Deductions from Salary

Deductions from salary or payments from employee to employer. These are only permitted in very restricted circumstances:

— where it is required by law;

— where it is stated in the contract of employment;

— where the employee has agreed in writing. This agreement must have been made in advance.

The exceptions to this are:

— for refunding overpayment of wages or expenses;

— as a result of disciplinary proceedings required by law;

— if it is legally demanded by a statutory authority;

— as part of an agreement to pay a third party direct;

— where it is required as a result of the employee having taken strike action;

— where there is a court order.

The employee may complain to an Industrial Tribunal (see also Industrial Tribunals) within 3 months of any deduction or as soon after as is reasonably practicable. The Tribunal may order repayment of the disputed sum.

"Wages" for this purpose are defined as including fees, bonuses, Statutory Sick Pay, maternity pay etc. They do not include pensions, expenses or redundancy payments.

Wages Act 1986

Equal Pay

The concept of equal pay is simple, that all employees doing the same job in similar circumstances should receive the same pay, regardless of their sex. In practice, however, this is extremely complex, in that it requires comparisons to be made between different jobs. If, for instance, all the secretarial staff are women and the accounts clerks are all men, it may be difficult to evaluate the two jobs for this purpose. In order for equal pay to be required it must be shown that:

— the job is the same as that done by a member of the opposite sex (remember that both men and women are covered);

— the job is of equal value, in terms of demands made on the employee of effort, skill and decision making, to that done by a member of the opposite sex;

The right to equal pay is open to all employees, with the following limitations:

— members of the opposite sex must employed in the same establishment;

— comparison must not be made with another employee of the same sex, ie the legislation must not be used to consider pay differentials between two men or two women;

— comparison must be made with employees of the same employer or of an associated employer. "Equal pay: a guide to the Equal Pay Act" produced by the Department of Employment says that two employers are associated if "one is a company of which the other has direct control or if both are companies controlled by a third person or company." Companies can be taken to include partnerships etc.

An employer can claim as a defence that there are other factors which cause the differential in pay such as seniority, market forces etc. This latter can only be used if it can be shown that different skills whilst, theoretically, of equal value, command different rates in the job market.

The right to equal pay also extends to fringe benefits, bonuses etc. If a man has extra benefits included in his conditions of employment compared with a woman doing the same job, the woman can act as if that benefit is included in her contract.

Errors in Statutory Sick Pay

The onus is on the employer to correct any errors made, including all of the records, and to inform the local social security office if the error has resulted in over or under payment of a state benefit. Precise guidance on the correction of errors is provided in the "Employer's guide to statutory sick pay" by the DHSS.

Social Security and Housing Benefits Act 1982 as amended by the Statutory Sick Pay (General) Regulations 1982, the Social Security Act 1985, the Statutory Sick Pay (General Amendment) Regulations 1985, the Statutory Sick Pay (Additional Compensation of Employers and Consequential Amendments) Regulations 1985 and the Statutory Sick Pay (Medical Evidence) Regulations 1985

Holidays

The law has no requirement for an employer to provide paid holiday for the employees, this is entirely a matter for negotiation. There is not normally even a requirement for an employer to give paid leave on Bank Holidays, although the Factories Act 1961 requires that young people are given paid leave on Christmas Day, Good Friday and Bank Holidays. When an employer has decided to grant paid holidays for the employees, however, there is a requirement to note the details in the statement of conditions (see also Conditions of employment: Contract of employment) and the way in which any holidays owed will be paid off when an employee leaves.

Factories Act 1961 as amended by Sex Discrimination Act 1986

Itemized Pay Statement

All employees must be given an itemized pay statement. This must include the following information:

— the gross amount payable;
— the amount of each and any deduction made, together with the reason for the deduction;
— the net amount payable - ie the gross amount less any deductions;
— if the wages are paid in different ways - ie part in cash and part by cheque, the amounts payable in each way.

Any conflict over pay statements must be taken to an Industrial Tribunal. If employment has been terminated, the complaint must be made within 3 months of the termination. The Tribunal may order compensation to be paid. If the complaint relates to unnotified deductions of pay, a refund may be made which does not exceed the amount deducted during the 13 weeks prior to the complaint being made.

Full details are given in ''Itemized pay statement'' by the Department of Employment.

Leaver's Statement

When an employee leaves an organisation, the employer must provide a leaver's statement if:

— the employee had a PIW (see also Period of incapacity for work) in the 56 days preceding the end of the employment contract
— SSP (see also Statutory sick pay) was payable for at least one week. The method of calculation is such that 3 days is rounded down and does not count. 4 or more days are rounded up to count as a week.

This statement must contain the following information:

— the date of the first day of the PIW. If this includes time carried forward on a leavers statement from a previous employer, the 1st day of that PIW must be shown;
— the number of weeks of statutory sick pay payable, including any paid by a previous employer;
— the last day on which SSP was payable.

The employer keeps one copy of this and must send the other copy to the employee within 7 days of the end of the employment contract. If the employer does not have an address for the employee or cannot hand it over for some other reason, the certificate should be kept for at least 3 years after the end of the relevant tax year, so that it may be given to the employee should it be demanded.

A new employee who is ill may give the form to the new employer who must accept it if it is received with 7 days of the PIW. If the PIW is within the first 8 weeks of the start of the job, the employer will have to consider the statutory sick pay record built up at the last place of employment.

Maternity Leave: Right to Return to Work

After the birth of the baby, even if it is still born, the woman has the right to ask that she be allowed to return to her job. To qualify for this, she must have told her employer that she intends to return at least 21 days before she begins her maternity leave or as soon after as is reasonably practicable. She must then inform her employer at least 21 days before the date of her intended return. Exceptions to this are:

— Companies employing 5 or fewer staff (including part-timers) and where the employer can show that it is not reasonably practicable for the woman to be allowed to return to her old job and that no suitable, alternative, job exists. This latter condition is, of course, liable to be decided before an industrial tribunal.

— Where the employer can convince the Tribunal that it is not reasonably practicable for her to return to the job that she previously occupied. If the woman refuses to accept a reasonable alternative job she will forfeit her right to be re-employed. A reasonable job is one which is suitable for her and in which she enjoys conditions of employment "not substantially less favourable".

— Where the woman cannot return to her job because of redundancy. The employer must offer suitable alternative employment if this is available. If it is not, the woman will be eligible for redundancy pay. If the woman rejects suitable alternative employment, she will forfeit her right to redundancy pay.

The employer has the right to postpone the woman's return for up to 4 weeks provided that she is given a date when she can return within the 4 weeks and that she is given a reason for the postponement. Similarly, the woman may delay her return for a further 4 weeks if she is ill and can produce a medical certificate.

The employer may write to the woman at least 49 days after the beginning of the expected week of her confinement or after the date of the confinement itself, asking her to confirm her intention to return to work. If she does not reply in writing within 14 days, or as soon as is reasonably practicable, she may forfeit her right to return to work. Complaints over maternity rights must be made to an Industrial Tribunal (qv) within 3 months of the cause of the complaint or as soon as is reasonably practicable.

Maternity Pay (SMP)

The Social Security Act 1986 introduced statutory maternity pay (SMP). This brought maternity pay into line with sickness pay and came into force on 6 April 1987. It applies to all women whose babies were due on or after 21 June 1987.

SMP will normally be payable to every woman who fits the following criteria:

— she must have completed 26 weeks of continuous employment (See also Conditions of employment: continuous employment) ending with the week immediately preceeding the 14th week before the week in which the baby is due: ie she must have started work approx 40 weeks before the baby is due;

— she must have average weekly earnings higher than the lower earnings limit for the payment of National Insurance contributions;

— she must normally be employed in the UK. There are several complicated regulations relating to women who work in any of the EEC countries. The DHSS should be consulted in any such case.

Evidence of pregnancy and the expected date of the birth must be given to the employer (the person responsible for paying SMP) by a doctor or registered midwife. The evidence must be given on the form included in the regulations or a similar document not earlier than 14 weeks before the expected date of birth.

The level of payment is variable, depending upon the woman's length of service. Two levels of payment have been established.

— A higher level, 90% of the average weekly earnings in the 8 weeks prior to the 14th week before the week when the baby is due, will be paid to women with 2 years of continuous employment (see also Conditions of employment: continuous employment). This will be paid for the first 6 weeks of absence.

— A lower level will be paid to all others eligible for SMP and will be reviewed annually.

Payment is for a maximum of 18 weeks, beginning 11 weeks before the week in which the baby is due. This period will include 13 weeks starting 6 weeks before the week in which the baby is due. The remaining 5 weeks may be either before or after the birth or a mixture of the two. The woman is free to chose within these limits.

Receipt of SMP will affect a woman's right to receive statutory sick pay (see also Payment of SSP). It should be added that a woman will also be affected in this way if she is pregnant but not claiming or not eligible to receive SMP. Full details of the new scheme may be found in ''Employer's guide to statutory maternity pay'' which is free from the Department of Health and Social Security.

Social Security Act 1986 as amended by Statutory Maternity Pay (General) Regulations 1986, Statutory Maternity Pay (Medical Evidence) Regulations 1987 and Statutory Maternity Pay (Persons Abroad and Mariners) Regulations 1987

Maternity Rights

Any woman who has been continuously employed (see also Conditions of employment: continuous employment) for more than 2 years has a right both to a period of paid maternity leave and to have her job held open for her should she wish to return to it. The actual requirement is that the woman should have worked for 2 years preceeding the 11th week before the week in which the baby is due. If she has had to give up work earlier due to incapacity or has left, but not been dismissed, for other reasons, she will still qualify if she would have worked for the required period but for this absence. She must have informed her employer of her proposed absence at least 3 weeks beforehand or as soon as is practicable. This must be in writing if the employer demands it. The employer can also require that she provides a medical certificate stating the date on which the baby is due.

Full details are given in "Employment rights for the expectant mother" by the Department of Employment

Part Time Staff: Sick Pay

Part time staff are covered in the same way as any other employees, although they are only paid SSP for the days on which they would normally have been at work (see also Qualifying days).

Payment in Cash

Following the introduction of the Wages Act 1986, there is no longer a right for any employee to be paid in cash, so that payment may be made in any way agreed between employer and employee.
Wages Act 1986

Payment of Statutory Sick Pay

Statutory Sick Pay (SSP) is now payable to all workers, with a number of exceptions including:

— those already being paid their normal salaries in spite of being absent due to illness;
— pensioners or people under 16;
— those employed on a contract of 3 months or less who have not worked for 13 weeks. For the purposes of calculating this period, 2 separate contracts may be added together if they are not separated by more than 8 weeks;
— anyone involved in "stoppage of work due to a trade dispute" at their place of employment;
— anyone who has reached the maximum sick pay entitlement, currently 28 weeks in any PIW (see also Period of incapacity to work);
— anyone who has a linked PIW which has reached 3 years;
— any employee whose leaver's certificate shows 28 weeks SSP already paid in a PIW and not more than 56 days since the last SSP was paid;
— anyone earning less than a specified amount;
— anyone who is pregnant, whether or not they are entitled to or are claiming statutory maternity pay. This covers a period of 18 weeks, starting 6 weeks before the expected date of confinement.

Payment will commence after 3 days off work and will continue:

— until the employee has recovered;
— until his contract is considered to have ended;
— until the maximum sick pay entitlement has been reached, currently 28 weeks in any PIW;
— until the "linked PIW" has lasted for 3 years;
— until the employee becomes ineligible by reason of pregnancy.

If an employee has two periods of sick leave of less than 3 days within any two week period, SSP is payable for the second period.

When an employee in receipt of SSP is to have the payment terminated, whatever the reason, he must be given one of the forms available from the local office of the DHSS. The special requirements for these should be checked with the DHSS.

The amount payable is subject to change at least annually. Full details can be obtained from the local office of the DHSS.

In the event of the employer being unable to pay due to bankruptcy, the DHSS will be responsible for paying the employees. If the employer fails to pay for some other reason, the DHSS will also make the relevant payments to the employees. The money will, of course, eventually be recovered from the employer but the legislation does not make the mechanism for doing this clear. It is extremely unwise to refuse to pay SSP!

Statutory Sick Pay (General) Amendment Regulations 1987

Period of Incapacity for Work

Known from here on as PIW. This is the basic unit around which statutory sick pay is organised. A PIW is any period of 4 days on which the employee is unfit to work. This includes non-working days (weekends etc) and days in which an employee is barred from work for reasons of prevention of infection (an employee who is fit to work but who has been in contact with an infectious disease). Complete days only count, not days in which an employee was taken ill during the working day.

PIWs may be "linked". This means that two periods of absence, each of 4 days or more, are separated by a period of less than 56 days. This concept is important in considering when SSP should or should not be paid.

Special regulations govern those who are absent regularly for reasons of ill health, eg those undergoing renal dialysis.

Qualifying Days

These are days for which the employee is paid statutory sick pay ie those days on which the employee would normally be paid to work. In most cases, there will be no doubt as to which these days are — Monday to Friday. Where there is a doubt, with part time staff, for instance, a formula is laid down:

— where employer and employee agree that no work would have performed in the week, Wednesday of each week should be specified as the qualifying day;

— where it is agreed that some days would have been worked but where no agreement can be reached as to which days, every day will be assumed to be a qualifying day unless it can be shown to be a normal rest day.

Reclaiming Statutory Maternity Pay

The employer's payments of SMP can be reclaimed in a manner similar to that established for the reclamation of Statutory Sick Pay (see also Reclaiming SSP).

Social Security Act 1986 as amended by Statutory Maternity Pay (General) Regulations 1986, Statutory Maternity Pay (Persons Abroad and Mariners) Regulations 1987 and Statutory Maternity Pay (Compensation of Employers) Regulations 1987

Reclaiming Statutory Sick Pay

The employer will normally recover all sums paid out in SSP, together with an additional sum to cover National Insurance contributions, by deducting the amount from the National Insurance payments made for the employee. If this is not a sufficient amount in any month, deductions may be made from the employee's PAYE. Should this, too, be insufficient, the employer may either carry the debt forward to the next month or make arrangements for a direct refund from the Collector of Taxes.

Social Security and Housing Benefits Act 1982 as amended by the Statutory Sick Pay (General) Regulations 1982, the Social Security

Act 1985, the Statutory Sick Pay (General Amendment) Regulations 1985, the Statutory Sick Pay (Additional Compensation of Employers and Consequential Amendments) Regulations 1985, Statutory Sick Pay (Medical Evidence) Regulations 1985 and Statutory Sick Pay (Additional Compensation of Employers) Regulations 1987.

Records of Sick Pay

The law now requires that the employer keeps detailed records of all absence due to sickness for 3 years after the end of each tax year. This record must contain:

—   dates of each period of incapacity;
—   details of agreed qualifying days;
—   details of SSP paid to each employee;
—   dates when an employee was refused SSP and the reasons;
—   leaver's statements given to the employer;
—   leaver's statements given by the employer to departing staff.

The DHSS has produced a sample form of record to assist the employer, although its use is not mandatory.
Social Security and Housing Benefits Act 1982 as amended by the Statutory Sick Pay (General) Regulations 1982, the Social Security Act 1985, the Statutory Sick Pay (General Amendment) Regulations 1985, the Statutory Sick Pay (Additional Compensation of Employers and Consequential Amendments) Regulations 1985 and the Statutory Sick Pay (Medical Evidence) Regulations 1985.

Salaries

The law does not dictate the amount that an employee must be paid but it does demand that an itemised pay statement is provided. This aspect of the law is on the point of changing (see also Payment in cash). The amount that must be paid is a matter for the contract between the employer and the employee and should be clearly described in the statement of conditions. This should include extra payments such as bonuses and overtime and, indeed, whether or not there is any requirement to work overtime should the employer so demand.

Sick Pay

This is divided into 2 areas, statutory sick pay (SSP), which is directly paid by the employer and then claimed back from the Government, and state sickness benefit, which is paid by the Goverment. The law relating to this is extremely complex and, where there is any doubt, advice should be sought from the local office of the DHSS.

If the employer continues to pay full salaries during absence due to illness, the legislation relating to payment of sick pay and recording of those payments may be ignored. The requirements relating to self-certification, however, still apply. (See also Certification of illness).

The DHSS produces a comprehensive guide to the subject. ''Employer's Guide to Statutory Sick Pay''.

Social Security and Housing Benefits Act 1982 as amended by the Statutory Sick Pay (General) Regulations 1982, the Social Security Act 1985, the Statutory Sick Pay (General Amendment) Regulations 1985, the Statutory Sick Pay (Additional Compensation of Employers and Consequential Amendments) Regulations 1985 and the Statutory Sick Pay (Medical Evidence) Regulations 1985

Time off for Jury Service

This is subject of separate legislation which, effectively, states that employees must be given time off for jury service. It is, however, possible to ask for the service to be delayed if it can be shown that losing an employee at a particular time would impose particular problems on the business. Employers are, of course, similarly affected. Once on jury service both employer and employee are paid by the court although employment conditions often contain a clause to the effect that the employer will make up this sum so that it is equal to the normal wage.

Juries Act 1974

Time off for Pre-Natal Care

All female staff, regardless of their period of continuous employment have the right to time off for pre-natal care. This is subject to the normal conditions as to taking only the amount of time that is reasonable and all appointments, after the first, must be covered by a certificate from a clinic, midwife etc.

Time off for Official and other Duties

An employer must allow an employee to take "reasonable" time off to perform certain public and trades union duties, the definition of "reasonable" ultimately resting with an Industrial Tribunal. The legislation suggests that the following factors be considered when making this assessment:

— how much time is actually required to perform the task;
— how much time has the employee already taken off for the purpose;
— what effect will the employee's absence have upon the running of the employers' business.

If the industrial tribunal thinks that "reasonable" time has not been permitted, the employee can be awarded compensation.

The duties specified are:

— as an official of a trades union recognised by the employer, both to look after industrial relations within the company and to undergo relevant training. This also includes duties as a safety officer under the Health and Safety at Work etc. Act 1974. (see also Health and safety: safety representatives and committees).

While the employee is engaged in these duties, he or she must be paid either the normal agreed wage or, if the wage is based upon performance, an average wage for the job.

— as a justice of the peace;
— as a member of a local authority;
— as a member of a statutory tribunal;
— as a member of a regional or area health authority;
— as a member of the governing body of a local authority run educational establishment;
— as a member of a water authority.

The legislation does not actually require that time off for these purposes is paid but decisions by the Industrial Tribunal have suggested that not to make payments similar to those required for trades union duties may be infringing the employee's legal rights.

Full details are given in "Time off for public duties" by the Department of Employment.

Time off for Those Facing Redundancy

An employee who has been given notice of redundancy has a similar right to time off in order to find work. This right only applies to those who have been continuously employed for two years, including the period of notice (see also Conditions of Employment: continuous employment). Employees should be paid the appropriate hourly rate during these absences.

Full details are given in "Facing redundancy? - time off for job hunting or to arrange training" by the Department of Employment.

Employment: Discrimination

Introduction

The law demands that certain groups of people are allowed equality of opportunity both during the selection process and after becoming employed. The simplest way of avoiding any problems in this area is to ensure that all employees and potential employees are treated equally. It has to be emphasised, once again, that the only way to achieve this is by the application of good faith on all sides. If this breaks down, common sense rather than the law is likely to be the best ally.

The basis for all employment law is contained in three acts: Employment Protection (Consolidation) Act 1978, as amended by Employment Act 1980 and the Employment Act 1982. The periods of continuous employment required to qualify for many of the rights discussed below have been amended by the Unfair Dismissal (Variation of Qualifying Period) Order 1985.

Convicted Criminals

The law requires that those with spent criminal convictions must not be discriminated against in employment. The precise details of a "spent conviction" are complex, depending upon the severity of the sentence and the length of time since it was served. If in doubt, consult the local office of the Department of Employment or a similar source. The one exception to this which might affect an architectural practice is for those working in prisons or similar security establishments. It is possible that this might extend to organisations with design or maintenance contracts in these establishments.

Rehabilitation of Offenders Act 1974 as amended by Rehabilitation of Offenders Act 1974 (Exceptions) Order 1975

Disabled People

The law actively encourages reverse discrimination in favour of disabled people and requires that any organisation with more than 20 employees must employ a minimum of 3% of registered disabled people. If an organisation believes that it would not be practicable for it to do so, it must apply to the Department of Employment for an exemption certificate. Organisations must keep records of all the disabled people that they employ and the Department of Employment has the right to enter the premises to inspect these records. An employer can be prosecuted both for failing to employ the correct number of disabled people and for failing to keep suitable records.

Disabled Persons (Employment) Act 1944 as amended by the Disabled Persons (Employment) Act 1958 and the Disabled Persons (Standard Percentage) Order 1946.

The Disabled Persons (Designated Employments) Order 1946 specifies that jobs as lift and car park attendants should be reserved for disabled people.

Race and Sex Discrimination

It is illegal to discriminate against an employee on the grounds of either race or sex. As with many other concepts in employment law, this is very simple to understand until it is put into practice, particularly as so much depends upon case law and upon the decisions of tribunals. The law essentially poses few difficulties for employers and employees who can co-operate in a reasonable manner. Problems only arise when one side or the other tries to use the law for their own ends.

The basic sources of advice in this area are the Department of Employment, the Equal Opportunities Commission, the Advisory, Conciliation and Arbitration Service and the Commission for Racial Equality. Two useful free guides to racial discrimination are produced by the Commission for Racial Equality: "A general guide: your rights to equal treatment under the Race Relations Act 1976" and "Employment: your rights to equal treatment under the Race Relations Act 1976". The Equal Opportunities Commission produces a similar guide on sex discrimination "Equal opportunities: a guide for employers to the Sex Discrimination Act 1975". It should be remembered when using this latter publication that the Sex Discrimination Act 1986 has not been covered. The main change brought in by this Act was the removal of the exemption for small firms.

The law requires that no person must be treated differently because of race, sex or marital status. There are certain exceptions to this, such as some staff in domestic service and other specified areas of employment. It seems unlikely that an architectural practice could be covered by any of these exclusions.

Exactly what constitutes discrimination is normally left to a tribunal to decide. What is important is that it is up to the claimant to prove the discrimination. Once discrimination has been proved, however, the employer must prove that being of a particular sex or race was an essential qualification for the job. It seems unlikely that this could apply to any job in an architectural practice.

Any employee wishing to complain of discrimination must apply to an Industrial Tribunal (see also Industrial Tribunals) within 3 months of the cause for complaint. Any case raised in this way may also consider incidents which happened before or after that date.

Sex Discrimination Act 1975
Race Relations Act 1976
Sex Discrimination Act 1986

Trades Union Members

All employees have the right to belong to an independent trades union or, alternatively, not to belong to one. The ''independent'' status essentially means any union which is not dominated by any employer or group of employers and is intended to exclude staff associations from these conditions. The employer must not discriminate against or dismiss any employee who is or who seeks to become a member of a trades union. Similarly, an employer may not dismiss an employee for failing to join or for resigning or being dismissed from a trades union. If a legally approved ''closed shop'' has been established it is possible to dismiss someone for not joining or for leaving the union. This is examined in more detail in the section on Dismissal.

As with race or sex discrimination, an employee who believes that discrimination has taken place must apply to an industrial tribunal within 3 months or within whatever period the tribunal considers appropriate if a complaint within 3 months was not reasonably practicable.

Employment: Dismissal

Introduction

Whilst most employers and employees co-exist in a state of relative harmony, it is wise to remember from the earliest stage of the relationship that problems may arise and that a framework for handling these must be established.

The basis for all employment law is contained in three acts: Employment Protection (Consolidation) Act 1978, as amended by Employment Act 1980 and the Employment Act 1982. The periods of continuous employment required to qualify for many of the rights discussed below have been amended by the Unfair Dismissal (Variation of Qualifying Period) Order 1985.

Dismissal: the Process

The law requires not only that the employer has a good reason to dismiss the employee but also that that reason is sufficient to justify dismissal. This effectively means that the employer must have followed the disciplinary provisions set out in the employee's conditions of employment and, if this is inadequate, has done whatever could be deemed ''reasonable''. The law requires that anyone dismissed who has been continuously employed for 6 months may ask the employer to provide a written statement of the reasons for dismissal. The employer must provide this within 14 days of it being requested.

Employment Protection Act 1975 as amended by the Employment Protection (Handling of Redundancies) Variation Order 1979. See also ''Procedure for handling redundancies'' by the Department of Employment.

Dismissal: what it Is

An employee is considered to have been dismissed if:

— His employment contract is terminated by the employer, either with or without notice.

— A fixed term contract, of more than 1 year's duration and which does not contain a clause agreeing not to claim compensation on dismissal, is not renewed in the same terms. This would not normally include an apprenticeship or similar training contract where it would not be considered reasonable to renew on the same terms.

— An employee terminates his contract, either with or without notice, because of a breach of that contract by the employer.

Case law has shown that there can be some doubt as to what actually constitutes dismissal. If the employer tells the employee to ''**** off'' this does not constitute dismissal, it merely suggests that he leaves the area. Similarly, if an employer informs an employee that dismissal, for any reason, is likely, and the employee then finds another job, the employee may not then claim compensation for either unfair dismissal or redundancy because the employment contract has not actually been terminated.

Because the date of dismissal can be crucial in deciding the level of compensation, period of notice, ability to lodge a claim of unfair dismissal etc, it is essential that all actions are fully recorded and documented. Never rely upon verbal statements and memory!

Disciplinary Procedures: the ACAS Code

As a guide to both employers and employees on what would be considered reasonable behaviour by both sides, the Advisory, Conciliation and Arbitration Service (ACAS) has produced a ''Code of practice on disciplinary practice and procedures in employment''. This is free from ACAS and is essential reading.

The code of practice is not the law but, as with other government sponsored codes, following its advice can be expected to be interpreted by an Industrial Tribunal as being ''reasonable'' behaviour. The basic advice given is that all disciplinary procedures are set out in writing. These should normally be in the employee's conditions of employment (see also Contract of employment). The procedures should specify:

— to whom they apply;
— what disciplinary actions may be taken by whom, ie who has the power of dismissal;
— how an employee should be informed of complaints made against him.

Good practice in this area will ensure that:

— No employee should be subject to dismissal by an immediate superior without recourse to senior management. This will, obviously, be difficult in a practice with a principal and two employees!
— No employee is dismissed for a first offence, unless this is one of gross misconduct, such as murdering the sole principal!
— Any decision is only taken after the facts have been carefully considered and after the employee has been allowed to appeal.
— The employee is given an explanation of any penalty imposed.

Ability of the Employee

The legislation provides a definition of this, which specifically includes health, both mental and physical, as well as the more obvious skills and qualifications. The employer must remember that a convincing case must be put before the Tribunal, which has to pass the test of both the letter of the law and the more difficult one of reasonable behaviour. Dismissing an employee on the grounds of ill health might be very difficult to justify as the act of a reasonable employer. The employer will have to show that the employee really is unable to do the job or that periods of continuous absence are imposing an unreasonable strain upon the organisation. The employee will have had to be consulted and medical evidence sought. The size of the organisation will, inevitably, play an important part in the decision as to what is reasonable.

Similarly, dismissing an employee because a lack of a skill, computer literacy for example, meant that he could not adapt to a new working process, could be seen as an attempt by the employer to change the employee's conditions of contract.

Change of Ownership

An employee may not be dismissed just because an organisation has changed hands. The new employer would have to show that organisational, technical or economic reasons required a change in the workforce. The employer must discuss with any recognised trades union the effect that this change of ownership might have upon the union's members, whether or not dismissal may result.

It is highly likely that such a change of ownership would result in redundancies rather than dismissals and the relevant legislation should be consulted (see also Redundancy Procedures).

Transfer of Undertakings (Protection of Employment) Regulations 1981 and Transfer of Undertakings (Protection of Employment) (Amendment) Regulations 1987. This is further explained in "Employment rights on the transfer of an undertaking" by the Department of Employment.

Conduct of the Employee

This is entirely the area of the Tribunal rather than of the letter of the law. The section on Notice covers some of the areas which have to be considered. Above all, it must be remembered that the offence must be serious enough to constitute a breach of contract.

Constructive Dismissal

An employee can claim to have been dismissed if the employer takes action which can be said to have forced the employee to resign. This is known as constructive dismissal and offers the same rights to the employee as if he had actually been dismissed. The action taken must be serious enough to be considered a breach of the contract of employment. Arbitrarily demoting the employee to a lower paid job would be an obvious example but any action which reduces the employee's conditions of employment could be seen in this light. A precise decision as to the merits of a claim of constructive dismissal will rest with the Industrial Tribunal.

Employment Protection Act 1975 as amended by the Employment Protection (Handling of Redundancies) Variation Order 1979. See also "Procedure for handling redundancies" by the Department of Employment

Dismissal without Notice

It is possible for either side to terminate the employment contract without notice if the conduct of the other side is considered sufficiently serious. This is a dangerous process and should only be followed in extreme circumstances. Always remember that what seems like an extreme circumstance in the heat of the moment may look entirely different when considered several months later by an Industrial Tribunal.

Dismissal without notice would come under the heading of unfair dismissal so that the onus would be on the employer to prove that the employee had acted in such an unacceptable manner as to break the contract of employment instantly. The decisions of Industrial Tribunals suggest that a single act of bad temper etc, on either side, does not constitute a breach of contract. If, however, this act of temper is the final act in a long running saga, it may be seen as breaching the contract. Should the single act of temper result in assault or arson, or should a single major theft occur, then it is highly likely that a Tribunal would accept that the contract had been broken.

Because dismissal without notice will breach the employment contract, it is always open to the employee to sue the employer on this basis, regardless of the actions of an Industrial Tribunal.

Fair Dismissal

For a dismissal to be deemed fair, the employer must show that:

— there is a good reason (the principal reason if there are several);

— the reason is sufficient to justify dismissal.

This two-stage definition of fair dismissal must be applied to every case and it is essential that both stages are satisfied if the dismissal is to be considered fair. If either is at all doubtful, the employer should swallow his pride and think again!

The legislation specifies 5 reasons which are considered to be sufficient to justify dismissal. They are not cast iron certainties, merely possible factors which may justify dismissal. Care must be taken to prove that one of them actually applies to the case in question and that the case is serious enough to warrant dismissal.

These are:

— the ability of the employee to do the job;
— the conduct of the employee;
— redundancy;
— a legal problem: eg a chauffeur who is banned from driving cannot be offered alternative employment;
— some other ''substantial'' reason sufficient to ''justify the dismissal of an employee holding the position which the employee held''.

Reasons which are specifically excluded are:

— in connection with trades union membership or activities;
— because of pregnancy;
— because the business changed hands;
— ''spent'' criminal convictions (See also Discrimination: Convicted criminals).

These ''reasons'' are simple on paper but complex in real life and will, where there is a dispute, depend upon a decision from an Industrial Tribunal rather than a statement in the legislation. There is, of course, a massive volume of case law in this area.

General guidance is given in ''Unfairly dismissed'' by the Department of Employment. The Employment Act 1980 provides guidance on the factors which must be considered by the Tribunal when coming to its decision. This must depend upon ''whether in the circumstances (including the size and administrative resources of the employer's undertaking) the employer acted reasonably or unreasonably in treating it as a sufficient reason for dismissing the employee''. Some more specific interpretations, however, may be given.

Industrial Disputes

If an employee is dismissed whilst either on strike or, as a result of industrial action, locked out by the employer, there is no recourse to an Industrial Tribunal unless it can be claimed that:

— not all of the employees involved have been dismissed;

— some of the employees, other than the claimant, previously dismissed have been offered reinstatement within 3 months of the date of dismissal.

This only applies to those on strike or actively engaged in the industrial dispute which led to the lock-out.
Employment Protection Act 1975 as amended by the Employment Protection (Handling of Redundancies) Variation Order 1979. See also ''Procedure for handling redundancies'' by the Department of Employment

Interim Relief

If an employee believes that he has been unfairly dismissed as a result of trades union membership or activities, he may apply for an interim relief order. This order is made by an Industrial Tribunal and requires the employer to reinstate the employee pending the Tribunal's decision upon the case. Such an order will only be made when the Tribunal considers it likely that it would uphold the case of unfair dismissal when it is given a full hearing. The employee must apply for the order not later than 7 days after the termination of employment and must include a signed statement from an official of the trades union supporting the claim.

The Tribunal can order the employer to reinstate the employee in his old job or in another job with conditions no less favourable than those previously enjoyed. In effect, the employer does not have to take the employee back into the workplace, merely to suspend him on full pay.
Employment Protection Act 1975 as amended by the Employment Protection (Handling of Redundancies) Variation Order 1979. See also ''Procedure for handling redundancies'' by the Department of Employment

Notice

All employees have the right to a period of notice after they have been continuously employed for more than 1 month. Details of this must be included in the employee's statement of conditions. The minimum periods of notice for employees who have served the following periods of continuous employment are:

— less than 2 years - 1 week
— more than 2 years but less than 12 - 1 week for each year of employment

— more than 12 years - 12 weeks.

Any employer may negotiate longer periods of notice with the employees. Equally, either side may agree to waive the right to notice.

Pregnancy

A woman can complain of unfair dismissal if she has complied with the legal requirements but is then refused permission to return (see also Payment and benefits: right to return). She can only be dismissed on the grounds of pregnancy if:

— her pregnancy makes it impossible for her to perform her job properly. This would, effectively, be subject to the same constraints as dismissing an employee on the grounds of ill health; (see also Dismissal: ability of the employee);
— it would be against the law for her to perform her job whilst pregnant.

The employer would also have to show that there was no alternative job that she could do.
Employment Protection Act 1975 as amended by the Employment Protection (Handling of Redundancies) Variation Order 1979. See also ''Procedure for handling redundancies'' by the Department of Employment

Redundancy

This means that there is no longer any requirement for the skills posessed by the employee. If all of the employees with such skills are dismissed simultaneously, there is no problem. If, as is normally the case, there is only a need to reduce the number of employees rather than to dispense with them all, the employer must be able to show that redundancy was the real reason for dismissal rather than an excuse for sacking someone, and that the person was selected in accordance with the customary or agreed procedure for selecting staff for redundancy. A Tribunal may still consider this to be unfair dismissal if the employer did not gave reasonable warning of the redundancy or did not make a reasonable attempt to find alternative work for those facing redundancy. See ''Procedure for handling redundancies'' by the Department of Employment.

Employment Protection Act 1975 as amended by the Employment Protection (Handling of Redundancies) Variation Order 1979

Redundancy: Length of Service

The period of service ends on the day on which the employee's period of notice expires. If less than the legal period of notice has been given (see also Dismissal: notice), the length of service will be calculated as if the employee had worked for the extra time. Days on which the employee was on strike should be deducted from this figure so that the employee will be considered to have started his employment on the appropriate number of days after the actual date. *Employment Protection Act 1975 as amended by the Employment Protection (Handling of Redundancies) Variation Order 1979.* See also ''Procedure for handling redundancies'' by the Department of Employment.

Redundancy Payments

Any employee who is made redundant is eligible for redundancy pay provided that:

— he has completed 2 years continuous employment;
— he has not unreasonably turned down an offer of alternative employment;
— he has not reached retirement age (65 for men and 60 for women.

Full details of the payments due are given in ''Redundancy payments'' by the Department of Employment. The calculation depends upon the employee's age, average wage and length of continuous employment.
For each year of continuous employment, up to a maximum of 20, the figures are:

— age 41 to 65 (60 for women) one and a half week's pay
— age 22 to 40   one week's pay
— age 18 to 21   half a week's pay

If the employee is within 1 year of the legal retirement age, 65 for men or 60 for women, the sum payable is reduced by $1/12$ for each complete month after the 64th or 59th birthdays.

Employment Protection Act 1975 as amended by the Employment Protection (Handling of Redundancies) Variation Order 1979. See also ''Procedure for handling redundancies'' by the Department of Employment

Redundancy Procedures

The law makes specific recommendations about the way in which consultations with the trades unions should take place. Consultations should begin at the earliest possible opportunity and not later than:

— if 10 to 99 employees to be dismissed in a period of less than 30 days at one establishment, consultations to begin at least 30 days before the first redundancy;

— if 100 or more to be dismissed in a period of less than 90 days at one establishment, consultations to begin at least 90 days before the first redundancy.

The employer has a similar requirement to inform the Department of Employment, even if the redundancies are all ''voluntary''. Failure to do so may result in a fine or in a reduction of the rebate of redundancy payments.

The union has the right to demand certain information in writing in order to be able to take a useful part in the consultation process. The employer must tell the union:

— the reasons for the proposed redundancies;

— numbers and descriptions of the employees proposed for redundancies;

— total number of employees of the types listed above employed at the establishment;

— the proposed method of selection for redundancy;

— the proposed method of implementing the redundancies, including the time scale.

The employer must consider any points raised by the Union and give written reasons for rejecting any of them. If the union does not reply to the employer, the employer need not take further action.

If there are special factors which prevent the employer from complying with the letter of the law, he must take all reasonable steps to comply.

A union may complain to an Industrial Tribunal within 3 months of the dismissals taking effect.

Employment Protection Act 1975 as amended by the Employment Protection (Handling of Redundancies) Variation Order 1979. See also "Procedure for handling redundancies by the Department of Employment.

Redundancy: Protective Awards

If the Tribunal finds a union's complaint justified, it may make a protective award which will safeguard the employees' wages. The employer will be required to pay all those affected their normal weekly wage for a specified period. This may not exceed:

— 90 days where 100 employees are to be made redundant over a period of 90 days or less;

— 30 days for 10 or more employees over a period of 30 days or less;

— 28 days in any other case, ie where less than 10 are involved.

The weekly wage is calculated in a similar manner to the sum for redundancy payments (See also Dismissal: redundancy payments). If the employer fails to pay, the employee may complain to an Industrial Tribunal within 3 months from the last day for which there has been a failure to pay. *Employment Protection Act 1975 as amended by the Employment Protection (Handling of Redundancies) Variation Order 1979.* See also "Procedure for handling redundancies" by the Department of Employment.

Redundancy: Reclaiming Payments

The employer may reclaim 41% of any payments made from the local Redundancy Payments Office. The remaining 59% may be set against tax. If the employer is unable to pay because of cash flow problems, the Department of Employment can pay the complete sum and then reclaim the employer's 59% at a later date. If the employer is insolvent, the Department will make the complete payment and then recover the sum owed from the assets of the business.

The onus is on the employer to pay the sum without the employee having to claim it. If the employer fails to pay, the employee may make a written request to the employer or may complain to an Industrial Tribunal within 6 months of being made redundant.

Employment Protection Act 1975 as amended by the Employment Protection (Handling of Redundancies) Variation Order 1979. See also "Procedure for handling redundancies" by the Department of Employment.

Redundancy: Short Time Working

An employee who has been laid off or whose wage has been cut by more than half as a result of short time working, may be entitled for redundancy pay if:

— he gives the employer notice in writing;

— the short time/lay off has lasted for 4 consecutive weeks;

— the short time/lay off lasted up to 6 weeks of which not more than 3 were consecutive in a period of 13 weeks;

— the last week was no more than 4 weeks before the notice in writing was given.

Employment Protection Act 1975 as amended by the Employment Protection (Handling of Redundancies) Variation Order 1979. See also "Procedure for handling redundancies" by the Department of Employment.

Redundancy: Week's Pay

This is the amount to which the employee is entitled in his contract of employment on the day on which notice was given. If less than the legal period of notice was given (see also Notice) the day on which the wage is calculated will be the day on which notice should have been given in order for the employee to finish on the actual day on which his contract was ended; ie if the employee was entitled to 3 weeks notice, the week's pay should be the one to which the employee was entitled 3 weeks before the day on which he finished employment, regardless of when he was actually given notice.

Employment Protection Act 1975 as amended by the Employment Protection (Handling of Redundancies) Variation Order 1979. See also "Procedure for handling redundancies" by the Department of Employment.

Replacement Staff

If an employee is engaged specifically as a temporary replacement for someone on maternity or sick leave, and is informed of the position in writing at the time of engagement, he may be fairly dismissed when the original employee is ready to return. In most circumstances, there would be no problem as the replacement employee would not have worked the minimum period required to qualify for a claim of unfair dismissal, currently 2 years. This would also solve the problem where the right to return after maternity leave is not taken up but where the employer does not wish to offer permanent employment to the temporary replacement.

Employment Protection Act 1975 as amended by the Employment Protection (Handling of Redundancies) Variation Order 1979. See also ''Procedure for handling redundancies'' by the Department of Employment.

Trades Union Membership

It is not normally legal to dismiss an employee because of membership of a trades union or because of a refusal to join a trades union. The issue of closed shops is a source of considerable confusion and complication and is unlikely to apply in most architectural organisations. Essentially, where an approved closed shop has been established, it is possible to dismiss an employee for refusing to join a union or for resigning from a union, provided that the employee is not covered by a number of exclusions. These include:

— refusal to join a union for reasons of religion, other deep seated convictions or professional conduct;
— because the employee has been expelled or excluded from the union without good reason;
— employees who were employed before the closed shop agreement took effect.

A full analysis of the closed shop is given in ''Union membership rights and the closed shop including the union labour only provisions of the Employment Act 1982'' by the Department of Employment.

Employment Protection Act 1975 as amended by the Employment Protection (Handling of Redundancies) Variation Order 1979. See also ''Procedure for handling redundancies'' by the Department of Employment.

Unfair Dismissal

Only those employees who have been employed for a period of 2 years can take action against the employer for unfair dismissal. There are two exceptions to this:

— dismissal on the grounds of race or sex discrimination or trades union membership is barred at all times (See also Discrimination);

— employees normally working under 16 hours but over 8 hours per week can claim similar rights after they have completed 5 years employment.

There are a number of excluded groups of employees, two of which are likely to affect the architectural profession:

— those who are normally employed outside Great Britain. If the employee is normally employed inside Great Britain but happens to be working outside the country for the same employer at the time of dismissal, compensation for unfair dismissal may be claimed.

— employees over the normal retirement age.

Employment: Industrial Tribunals

Introduction

Employment law is civil rather than criminal and almost all cases are decided by an Industrial Tribunal rather than in one of the normal courts of law. The Tribunals have permanent offices in the larger centres of population and consist of a legally qualified chairman and two other members appointed by the Secretary of State for Employment after consultations with, respectively, organisations representing employers and organisations representing employees.

Their activities are governed by Industrial Tribunals (Rules of Procedure) Regulations 1985. In the following sections, this is the relevant legislation unless otherwise stated. The Department of Employment has produced a booklet entitled "Industrial Tribunals: procedure for those concerned in Industrial Tribunal proceedings".

Applicants

An application form may be obtained from any Job Centre or unemployment benefit office. Legal aid may be obtained, depending upon the financial status of the applicant. In appropriate cases, the Equal Opportunities Commission or the Commission for Racial Equality will help with the preparation of the case. The applicant may name a representative in the application, in which case, all future communications will be sent to him. If the Tribunal is prepared to consider the case, it will be "registered" and a copy will be sent to the respondent. If the applicant wishes to withdraw the application before the hearing, the appropriate Tribunal office must be informed in writing as soon as possible.

Costs

Normally, each party will be responsible for its own costs. The ultimate result of the case will not affect this. Legal aid is, in theory, available to cover the costs of having a solicitor prepare an application. Experience suggests, however, that it is seldom granted. Expenses for travel, subsistence, loss of earnings etc may be reclaimed by each of the parties and their witnesses and representatives, except for:

— full time officials of a trades union;
— full time officials of an employers' organisation;
— paid representatives such as a barrister or solicitor;
— anyone against whom the Tribunal has awarded costs.

Travel warrants may be issued to anyone unable to afford the fare to a hearing. The Tribunal should be given notice if this is required.

If the Tribunal decides that a case has been brought frivolously, vexatiously or unreasonably, it may order the offending party to pay its own expenses and, sometimes, the expenses of the other party. Either party can claim expenses from the other.

Decisions

This will either be given at the hearing or shortly afterwards, together with a document containing the reasons for it. This will normally be a summary only but either party may request a full explanation. This will automatically be given if the case relates to a number of matters such as race or sex discrimination, equal pay or trades union activities.

Hearings

Both sides will be informed of the date at least 14 days in advance. If either is unable to attend, the Tribunal may postpone the hearing, provided that the reason is considered good enough. A pre-hearing assessment may be held to assess whether or not either party has a case which has no chance of succeeding. Normally, only the party whose case is being considered will be asked to attend, although the other party may attend if he wishes. The Tribunal cannot order the case to be dismissed although it may warn the party with the weak case that they may be made liable for the costs of the other party if the case is continued. The final decision on this will be made at the full hearing.

The hearing is, basically, an informal court of law, with evidence being given by both parties and by any witnesses who have been called. The Tribunal can grant an order requiring someone to attend as a witness but this order will have to be served by the party requiring the presence of the witness. It may also require documents to be supplied. The evidence may have to given under oath, at the discretion of the Tribunal.

The Tribunal may consider matters which have not actually been raised in the application, provided that they relate to the case being heard. In the event of a postponement being required because of a failure to provide evidence by one of the parties of for a similar reason, the offending party may have to pay the extra costs incurred.

Joinder

If either party considers that the case results from pressure exerted by a third party, either the applicant or the respondent may request that party to attend the proceedings. This must be done before the start of the hearing. In certain cases, the Tribunal may request attendance by a third party.

Respondents

Once an application has been registered, the respondent will be sent a copy, together with a ''notice of appearance''. This requires the respondent to state whether or not the case will be contested and, if it will be, the reasons for doing so. This must be returned to the Tribunal within 14 days of receipt. The Tribunal may be prepared to extend this period if the respondent has a good reason. As for applicants, the respondent may name a representative, who will receive all future communications. If the notice of appearance is not returned, the respondent will not be able to participate in the Tribunal's proceedings although the respondent may be called as a witness. The respondent will continue to be informed about the progress of the case even if the notice of appearance is not returned. At any stage, a voluntary settlement may be reached between the parties which will then be acknowledged by the Tribunal.

Reviews and Appeals

The Tribunal may reconsider its decision for a number of reasons:

— error by the tribunal staff resulting in an incorrect decision;
— a party did not receive notice of the hearing;
— the decison was made in the absence of one of the parties or of someone else entitled to be heard;
— new evidence has emerged since the hearing;
— the interests of justice require the review.

Any party seeking a review of a decision must apply at the hearing or, in writing, within 14 days of the decision being sent out.

Appeals may only be made on a point of law or, where the case relates to expulsion from a trades union in a closed shop, on points of both law and fact. Appeals must be sent to the Employment Appeals Tribunal within 42 days of the decision being sent out. Information on how to appeal is enclosed with each Tribunal decision.

Table of Statutes

1968	c 62	Clean Air Act
1969	c 25	Public Health (Recurring Nuisances) Act
1969	c 42	Architects Registration (Amendment) Act
1969	c 59	Law of Property Act
1970	c 44	Chronically Sick and Disabled Persons Act
1971	c 40	Fire Precautions Act
1971	c 78	Town and Country Planning Act
1972	c 35	Defective Premises Act
1972	c 61	Land Charges Act
1972	c 70	Local Government Act
1973	c 26	Land Compensation Act
1973	c 35	Employment Agencies Act
1973	c 37	Water Act
1973	c 57	Badgers Act
1973	c 60	Breeding of Dogs Act
1974	c 23	Juries Act
1974	c 32	Town and Country Amenities Act
1974	c 37	Health and Safety at Work Etc. Act
1974	c 40	Control of Pollution Act
1974	c 53	Rehabilitation of Offenders Act
1975	c 50	Guard Dogs Act
1975	c 52	Safety of Sports Grounds Act
1975	c 56	Coal Industry Act
1975	c 65	Sex Discrimination Act
1975	c 71	Employment Protection Act
1975	c 76	Local Land Charges Act
1976	c 38	Dangerous Wild Animals Act
1976	c 49	Chronically Sick and Disabled Persons (Amendment) Act
1976	c 57	Local Government (Miscellaneous Provisions) Act
1976	c 74	Race Relations Act
1976	c 83	Health Services Act
1977	c 29	Town and Country Planning (Amendment) Act
1978	c 44	Employment Protection (Consolidation) Act
1978	c 47	Civil liability (Contribution) Act
1978	c 50	Inner Urban Areas Act
1979	c 13	Arbitration Act
1980	c 5	Child Care Act
1980	c 42	Employment Act
1980	c 51	Housing Act
1980	c 53	Health Services Act
1980	c 58	Limitation Act
1980	c 65	Local Government, Planning and Land Act
1980	c 66	Highways Act
1981	c 18	Disused Burial Grounds (Amendment) Act
1981	c 36	Town and Country Planning (Minerals) Act
1981	c 43	Disabled Persons Act
1981	c 69	Wildlife and Countryside Act
1982	c 21	Planning Inquiriess (Attendance of Public) Act
1982	c 24	Social Security and Housing Benefits Act
1982	c 29	Supply of Goods and Services Act
1982	c 30	Local Government (Miscellaneous Provisions) Act
1982	c 42	Derelict Land Act
1982	c 46	Employment Act
1983	c 35	Litter Act
1983	c 42	Copyright (Amendment) Act
1984	c 3	Occupiers Liability Act

Table of Statutory Instruments

1982/ 1112	Housing (Payments for Well-Maintained Houses) Order 1982
1982/ 1205	Grants by Local Authorities (Repair) Order 1982
1982/ 1357	Notification of Installations Handling Hazardous Substances Regulations 1982
1983/ 23	Public Path Orders and Extinguishment of Public Right of Way Orders Regulations 1983
1983/ 978	Factories Act 1961 etc.(Metrication) Regulations 1983
1983/ 1615	Town and Country Planning General Development (Amendment) Order 1983
1983/ 1649	Asbestos (Licensing) Regulations 1983
1983/ 1674	Town and Country Planning (Fees for Applications and Deemed Applications) Regulations 1983
1984/ 421	Town and Country Planning (Control of Advertisements) Regulations 1984
1984/ 838	Homes Insulation Grants Order 1984
1984/ 1015	Town and Country Planning (Crown Land Applications) Regulations 1984
1984/ 1285	Operations in Areas of Archaeological Importance (Forms of Notice etc.) Regulations 1984
1984/ 1286	Areas of Archaeological Importance (Notification of Operations) (Exemption) Order 1984
1984/ 1933	Builders Skips (Markings) Regulations 1984
1984/ 1992	Control of Noise (Codes of Practice for Construction and Open Sites) Order 1984
1985/ 1	Supply of Services (Exclusion of Implied Terms) Order 1985
1985/ 16	Industrial Tribunals (Rules of Procedure) Regulations 1985
1985/ 126	Statutory Sick Pay General (Amendment) Regulations 1985
1985/ 698	Town and Country Planning (Compensation for Restrictions on Mineral Working) Regulations 1985
1985/ 708	Control of Pollution (Radioactive Waste) Regulations 1985
1985/ 782	Unfair Dismissal (Variation of Qualifying Period) Order 1985
1985/ 910	Asbestos (Prohibitions) Regulations 1985
1985/ 1011	Town and Country Planning General Development (Amendment) Order 1985
1985/ 1012	Town and Country Planning (National Parks, Areas of Outstanding National Beauty and Conservation Areas etc) Special Development Order 1985
1985/ 1065	Building Regulations 1985
1985/ 1066	Building (Approved Inspectors Etc) Regulations 1985
1985/ 1182	Town and Country Planning (Fees for Applications and Deemed Applications) (Amendment) Regulations 1985
1985/ 1411	Statutory Sick Pay (Additional Compensation of Employers and Consequential Amendments) Regulations 1985
1985/ 1493	Secure Tenancies (Right to Repair Scheme) Regulations 1985
1985/ 1576	Building (Prescribed Fees etc) Regulations 1985
1985/ 1579	Town and Country Planning (New Towns) Special Development (Amendment) Order 1985
1985/ 1604	Statutory Sick Pay (Medical Evidence) Regulations 1985
1985/ 1884	Waste Regulations and Disposal (Authorities) Order 1985
1985/ 1936	Building (Inner London) Regulations 1985
1985/ 1981	Town and Country Planning General Development (Amendment) (No 2) Order 1985
1985/ 1982	Town and Country Planning (National Parks, AONB and Conservation Areas etc.) Special Development (Amendment) Order 1985
1985/ 2023	Reporting of Injuries, Diseases and Dangerous Occurences Regulations 1985

Selected Bibliography

Architects and Builders Handbook, ed. by Architects Information Services (Dataday 1987)

Bowyer, J., *Guide to Domestic Building Surveys*, 4th edition (Architectural Press 1988)

Building Employer's Federation, *Construction Safety Manual*, (Construction Safety, updating service)

Building Research Establishment Digests, (BRE)

British Standards and Codes of Practice, (BSI)

Croner, *Health and Safety at Work* (Croner, updating service)

Cross, C., and Bailey, S., *Cross on Local Government Law*, 7th edition (Sweet and Maxwell 1986)

Cutler, D.F. and Richardson, I., *Tree Roots and Buildings*, (Construction Press 1981)

Department of the Environment Circulars, (HMSO)

Encyclopedia of Environmental Health Law and Practice, ed. by Cross (Sweet and Maxwell, updating service)

Encyclopedia of Health and Safety at Work, ed. by Goodman and Walker (Sweet and Maxwell, updating service)

Encyclopedia of Highway Law and Practice, ed. by Cross (Sweet and Maxwell, updating service)

Encyclopedia of Housing Law and Practice, ed. by Arden and Cross (Sweet and Maxwell, updating service)

Encyclopedia of Planning Law and Practice, ed. by Heap and Brown (Sweet and Maxwell, updating service)

Flint, M., *User's Guide to Copyright*, 2nd edition (Butterworth 1984)

Grant, M., *Planning Law Handbook*, (Sweet and Maxwell 1981)

Green, R., *Architect's Guide to Running a Job*, 4th edition (Architectural Press 1986)

Heap, D., *Outline of Planning Law*, 8th edition (Sweet and Maxwell, 1982) 9th edition now available.

Morse, G., *Partnership Law* (Financial Training Publications 1986)

Mynors, C., *Planning Applications and Appeals*, (Architectural Press 1987)

Neufert's Architect's Data, ed. Vincent Jones and John Thackara, 2nd edition (Neufert 1980)

Pitt, P.H., *Guide to Building Control in Inner London 1987*, (Architectural Press 1987)

Pitt, P.H., *Guide to Building Control by Local Acts 1987*, (Architectural Press 1987)

Planning Applications, the RMJM Guide, (Blackwell Scientific Publications 1987)

Powell-Smith, V., and Chappell, D., *Building Contracts Compared and Tabulated* (Architectural Press 1987)

Powell-Smith, V., and Chappell, D., *Building Contract Dictionary*, (Architectural Press 1985)

Redgrave and Fife, *Health and Safety in Factories*, 2nd edition (Butterworth 1982)

Sandys-Winsch, G., *Animal Law* (Shaw)

Sandys-Winsch, G., *Garden Law* (Shaw 1982)

Speaight, A., and Stone. G., *AJ Legal Handbook*, 4th edition
(Architectural Press 1984)
Spon's Landscape Handbook, ed. by Derek Lovejoy, 3rd edition (E & F
Spon 1986)
Stratton, I., *Building Land and Estates* (Oyez 1987)
Tolley, *Health and Safety at Work Handbook* (Tolley 1983)
Uff, J., *Construction Law*, 4th edition (Sweet and Maxwell 1985)
Underwood and Holt, *Professional Negligence* (Format 1981)

Index

Figures in bold type indicate main
entries